WHAT FAMILY LAW FOR EUROPE?

WHAT FAMILY LAW FOR EUROPE?

Edited by
Katharina Boele-Woelki
Maarit Jänterä-Jareborg

INTERSENTIA
LEFEBVRE GROUP

Intersentia
Lefebvre Belgium SA
Avenue Jean Monnet 4
1348 Louvain-la-Neuve
Belgium
Email: contact@larcier-intersentia.com

Distribution for the UK, Ireland and
Rest of the World (excl. France, Belgium and Luxembourg)
Ingram Publisher Services UK
1 Deltic Avenue, Rooksley
Milton Keynes MK13 8LD
United Kingdom
Tel: +44 1752 202 301 | Fax: +44 1752 202 331
Email: ipsuk.customercare@ingramcontent.com

Distribution for France and Rest of the World (excl. Ireland and the UK)
Interforum Editis
92 avenue de France
75013 Paris
France

Distribution for Belgium and Luxembourg
Larcier-Intersentia
Avenue Jean Monnet 4
1348 Louvain-la-Neuve
Belgium

What Family Law for Europe?

ISBN 978-1-83970-548-9
D/2025/06040/0409
NUR 820

British Library Cataloguing in Publication Data. A catalogue record for this book is available from the British Library.

CONTENTS

ABBREVIATIONS

AcP	Archiv für die civilistische Praxis
ART	Assisted Reproductive Technologies
AI	Artificial Insemination
BGB	Bürgerliches Gesetzbuch (German Civil Code)
BGBl.	Bundesgesetzblatt
BGHZ	Entscheidungen des Bundesgerichtshofes in Zivilsachen
BOE	Boletín Oficial del Estado
BMJ	Bundesministerium der Justiz
BT-Drucks.	Bundestags-Drucksachen
BVerfG	Bundesverfassungsgericht (German Constitutional Court)
CC	Code Civil
CDADI	Steering Committee on Anti-discrimination, Diversity and Inclusion, Council of Europe
CEFL	Commission on European Family Law
CJEU	Court of Justice of the European Union
CRPD	Convention on the Rights of Persons with Disabilities
Convention on IC	Convention on Preventing and Combating Violence Against Women and Domestic Violence, commonly known as the "Istanbul Convention"
CRC	Convention on the Rights of the Child
DJI	Deutsches Jugendinstitut
ECHR	European Convention of Human Rights
ECLI	European Case-Law Identifier
ECtHR	European Court of Human Rights
EEA	European Economic Area

ELI	European Law Institute
EU	European Union
Eur. Rev. Priv.Law	European Review of Private Law
ERPL	European Review of Private Law
FamPra.ch	Die Praxis des Familienrechts
FamRZ	Zeitschrift für das gesamte Familienrecht
FL-EUR	Family Law in Europe: Academic Network
GIGESC	Gender Identity, Gender Expression and Sex Characteristics Act
GRC	Gender Recognition Certificate
GRP	Gender Recognition Panel
ICON	International Journal of Constitutional Law
ILGA	International Lesbian, Gay, Bisexual, Trans and Intersex Association
IVF	In vitro fertilisation
JORF	Journal official de la République Française
LGR	Legal gender recognition
LGBTQI+	Lesbian, gay, bisexual, transgender, queer or questioning, intersex and others
LPartG	Gesetz über die Eingetragene Lebenspartnerschaft (Lebenspartnerschaftsgesetz)
MP	Member of Parliament
NJB	Nederlands Juristenblad
NJW	Neue Juristische Wochenschrift
Nord	Nordiska ministerrådet
NorFam	Nordic Centre for Comparative and International Family Law
NS	National Socialism
PACE	Parliamentary Assembly of the Council of Europe
PStG	Personenstandsgesetz (German Civil Status Act)
PStV	Verordnung zur Ausführung des Personenstandsgesetzes (Personenstandsverordnung)

RabelsZ	Rabels Zeitschrift für ausländisches und internationales Privatrecht
SBGG	Gesetz über die Selbstbestimmung in Bezug auf den Geschlechtseintrag und zur Änderung weiterer Vorschriften
SOU	Statens offentliga utredningar
StAZ	Das Standesamt
TFEU	Treaty of the Functioning of the European Union
UCiLER	University of Coimbra Institute for Legal Research
UN	United Nations
UNCRPD	United Nations Convention on the Rights of Persons with Disabilities
ZRP	Zeitschrift für Rechtspolitik

LIST OF AUTHORS

Masha Antokolskaia
Professor of Family Law at the Free University of Amsterdam

Katharina Boele-Woelki
Professor Emerita of Comparative Law at Bucerius Law School, Hamburg; Chair of the Commission on European Family Law

Nina Dethloff
Professor of Private Law, Private International Law, Comparative Law and European Private Law at Bonn University

Hrefna Friðriksdóttir
Professor of Family and Inheritance Law at the University of Iceland

Cristina González Beilfuss
Professor of Private International Law at the University of Barcelona

Elisabeth Hartley
Judge at the Svea Court of Appeal, Sweden

Maarit Jänterä-Jareborg
Professor Emerita of Private International Law and International Procedural Law at Uppsala University

Katja Karjalainen
Professor of Law and Welfare, University of Lapland

Felix Leven
Research Assistant at the Institute for German, European and International Family Law at Bonn University

Nigel Lowe
KC (Hon), Emeritus Professor of Law, Cardiff University

Ingrid Lund-Andersen
Professor Emerita of Family and Succession Law at the University of Copenhagen

Jane Mair
Professor of Private Law at the University of Glasgow

Dieter Martiny
Professor Emeritus of Private Law, Private International Law and Comparative Law at the European University Viadrina

Charlotte Mol
Assistant Professor of Family Law at Utrecht University

Barbara Novak
Professor of Civil and Commercial Law at the University of Ljubljana

Jordi Ribot Igualada
Professor of Civil Law at the University of Girona

Susanna Roßbach
Senior Research Fellow at the Max-Planck-Institute for Comparative and International Private Law, Hamburg

Nils-Eric Sahlin
Professor of Medical Ethics at Lund University

Jens M. Scherpe
Professor of Comparative Law at Aalborg University, Director of NorFam

Wendy Schrama
Professor of Family Law and Comparative Law at Utrecht University

Salla Silvola
Senior Ministerial Advisor Ministry of Justice, Finland

Tone Sverdrup
Professor Emerita of Private Law at the University of Oslo

Frederik Swennen
Professor of the Law of Persons and Family Law at the University of Antwerp

Paula Távora Vítor
Professor of Law at the University of Coimbra, University of Coimbra Institute for Legal Research (UCILeR)

Velina Todorova
Professor of Law at Plovdiv University, Member of the UN Committee on the Rights of the Child

Laima Vaigė
Associate Professor and Senior Lecturer in Private International Law at Uppsala University

Tim Wuyts
Professor of Law at the University of Hasselt

PART I

INTRODUCTION

THE ENIGMA OF FAMILY LAW COOPERATION IN EUROPE

Maarit Jänterä-Jareborg

1. CONFERENCE GOAL

The goal of the conference 'What Family Law for Europe?', held on the initiative of the Commission on European Family Law (CEFL), was to bring together leading European family law comparatists to present their ongoing and planned research, to discuss the latest developments in European family law and to evaluate what role comparative family law can play now and in the future. The programmes for harmonisation of European family law were discussed in depth, in respect of both the methods applied and the results achieved. Evolving research issues, for example new ways of approaching core concepts such as 'the family', 'parentage' and each individual's right to self-determination in respect of gender identity or in case of disabilities, generated lively debates. How is the shaping of European family law legislation impacted by more recent societal changes and the increased demands to take human rights in into account? Can we observe any emerging common cores and agree on any exemplary models? The programmes and the research groups involved are briefly introduced in the next chapter of this volume.

The need for the adoption of joint legal and ethical standards was another special concern during the conference, not least in respect of new methods enabling artificial creation of human life. Research in biotechnology is developing rapidly, and novel techniques that for both lawyers and humanists were previously unimaginable are in place which could be used for this purpose. How can the best interests of a not-yet-fertilised (future) individual be met in relation to the never-ending demands for babies? Where and how should law set the limits?

Dissemination of research and, in particular, the need to reach the lawmakers' attention is of increased importance. With this in mind, government officials in charge of family law in each of the Nordic countries were invited. This category of experts exercise a considerable influence in the drafting of the law proposals presented to the national parliaments. They also represent their countries in intergovernmental organisations, such as the EU, the Council of Europe, the Nordic Council and the Hague Conference on Private International Law.

The organisation of this conference was made possible through generous funding by the Royal Swedish Academy of Letters, History and Antiquities and by the Swedish foundation Riksbankens Jubileumsfond, both of which support research in Sweden in the humanities and social sciences. The conference took place in Stockholm in the historic premises of the Academy, with excellent administrative assistance from the Academy.

2. FAMILY LAW COOPERATION BETWEEN THE NORDICS: AN EXAMPLE FOR OTHERS TO FOLLOW?

It was a strategic decision to hold the conference in one of the Nordic capitals. The five Nordic states, consisting of Denmark, Finland, Iceland, Norway and Sweden, have a long tradition of legislative cooperation in law, dating back to the 1870s.[1] This cooperation has resulted in the harmonisation of parts of the states' civil law, in the simple form of the states agreeing on harmonised law without the need to adopt special Conventions for this purpose. The most remarkable result in family law was achieved in the 1920s, through the harmonisation of substantive marriage law, in terms of essentially similar rules on marriage conclusion, marriage dissolution and marital property.[2] The conclusion of inter-Nordic Conventions on Private International Law (PIL), on issues of marriage and inheritance, counts as the other most significant result.[3]

---

1 At this time, Finland was a part of the Russian Empire but with the status of a Grand Duchy of its own, having previously been a part of Sweden. In the 1809 Peace Treaty between Sweden and Russia, following the Napoleonic Wars, Sweden was forced to cede Finland to Russia. However, Finland was granted the right to maintain the laws of Sweden. After declaring its independence in December 1917, Finland joined the Nordic civil law cooperation. This was facilitated by the fact that Sweden's 1734 codification on, for example, marriage law was still in force in Finland. Iceland, on the other hand, was part of Denmark until its independence in 1918, and remained in union with Denmark until 1944.

2 The term 'Nordic legal family' occurs in comparative law research in another sense, not limited to harmonised family but referring to similarities and similar developments in the Nordic states' legal systems, thus qualifying them as a 'legal family' of their own, within the continental European legal systems. See e.g. K. Zweigert and H. Kötz, *Introduction to Comparative Law*, 2nd revised ed., Clarendon Press, Oxford 1987, pp. 286–295. Nevertheless, this kind of a classification is a generalisation hiding differences. It is also a generalisation when the concept of 'Nordic family law' (or Scandinavian family law) is used as a collective term covering family law in all five states. This can be misleading, as Ingrid Lund-Andersen emphasises in her contribution in this book.

3 This cooperation required the conclusion of Conventions, due to Sweden's active participation in the work of the Hague Conference on Private International Law. Sweden had ratified the early Hague Conventions on marriage. Legal cooperation with the Nordic states required special solutions that did not conflict with Sweden's obligations under the Hague Conventions.

Legal cooperation between the countries, and the impact they have on each other's laws, has other expressions, too. Usually, when a Nordic state enacts legislation of its own, the other Nordic states' solutions are carefully analysed. This applies, in particular, in respect of more recent law reforms in the other states.[4] In legal research, including doctoral dissertations, legal comparisons focus primarily on the other Nordic states' laws. Several inter-Nordic fora exist for regular meetings and conferences between judges, practitioners, researchers and legal experts at the government offices, and contribute to professional cooperation and to close personal links. The many inter-Nordic legal journals enable publishing in Danish, Norwegian or Swedish, in addition to English, which has become an increasingly popular tool of legal communication between Nordic scholars.[5] Occasionally, the Supreme Courts of the Nordic states refer to judgments rendered in another Nordic state, in support of their own reasoning.[6]

In her contribution to this book, Ingrid Lund-Andersen describes the political history of the Nordic states and the various fora where the legal cooperation takes place, giving special attention to the cooperation between Nordic family law scholars. I will add a few words about the Nordic states' cooperation within PIL, in family law.

In 1931, the states adopted an inter-Nordic PIL Convention on issues of marriage, in order to overcome the remaining differences in the states' substantive marriage law. In 1934, the states concluded another inter-Nordic Convention, now on matters of inheritance.[7] The application of these Conventions is restricted to Nordic citizens habitually resident in a Nordic state, but who have made use of the free movement between the Nordic states and taken residence in another Nordic state.[8] Both Conventions remain in force, but have recently been adjusted to the European Union's corresponding regulations.[9] In 1962, the Nordic states

4 Legislative reforms are prepared by special law committees which are not necessarily parliamentary. Each committee is led by a government-appointed investigator, often a specialist in the working field. Likewise, the other committee members are appointed by the government, often academics. Academic experts tend to exercise a considerable influence in the investigations, including through comparative law perspectives, and in the drafting of the proposed provisions.

5 The Icelandic language is too difficult for others to follow, whereas the Finnish language belongs to a totally different language group.

6 It is much more unusual that a court in a Nordic state would refer to judgments rendered outside the Nordic states. References to judgments from the European Court on Human Rights are, on the contrary, becoming more and more common. The same applies to preliminary rulings of the European Court of Justice, in the Nordic Member States of the European Union.

7 The Nordic states failed to harmonise their substantive law on inheritance. The differences were considered to be too big for compromises. For this reason, the adoption of the 1934 inter-Nordic Convention on inheritance was a significant event.

8 The Nordic states have had a joint labour market since 1955. Even before the 1950s, there was a lot of mobility between the states among the states' citizens.

9 These adjustments took place as late as during the first two decades of the 21st century. Finland's and Sweden's obligations towards the European Union as Member States participating

concluded a PIL Convention on the Recovery of Maintenance when ordered in another Nordic State.[10] The Nordic PIL Conventions' continued simple and clear structure, as well as the modest number of provisions, illustrate how similar approaches in substantive law and mutual trust enable PIL regulations to be kept very short. The states' agreement to maintain these Conventions, but with modernised content and a strong external influence through the EU's corresponding regulations, confirms the continued relevance of PIL in matters of the family, including inheritance law.[11] A close cooperation has existed between Nordic scholars in PIL since some generations back. The Nordic Group on Private International Law was established in 2002.

3. POLITICAL SUPPORT FOR CONTINUED NORDIC LEGAL COOPERATION

In 1962, the five Nordic states concluded an agreement on continued legal cooperation in private law. According to Article 4 of this so-called Helsinki Treaty,[12] which applies unchanged, the states parties commit themselves to continued legal cooperation, in order to achieve conformity to the extent possible in the field of civil law (private law).

In practice, the obligations created by the Helsinki Treaty have been interpreted in a flexible manner. Periodically, within family law, the pace and direction of law reforms have differed a lot. In the end, family law in the Nordic states turns out to have moved in the same direction, but not always in similar ways.[13] Being first does not necessarily mean being best.

---

in the EU's civil law cooperation required adjusting the main principles of the Conventions to those chosen by the EU in its corresponding regulations. On this and the background to the adoption of the so-called 'Nordic exceptions' in the EU's family law regulations, see M. Jänterä-Jareborg, 'The Nordic Input on the EU's Cooperation in Family and Succession Law: Exporting Union Law Through "Nordic Exceptions"' in B. Hess, M. Bergström and E. Storskrubb (eds), *EU Civil Justice: Current Issues and Future Outlooks*, Bloomsbury/Hart, Oxford 2016, pp. 143–159. See also M. Jänterä-Jareborg, 'Inter-Nordic Exceptions in EU Regulations on Matters of Family and Inheritance Law' in A. Verbeke, J.M. Scherpe, C. Declerck, T. Helms and P. Senaeve (eds), *Confronting the Frontiers of Family and Succession Law: Liber Amicorum Walter Pintens*, Intersentia, Cambridge 2012, pp. 733–752.

10 According to Article 69(3) of the EU's Maintenance Regulation, the Regulation does not preclude the application of the 1962 Nordic Convention, due to the Convention's 'simplified and more expeditious procedures', and its system on 'legal aid which is more favourable than that provided in the Regulation'.

11 In addition, in 1979 the Nordic states agreed on unified PIL legislation on the recognition of confirmations and court orders on paternity rendered in another Nordic State. Since 2005, these rules cover parentage in same-sex relationships.

12 *Samarbetsöverenskommelse mellan Danmark, Finland, Island, Norge och Sverige*, concluded in Helsinki, Finland, on 23 March 1962.

13 See M. Helin, 'The Story of the Nordic Family Conventions – Approaching Its End?' in M. Linton and M. Sayed (eds), *Festskrift till Maarit Jänterä-Jareborg*, Iustus Förlag, Uppsala 2022, p. 163.

Sweden took the lead in the early 1970s. The rules on divorce were modernised in 1973, unilaterally, much to the irritation of the other Nordic states. Legislation on unmarried cohabitation was introduced the same year, in order to provide some form of protection for the increasing number of couples who refrained from marriage. In 1989, Denmark was first – in the world – to introduce the legal concept of registered partnerships for the formalisation and legal recognition of same-sex relationships.[14] Denmark was also the first Nordic country to introduce legislation strengthening the rights of a child born abroad through a surrogacy agreement for intended parents in Denmark. On the condition that at least one of the intended parents has a genetic connection to the child, they can acquire legal parentage from the child's birth and without the need for adoption proceedings.[15]

Iceland stands out, inter alia, for its recent progressive legislation on gender identity.[16] Law reforms in Finland tend to follow Swedish enactments in particular, perhaps decades later, after deep-ploughing analyses and observations on how the Swedish rules work in practice. Consequently, the drafting is often more elegant and better 'thought through'.[17] Due to their previous joint family law legislation and continued similarity in family law, Sweden and Finland form the 'East Nordic' group in Nordic family law cooperation,[18] whereas Denmark, Iceland and Norway form the 'West Nordic' group. This applies both to substantive family law and to international family law.

The Nordic states' family law legislation is based on the same visions, such as equal rights for women and men, non-discrimination on the basis of sexual identity, self-determination of the individual, strengthening of children's rights, and the need to protect the vulnerable. Importantly, the shaping and application of rules on family law can be claimed to have a direct impact on the concerned individuals' quality of life. Year after year, in the World Happiness Index, the Nordic states rank highest among the 143 states, in terms of how the inhabitants evaluate their well-being.[19] Nevertheless, as several contributions in this book

---

14 The Danish Act on Registered Partnerships was repealed in 2002, when the concept of marriage was extended to cover same-sex couples.

15 Act no. 1687 of 30 December 2024. The Act applies as of 1 January 2025.

16 On this, see the contribution in this book by J.M. Scherpe, 'Legal Genders and Identities from a Nordic and German Perspective'.

17 One explanation for the high level of drafting of Finnish family law legislation could be the experts' academic background. It is not uncommon for the government officials in charge to have a background as university teachers and researchers in law. Otherwise, in the Nordic states, it is usual for the legal experts to have a background as court judges, and for work at the Ministry to be only one, but an important, stage in their court-centred career development.

18 According to its Constitution, Finland is a bilingual state with Finnish and Swedish enjoying equal status. Each citizen has the right to use either one of these languages in any contacts with public authorities, and public education is available in both languages. All legislation in Finland is officially published in both Finnish and Swedish.

19 See J.F. Helliwell, R. Layard, J.D. Sachs, J.-E. De Neve, L.B. Aknin and S. Wang (eds), *World Happiness Report 2024*, University of Oxford, Wellbeing Research Centre, www.

demonstrate, in many issues of substance the Nordic states can have much to learn from other European states' more recent enactments.

4. TOWARDS A MORE HARMONISED EUROPEAN FAMILY LAW?

In European family law research, harmonisation of family law enjoys wide support.[20] Comparative family law studies are popular. The initiatives taken and the work of the CEFL have been a vital source of inspiration. This development is in marked contrast to the previously nourished ideas on cultural strains of family law, rooting family law deeply into each state's history, culture and its own unique values, rendering it unreceptive to external influences.

Harmonisation of law can have different meanings and take different expressions. It can refer to an agreement, explicit or implied, on underlying basic principles, or to the adoption or application of basically similar rules in a specific area or field of law. Harmonisation can be a top-down or a bottom-up process. In the first case, it is a steered procedure, sanctioned or initiated by the states involved, or modelled on rules previously adopted by another state's legislature. In the second case, it is a spontaneous development whereby solutions promoted by national legislators or case law become increasingly similar, without conscious intentions to this effect.

In the European family law context, all these expressions and forms are present, besides the partly already achieved unification of PIL rules for cross-border family relations in the form of EU Regulations that are directly applicable and binding in the Member States.[21] Similar societal developments and the increased impact of human rights thinking are the major driving forces.

---

worldhappiness.report. Finland ranks as no. 1, Denmark as no. 2, Iceland as no. 3, Sweden as no. 4 and Norway as no. 7. In the measuring of welfare and quality of life, the Nobel Prize Laureate Amartya Sen's 'capabilities theory' is widely used. The focus lies on the individual's prospects to fulfil his or her own life choices. Factors such as poverty, inequality and lack of access to education are obstacles.

20 While many European scholars specialising in international family law were initially opposed to the EU's choice to enact uniform provisions of its own for cross-border family relations, many have reconsidered their opposition. The benefits of Member States applying the same rules are acknowledged, in spite of the common provisions' complexity.

21 The EU's enactments in family law introduce *uniform rules* for the Member States, applicable to cross-border situations. In a few cases, when not all Member States have been in favour of the enactment of a new cross-border family law EU Regulation, the Regulation has been adopted in the form of enhanced cooperation between the Member States in favour, a solution enabled by Article 81(3) of the Treaty on the Functioning of the European Union. This applies to the EU's Regulation on the law applicable to divorce and legal separation (No. 1259/2010) and the Regulations on jurisdiction, applicable law and the recognition and enforcement of judgments on property aspects of marriages (No. 2016/1103) and registered partnerships (No. 2016/1104). Most of the Member States participate in these Regulations.

All European states (save Russia) are bound by the European Convention on Human Rights and Fundamental Freedoms (1950). It would be an enigma and a lost opportunity if the states, under the current global threats to democracy and fundamental rights, fail to take seriously family law's potential to improve citizens' needs for fairness, protection and the recognition of their family lives and personal identities. To succeed, it is necessary to increase the funding for comparative family law research. Apart from cases where a considerable number of European states choose to accede to a convention covering issues of family law and which then needs to be properly implemented in their own legal systems, probably only an informal cooperation can be achieved. Factors such as time, costs, differences in resources and regular changes in states' governmental and parliamentary compositions cannot be disregarded. Nevertheless, once states decide to take joint actions, they will have access to extensive, up-to-date information and analyses, thanks to comprehensive European family law research.

A European-minded family law signals joint, democratic and liberal European values and stands as a symbol for togetherness. It provides a valuable tool to distance Europe from current authoritarian trends in many other states, where words such as gender and abortion are banned, as well as the contents of the abbreviation LGBTQ.

ACADEMIC COMMISSIONS AND EXPERT GROUPS IN THE FIELD OF FAMILY LAW IN EUROPE

This overview contains brief presentations of the organisation, objectives and working methods of six different commissions and groups. They meet regularly, undertake specific projects and all carry out comparative research in the field of family law.

CEFL – The Commission on European Family Law

Katharina Boele-Woelki

The Commission on European Family Law (CEFL)[1] is an independent academic network established in 2001, with the primary aim of fostering a harmonised approach to family law throughout Europe. It serves as a hub for leading legal scholars and practitioners who specialise in various aspects of family law. The CEFL's goal is to provide a structured framework for understanding and comparing family law systems across different European countries, and to propose common principles that can be adopted across jurisdictions to improve coherence, predictability and fairness in family law matters.

The CEFL was founded by a group of family law scholars who recognised the need for greater consistency in the field of family law across European nations. The founders envisioned a collaborative environment where experts could conduct comparative research and develop shared legal principles. Today, the CEFL operates as a non-governmental and non-profit organisation, with an Organising Committee and an Expert Group. This broad network consists of around 30 academics from a variety of European countries. The CEFL works through themes that focus on specific areas of family law. This structure enables the CEFL to conduct in-depth research and analysis in targeted areas, resulting in robust comparative studies and recommendations.

1 www.ceflonline.net.

The CEFL's mission is to advance the understanding, harmonisation, and development of family law in Europe. To achieve this, it has set out several key objectives:

1. *Comparative research:* Conducting in-depth comparative research on national family law systems, highlighting similarities and differences between them. This helps to identify areas where harmonisation could be most beneficial.
2. *Development of common principles:* Formulating common principles for European family law based on comparative analysis. These principles provide a reference point for countries looking to modernise or reform their domestic family law systems, ensuring that new laws are in line with broader European trends.
3. *Policy guidance:* Offering guidance to European institutions, national governments and legal practitioners on family law reforms. The CEFL's work is intended to inform legislative processes, ensuring that family law reforms are well grounded in comparative research and international best practices.
4. *Facilitating legal coherence:* Promoting greater legal coherence and understanding across Europe, thereby reducing the complexities that arise when family law matters involve cross-border elements, such as international divorce or childcare cases.

One of CEFL's most significant contributions to the field of family law is the development of Principles of European Family Law. These Principles serve as a model for national legislators and can be used by courts and practitioners when dealing with cases that have cross-border elements. The Principles provide a coherent framework that balances flexibility with consistency, allowing for variations in national traditions while encouraging alignment with shared European values.

The CEFL has published several volumes of Principles, covering various aspects of family law, including:

- Principles of European Family Law regarding Divorce and Maintenance Between Former Spouses (2004)
- Principles of European Family Law regarding Parental Responsibilities (2007)
- Principles of European Family Law regarding Property Relations Between Spouses (2013)
- Principles of European Family Law regarding Property, Maintenance and Succession Rights of Couples in *de facto* Unions (2019)

These Principles are the result of years of comparative research and discussions among CEFL members, aiming to create a body of work that is practical, accessible and respectful of national legal traditions while fostering a shared European perspective.

Additionally, the CEFL organises conferences, workshops and seminars, providing platforms for dialogue between academics, legislators and practitioners. These events foster a deeper understanding of the evolving landscape of European family law and encourage the exchange of ideas and best practices.

ELI – European Law Institute and Family Law

Wendy Schrama

The European Law Institute (ELI)[2] was established in 2011 and is inspired by the American Law Institute. It is funded by the EU and Vienna University and has its own secretariat based in Vienna. It is a large society with around 1,700 members, mostly from Europe. There is a strong institutional connection with institutional members such as the European Parliament and the European Court of Justice. A wide variety of legal professionals are members, including academics, judges, notaries and lawyers. The society has a well-developed governance structure, consisting of a large council, a president and a senate. Its financial resources, permanent staff and advanced organisational framework distinguish the ELI from the other five networks, which primarily operate with minimal or no funding and largely rely on the international collaboration of dedicated academics. What also sets the ELI apart is that it does not focus on family law, but on law in Europe. The ELI aims to initiate, conduct and facilitate research, make recommendations and provide practical guidance in the field of European legal development in a global world. Its mission is the harmonisation, integration and improvement of European legal systems. It aims to provide a European perspective on legal matters, seeking common ground and solutions that work across the diverse legal traditions of Europe (civil law, common law and other legal systems). The ELI's work is not limited to a specific field of law and has projects and members from all areas of law. The ELI operates primarily through projects, involving the collaboration of legal scholars, practitioners and judges to draft legislative proposals, model laws or legal guidelines. It has an advisory role for EU institutions.

The ELI has a Special Interest Group (SIG) on family and succession law. Members of this SIG are currently involved in several projects. One of these projects concerns the proposed EC Regulation on jurisdiction, applicable law and the recognition of decisions in matters of parenthood. The project 'Enhancing Child Protection: Private International Law on Filiation and the European Commission's Proposal COM/2022/695' will scrutinise the proposed

---

2 www.europeanlawinstitute.eu.

Regulation from four perspectives: children's, LGBTI persons' and women's fundamental rights, and the underlying EU primary law, especially concerning the free movement of citizens. This analysis will be the basis for a Position Paper and Model Rules in the form of desirable amendments.

The project 'Extra-Judicial Administration of Justice in Cross-Border Family and Succession Matters' is nearing its final stage with the publication of a book and a conference. This project concerns EU private international law relating to the increasing de-judicialisation in family law. Apart from a policy statement, a comparative analysis identifies out-of-court proceedings and non-judicial bodies in family and succession law at a national level. This analysis is used to develop a harmonised concept of the court in family and succession matters and adjust existing European private international law instruments.

The 'Empowering European Families' project was aimed at reducing obstacles faced by international families in Europe and at facilitating the free movement of citizens by developing an ELI instrument with an information sheet. Moreover, three toolkits were produced for legal experts advising married couples, registered partners and couples in informal relationships. In particular, the project looked into rules on the applicable law, jurisdiction, recognition and enforcement in family law, as well as at succession law. Currently, the EEF team aims to publish three books, the first one including many country chapters on private international law options for a legal choice and autonomy for international couples (married, registered partners and informal relationships). It will cover divorce, matrimonial property, maintenance and pension rights.

FL-EUR – Family Law in Europe: An Academic Network

Masha Antokolskaia

Family Law in Europe: An Academic Network (FL-EUR)[3] was established in Amsterdam in 2019. Its primary objective is to promote the spontaneous, bottom-up harmonisation of the law of persons and family law across Europe. This is achieved through the collection, systematisation, analysis and dissemination of knowledge concerning relevant national laws from the jurisdictions covered. FL-EUR focuses exclusively on substantive law, encompassing law in the books, law in action and law in context. The initiative also seeks to advance comparative and multidisciplinary research and education, thereby fostering mutual learning from diverse experiences. The target audience includes academics, practitioners, national and supranational governments, and international organisations.

As a purely academic initiative, FL-EUR operates independently of governments or international organisations. All participants contribute in their

[3] https://fl-eur.eu/.

personal capacities, maintaining full academic independence. Currently, the network comprises 34 leading experts – academics, judges and government officials – representing 31 European jurisdictions, both within and beyond the EU.

At present, FL-EUR is working on its first research topic: 'The Empowerment and Protection of Vulnerable Adults'. Experts from 30 jurisdictions were invited to contribute country-specific reports based on a systematically designed questionnaire. These national reports, completed in 2023,[4] provide a comprehensive foundation for further analysis. Through the analysis of these reports, FL-EUR aims to identify commonalities, best practices and challenges in the field of vulnerable adults' empowerment and protection. The ultimate goal is to propose a range of potential solutions that could be useful for national governments, European and international organisations, professionals, and their associations.

The Nordic Expert Group on Family Law

Salla Silvola and Elisabeth Hartley

1. General

The Nordic Expert Group on Family Law is a forum for cooperation in matters of family and succession law between the Nordic countries. Originally, the participants consisted of government officials from Denmark, Finland, Iceland, Norway and Sweden in addition to academic experts. In 2018, the Expert Group was pleased to welcome a new member: the Faroe Islands. The participating officials represent the ministries or departments involved in drafting family and succession law in the Nordic countries, typically the departments of justice and of social affairs and health. The participating states take turns in hosting the meetings. Financial support for the organisation of the meetings is provided by the hosting country and by the Nordic Council of Ministers.

2. Forms of Cooperation

The group does not have any charter or written code of conduct, but the forms of cooperation and the structure of the meetings remain relatively consistent. Originally, the principal tasks of the Expert Group were to develop and harmonise the private international law rules of Nordic family and succession law and to exchange information on national legislative projects. Already in the 1930s, three Nordic Conventions were introduced: the Nordic Convention on the Recovery of Maintenance (1931), the Nordic Marriage Convention (1931) and the Nordic

---

4 www.familyandlaw.eu/pagina/country_reports.

Inheritance Convention (1934). All three have since been amended. Model laws were drafted in other areas, which were then introduced as national legislation in each of the Nordic countries. Hence, already since the 1980s, all Nordic countries have similar legislation on the recognition of Nordic paternity decisions. This collaboration naturally required excellent knowledge of the existing national laws and their interpretation, which in turn demanded an active interaction with Nordic academia. Hence, academic seminars and presentations are arranged in connection with the Expert Group meetings.

3. Challenges and the Way Forward

When the EU started its work on private international family law at the beginning of the 21st century, the coordination of the Nordic and European instruments was put on the agenda. Although Denmark had already joined the EC in 1973, it has opted out of civil law cooperation. Following Finland's and Sweden's membership of the EU in 1995, one of the principal tasks has been to adjust the inter-Nordic Conventions on family law to the EU's corresponding regulations. Although Iceland and Norway are not members of the European Union, they are also impacted by the EU law via their membership of the EEA.

The increasing activity of the European Union in the area of family and succession law has often meant that the private international law rules drafted in the EU are taking priority over the rules drafted for the Nordic area. From the point of view of Nordic cooperation, this can be seen as a setback. However, as the migration of the Nordic population increasingly takes place beyond only the Nordic countries, it may also be viewed as a well-founded manoeuvre to adapt our legal toolbox to correspond with the social reality.

The long tradition of Nordic intergovernmental expert groups on family law and the informal atmosphere of its annual meetings have fostered solid, mutual trust and understanding. This is a source of strength and inspiration. It is frequently surprising how similar the Nordic countries and the emerging challenges still are. Hence, as the Expert Group is currently trying to adjust its role to the changing circumstances, it is clear that there is a well-founded need for continued Nordic cooperation and for the Nordic Expert Group on Family Law as a forum for exchanging information and for seeking the best practices to solve the issues that are common to us.

NorFam – The Nordic Centre for Comparative and International Family Law

Jens M. Scherpe

The Nordic Centre for Comparative and International Family Law (NorFam)[5] was launched in April 2023 and is intended to be a focal point for comparative

[5] See www.norfam.org for further information.

and international research in the Nordic Countries in the area of family law as well as in related areas such as succession law as well as private international law, social law and medical law.

Nordic legal scholarship in the fields of family and succession law is often underrepresented in international debates, and NorFam's core mission is thus to make Nordic law and Nordic legal scholarship globally available in the English language. As such, NorFam is not intended to be competition for existing Nordic initiatives but rather aims to be complementary and collaborative. Another key aim of NorFam is to provide in-depth comparative research for law reform discussions within the Nordic countries and beyond.

Even though NorFam is administratively based at Aalborg University in Denmark, its members are from all over the Nordic countries. NorFam has co-directors from all major Nordic jurisdictions and an Advisory Board consisting of eminent scholars in this field. But the true driving force is made up of NorFam's corresponding members, and the aim is to have at least one from every single Nordic institution where law is taught. In this way, NorFam hopes to maintain contact with all colleagues working in family law and related areas and especially also PhD students from these institutions. The corresponding members disseminate NorFam's information and encourage colleagues to participate in NorFam's activities. In addition, NorFam has international corresponding members who fulfil the same function internationally. Finally, NorFam is developing a network of institutional collaborations, and the first of these was agreed with RETHINKIN_.

NorFam's work, which is supported by a generous network grant from NordForsk,[6] can be summarised by its three aims: Nordic participation, Nordic scholarship and Nordic education.

1. Nordic Participation

NorFam includes scholars from all Nordic jurisdictions and at all stages of their careers in the work of NorFam and wants to stimulate collaboration through joint projects but also through the facilitation of research stays at Nordic institutions.

2. Nordic Scholarship

NorFam wants to promote collaborative research between scholars from the Nordic countries with the express aims of (a) generating genuinely inter-Nordic research, and (b) making accessible Nordic scholarship in the English language so that Nordic voices can be heard internationally.

6 On NordForsk see www.nordforsk.org/about; on its support for NorFam see www.nordforsk.org/news/new-family-constellations-are-questioning-current-family-laws-they-were-made-time-when-family.

At the time of writing, NorFam is undertaking a comparative project on assisted reproduction, gender and parenthood in collaboration with RETHINKIN_ and involving all five major Nordic jurisdictions as well as the jurisdictions of Germany, Belgium, the Netherlands and the United Kingdom. Another ongoing international project on the criminalisation of surrogacy involves some 27 jurisdictions and is conducted in collaboration with the University of Hong Kong's Centre for Medical Ethics and Law (CMEL).[7] A project on comparative Nordic pension law is scheduled to start in 2025, and several others are in their early planning stages.

3. Nordic Education

NorFam supports the next generation of scholars in the fields of family and succession law and promotes the fact that their work not only has a national but also a genuine Nordic focus, i.e. taking into account the legal and other developments in the other Nordic jurisdictions and beyond. For this, NorFam is organising Nordic Early Career Colloquia, the first of which was held in Copenhagen in June 2024 in collaboration with the University of Eastern Finland. Here young scholars met each other and began forming their own networks. The next colloquium will take place in collaboration with the Max Planck Institute for Comparative and International Private Law in Hamburg in June 2025.

RETHINKIN_ – Rethinking Family and Family Law in the Low Countries

Frederik Swennen

RETHINKIN_[8] was established in 2015 as a joint research programme on family law in the Low Countries. Both Belgium and the Netherlands had been international pioneers in the 2000s in the legal recognition and protection of post-marital family constellations, both horizontally (adult unions) and vertically (parents and children). The aim of RETHINKIN_ was to jointly promote further innovative legal developments and the academic redefinition of family law in the Low Countries at an international forum.

During the first lustrum, RETHINKIN_ consisted of all Flemish academic research units and the leading Dutch units that had formed the Family & Law Alliance. In the second lustrum, RETHINKIN_ was extended to include a representative of the Belgian French-speaking Famille & Droit Alliance. In its third lustrum, RETHINKIN_ is seeking to establish strategic collaborations with partners in all geographical directions, such as NorFam, to act as a two-way gateway for academic contacts in their region. It has also teamed up with the

7 On CMEL see https://cmel.hku.hk/.
8 www.rethinkin.eu.

Centre for Family Studies at the Odisee University of Applied Sciences to include practice-oriented, policy-preparatory and advisory scientific research dimensions.

RETHINKIN_ is coordinated by the Personal Rights & Property Rights Research Group at the University of Antwerp (Belgium).

During the first and second lustra, RETHINKIN_ was funded as a Scientific Research Network by the Research Foundation – Flanders.

For each lustrum, RETHINKIN_ focuses on selected research topics that allow its partners to develop and combine their respective strengths. The objectives of RETHINKIN_ are based on traditional basic research outputs, such as well-specified research projects, publications and conferences. It does not aim to develop principles or proposals for the harmonisation of law.

During the first lustrum, it focused on solidarity between partners according to the form of their union, solidarity between generations and the status of incapacitated adults, and non-traditional kinship formations and the law. Transversally, the respective roles of the state, families and individuals (the market) informed the research.

In the second lustrum, RETHINKIN_ continued to focus on the autonomy and protection of vulnerable persons, both adults and children, given the involvement of some of its members in FL-EUR. Another focus was the international migration of family form(ation)s, such as polygamy and international surrogacy.

Research topics from 2025 onwards are the construction and role of gender in family law, the 'dual system' of family law – where the primary family law in the Civil Code is confronted with secondary family law rules in tax and social law, among other areas; digital technologies and family (property) law, such as the application of AI for the division of property; and children and their trusted adults.

RETHINKIN_ primarily consists of and is aimed at family law academics. For each research topic, a Flemish and a Dutch coordinator are appointed to develop the programme. The groups apply (combined) socio-legal and comparative research methods. Interdisciplinary cooperation is usually included in order to provide a theoretical basis for the research. And societal perspectives are included through transdisciplinary collaboration, both during the research phase, for example through focus groups, and in the dissemination phase, such as through the organisation of a States General of the Families.

PART II

THE SUCCESS STORY AND FUTURE OF NORDIC FAMILY LAW COOPERATION

United or Separate Actors?

NORDIC FAMILY LAW
HISTORICAL OVERVIEW OF NORDIC COOPERATION IN ACADEMIA

Ingrid LUND-ANDERSEN

1. INTRODUCTION

In illustrations, the five Nordic countries – Denmark, Finland, Iceland, Norway and Sweden – are often depicted as five swans flying in the same direction. However, this idyllic scene conceals the fact that these countries vary greatly in size, in their affiliation with the European community and in their historical power.

The legal cooperation that occurs among the Nordic countries today cannot be understood without looking back in time. Both before and after the Middle Ages, wars between these countries led to territories changing hands among different Nordic kingdoms. The close connections between these countries fostered mutual influence in language, culture and legal traditions.

Denmark and Sweden have historically been the dominant countries. Norway has been in union with Denmark, and Iceland has been part of Denmark as well. Therefore, these three countries, forming the western region, share legal roots in terms of principles and details. Historically, Finland was a province of Sweden, and today the two countries form an eastern axis with very similar legislation.

Especially with regard to family law, during certain periods there has been intense Nordic cooperation for more than 100 years. This chapter will provide a brief historical overview and have a focus on collaboration in academia. Along the way, similarities and differences between the Nordic countries will be highlighted, as well as both successful results and challenges.[1]

---

1 See also I. LUND-ANDERSEN, 'Approximation of Nordic Family Law within the Framework of Nordic Cooperation' in M. ANTOLKOLSKAIA (ed.), *Convergence and Divergence of Family Law in Europe*, Intersentia, Antwerp/Oxford/Amsterdam 2007, pp. 51–61; P. LØDRUP, 'The Reharmonisation of Nordic Family Law' in K. BOELE-WOELKI and T. SVERDRUP (eds), *European Challenges in Contemporary Family Law*, Intersentia, Antwerp/Oxford/Portland 2008, pp. 17–26.

2. HISTORICAL RETROSPECTIVE

In 1380, Denmark and Norway were united under a Danish king. Iceland had belonged to Norway as a province, and the island became part of the new community. In 1874, Iceland was granted its own legislative authority. At the beginning of the 20th century (1918), Iceland became an independent state but remained in union with Denmark. This union was terminated by Iceland in 1944.

Denmark–Norway supported Napoleon in his campaign but lost the war to England. Consequently, in 1814, during the peace negotiations in Kiel, the victorious countries forced the Danish king to cede Norway to Sweden. However, Norway gained significant independence, with its own constitution, laws and parliament. The union with Sweden lasted until 1905, when Norway became an independent state. The cohesion with Denmark was demonstrated by the fact that the parliament elected the Danish king's second oldest son as Norway's first king.

Similar to Norway belonging to Denmark from the 15th to the 19th century, Finland was linked to Sweden, although Finland was more of a province to Sweden than Norway was to Denmark. Russia had occupied parts of Finland during several periods, and in 1809, the eastern part of Finland was ceded to Russia. The rest of Finland became a Russian dominion, but Swedish civil and family law remained in force. In 1917, shortly after the Russian Revolution, Finland declared independence.

The complicated relationship among the five countries can be compared to that of siblings, where there can be love and inspiration, but also dominance and a desire to distance oneself from the others. In recent years, the positive feelings have clearly prevailed. Denmark took over the chairmanship of the Nordic Association in 2023, and the new general secretary, Karen Ellemann, declared that if our relationship with Europe can be characterised as a marriage of convenience, our relationship with the Nordic countries is a love relationship.

3. DATA ON THE NORDICS

In the Nordic region, there are almost 28 million inhabitants, with 10.4 million in Sweden, 6 million in Denmark, around 5.5 million in both Norway and Finland, and 393,000 in Iceland.

All Nordic countries are modern welfare states with a high level of social benefits and free schools, universities and hospitals. There is public support for childcare in nurseries and kindergartens, providing good opportunities for women to enter the labour market. The legislation is based on gender equality.

The Danish National Church is Protestant, more specifically Evangelical Lutheran. It plays a modest political role.

The Danish, Norwegian and Swedish languages share many similarities, though their pronunciation are quite different. This means that it is usually possible – albeit sometimes with some difficulty – for the people of these three countries to understand each other. Written language is easier to understand than spoken language.

Using one of the Scandinavian languages is more challenging in Finland and Iceland, as their native languages differ greatly from those of the three Scandinavian countries. The Finnish language is a branch of the Uralic language family, also found in Estonia and Hungary. Due to Finland's close connection with Sweden, around 5% of Finnish children have Swedish as their mother tongue. The remainder of the children learn Swedish in school. In Iceland, the population speaks the old Nordic language, Icelandic, which cannot be understood in the rest of the Nordics. The close connection to Denmark means that Icelandic children learn Danish in school.

Both for historical reasons and due to the similarity in languages, the closest community exists between the three Scandinavian countries: Denmark, Norway and Sweden. However, there is another dividing line in the Nordic countries, namely in their membership of the European Union (EU). Only Sweden and Finland are full members and the two countries have a close collaboration within the EU. Denmark is a member of the EU but has a number of reservations; in particular, the country does not participate in judicial cooperation. Norway is not a member of the EU, as a majority of Norwegians in two referendums have voted 'no' to becoming a member. Iceland is not a member either. These two countries participate in other European cooperation, such as the European Economic Area (EEA) together with the rest of the Nordic region.

4. IMPORTANT YEARS IN NORDIC COOPERATION

In 1872, the first so-called 'Nordic Lawyers' Meeting' was held in Copenhagen. The background was the rise of industrialisation, which had led to a number of social problems and unresolved legal issues. The Nordic countries found that it was time to reduce the strong influence from Germany and to find solutions better suited to the smaller countries in Northern Europe. The goal was to base new legislation on common values and make it easier for citizens to move between the countries. Solutions should be developed in a uniform direction. Therefore, it was important to bring together the best legal experts – professors, judges, attorneys, etc. – to ensure that discussions on future legislation were at the highest level.

Since then, every third year the local committees have been responsible for organising meetings and social events for three days, alternating between the Danish, Norwegian and Swedish capitals. When Finland and Iceland became independent states, meetings were also held and continue to be held in Helsinki and Reykjavik. In August 2024, Copenhagen hosted the latest meeting, with over 1,000 participants. After a two-year delay, the assembled lawyers celebrated 150 years of cooperation.[2]

At the first Nordic Lawyers' Meeting, the community of property between spouses was one of the topics. However, it was not until 1910 that the Scandinavian countries established family law committees (see more about this collaboration below in section 6).

Nordic cooperation also takes place at a political level. The Nordic Council, established in 1952, has 87 members who are also Members of Parliament from different political parties. The members work mostly in one of the four committees, which include culture and welfare. Another Nordic organisation is the Nordic Council of Ministers, established in 1971, which works at the ministerial level on common solutions in the Nordic countries.

5. COOPERATION IN ACADEMIA

A formalised collaboration in academia began around 1980. This initiated a tradition of inviting participants to a Nordic family law seminar at a Nordic university. The purpose is to strengthen academic cooperation and initiate discussions on current topics that could lead to legal reforms. The idea is to inform and inspire, including providing information about new research projects. In addition to university employees, a small number of lawyers and ministry employees are invited and there are usually around 40 participants. The last seminar took place in the spring of 2023 in Lillehammer, Norway.

These Nordic seminars are held every second or third year. The frequent meetings have led to collaborations between Nordic universities on all levels, including the exchange of research stays for PhD students, memberships of assessment committees for university positions, and joint book and article projects.[3]

Moreover, in doctoral theses, there is a long tradition of describing the legal position of at least one Nordic country and thereby placing one's own country's legal position in perspective.[4] Therefore, assessment committees appoint members from other Nordic countries with expert knowledge of the thesis topic.

---

2 The history of the Nordic Lawyers' Meetings is described in a new book, D. Tamm, *Variationer over et nordisk tema*, De Nordiske Juristmøder, Copenhagen 2024, available at: https://jura.ku.dk/jurabog/pdf/juridiske-monografier/VariationerOverEtNordiskTema.pdf.

3 E.g. the double issue of (2021) 3–4 *Tidsskrift for familierett, arverett og barnevernrettslige spørgsmål* on the theme of 100 years of Nordic family law, celebrating Nordic cooperation, with articles by Professors Tone Sverdrup, Margareta Brattström, Katrine Kjærheim Fredwall, Ingrid Lund-Andersen, Anna Singer and John Asland. See also about the book *Nordic Cohabitation Law* below sections 6 and 7.4.

4 E.g. S. Danielsen, *Skilsmissesagen, skandinaviske synsvinkler*, Jurist- og Økonomforbundets Forlag, Copenhagen 1989. This Danish dissertation is a comparative study of divorce with detailed descriptions and analyses of Danish, Norwegian and Swedish law.

A new organisation from 2023 is the Nordic Centre for Comparative and International Family Law (NorFam) at Aalborg University in Denmark, with Professor Jens Scherpe as its director.[5] The Centre has affiliated several academic bodies: it has five co-directors from all the Nordic countries, an Advisory Board of Nordic senior scholars, and a large group of corresponding members from almost all Nordic universities, plus international corresponding members.

The central topics of NorFam are family law and succession law. However, the group that will benefit from the Centre also includes legal scholars and family-related researchers from other academic fields such as sociology, psychology, theology, medicine, gender studies, etc.

NorFam organises various international and Nordic conferences. In 2024, NorFam was responsible for the planning of the 2nd International Surrogacy Forum and an Early Career Colloquium, both of which took place in June 2024 in Copenhagen.

NorFam is particularly interested in Nordic projects which:

- generate genuine inter-Nordic research to stimulate scholarly and political debates in the Nordic countries; and
- make accessible and disseminate Nordic scholarship in the English language so that Nordic voices can be heard in European and international debates. For the latter, lecture series are organised by NorFam to show Nordic research and bring international scholarship and debate to the Nordic countries.

6. LEGAL COOPERATION IN FAMILY LAW IN FOUR PHASES WITH SPECIAL EMPHASIS ON THE ROLE OF ACADEMIA

The developments since 1909 can be divided into four phases.[6]

Phase 1: 1909–1927 – Major Reforms

At the beginning of the 1900s, it was a time for significant reforms regarding the legal status of spouses in family law. A Nordic conference held in Stockholm in 1909 initiated the establishment of expert committees in Denmark, Norway and Sweden, tasked with drafting new marriage laws. These expert groups, each comprising three members, included a law professor as the chairman and Supreme Court judges as members. The cooperation between the three

---

5 https://www.law.aau.dk/forskning/forskningsgrupper/nordic-centre-for-comparative-and-international-family-law-norfam.

6 See more in detail I. Lund-Andersen, above n. 1, pp. 53–56. See also I. Lund-Andersen and A. Kronborg, 'Marriage and Family Relations' in P. Letto-Vanamo, D. Tamm and B.O. Gram Mortensen (eds), *Nordic Law in European Context*, Springer, Cham 2019, pp. 99–101.

committees was intensive, with long meetings lasting up to four or five weeks in a hotel in Sweden.[7]

This period of Nordic cooperation is considered to be the most fruitful.[8] This is likely due to the fact that entirely new laws had to be introduced, and the committee members had the time to discuss common solutions without political interference. Moreover, the committees had few members, were led by law professors, and the members agreed on the fundamental principles on which the legislation should be based: equality between husband and wife, strengthening women's rights after the dissolution of marriage, and facilitating the dissolution of marriage, mainly on the basis of the irretrievable breakdown of the relationship. The focus was on creating forward-looking rules and ensuring new legal rights and self-determination for each spouse.

The objective was to achieve harmonisation, and the committees concurred on most aspects, although solutions to individual issues varied.[9] The parliaments adopted the submitted draft laws with minimal changes during the period 1915–1927. In Denmark, the Act on Contraction and Dissolution of Marriage was enacted in 1922, and the Act on Legal Effects of Marriage followed in 1925. The most significant revision was the introduction of deferred community of property.[10] Under this matrimonial property regime, the default position is that there is separate ownership and separate liability during the marriage. The assets of the spouses are to be divided upon the dissolution of the marriage in cases of separation or divorce, and upon death. With this division rule, the wife's household and care work and the extensive community between spouses are recognised. However, it became possible for spouses in a prenuptial agreement to divide separate property in the case of divorce and death.

Phase 2: 1955–1967 – Minor Reforms

For many years, there was no need to revise the marriage laws. It was not until around 1955 that minor reforms were recommended by the Nordic Council, partly based on discussions at the Nordic Lawyers' Meetings in 1954. By then, Finland and Iceland had become independent countries, leading to cooperation between five countries. Although the committees still had relatively few members, the collaboration became less intensive. The committees focused on resolving technical issues, resulting in only partial harmonisation.

---

7 Lecture by M. Jänterä-Jareborg, 'Nordic Family Law and Academia', NorFam centre launch, https://www.law.aau.dk/forskning/forskningsgrupper/nordic-centre-for-comparative-and-international-family-law-norfam#8861ce99-c90e-4049-b34f-38928a202393.

8 M. Antokolskaia, *Harmonisation of Family Law in Europe: A Historical Perspective*, Intersentia, Antwerp/Oxford 2006, p. 243.

9 See more about the work of the committees S. Danielsen and P. Lødrup, 'Det nordiske samarbeidet på familierettens område' (1988) 4 *Tidsskrift for Rettsvitenskap* 567.

10 The deferred community of property regime was later introduced in Finland and Iceland.

Law professors were appointed as chairmen in Denmark, Norway and Iceland, allowing academia to maintain a substantial influence. Conversely, in Sweden, the committee was without expert knowledge from a law professor. The chairman was a Supreme Court judge, and some politicians had become members of the committee.

Phase 3: 1969–1998 – Sweden Withdraws from Cooperation

The 1968 youth uprising led to major societal changes, especially regarding new family forms and altered social habits. The key issue during these years was the regulation of unmarried cohabitation, which was rapidly increasing. Family law suddenly became politically interesting. In Sweden, the desire for radical reforms was strongest, resulting in very modest interest in cooperation. In 1972, the guidelines for Sweden's new policy of neutrality were outlined by the Minister of Justice, who stated that the law should be neutral concerning different forms of cohabitation and moral views.[11] Marriage was to retain a central role, with an emphasis on autonomy. As the Swedish politicians aimed to implement reforms quickly, they deemed it unrealistic to introduce the same rules in all the Nordic countries. Sweden concluded that there was no reason to wait for the last country to finish.[12] Within the Swedish committee's work, politicians began to play a significant role. The committee now consisted of six politicians – three Social Democrats and three from the right or centre parties – with a lawyer as the chairman. In 1973, a Swedish Act on Unmarried Cohabitants' Joint Dwelling was introduced, regulating which cohabitee, upon the termination of the relationship, had the right to take over the joint dwelling. The decision was based on need, similar to spouses, and the Act covered leased property or dwellings owned by the cohabitees or one of them on a tenant basis.

In 1969, a Danish committee dealing with marriage and unmarried cohabitation was established, consisting of equal numbers of lawyers and politicians from each party in Parliament. The committee ended up with 18 members, 11 of whom were politicians. A district court president was appointed as chairman, but a family law professor as a member was lacking. Following the committee's proposal, a new rule was introduced in 1982 in the Tenancy Act.[13] This rule applied to parties living in the same household including cohabitants. The decision on taking over the lease was based on need considerations, but they were not the only criterion as in Sweden. In cases where cohabitation was terminated after two years, a court could decide which party should be entitled to continue the tenancy, considering any special circumstances, including the welfare of any minor children.

Regarding the division of property after the termination of cohabitation, the legal position in the Nordic countries developed at different paces and provided very different legal protections for the weaker party, see further details below in section 7.1.

11 See Swedish Report SOU 1972:41, p. 57.

12 See K. Boele-Woelki and T. Sverdrup (eds), above n. 1, p. 21.

13 See Danish Report No. 915/1980, p. 90.

Denmark amended its marriage acts several times, while the other four countries introduced new acts on marriage in the 1980s and 1990s.[14]

Phase 4: 1998 – Cooperation in Academia

Around 1998, academia was given the task of collaborating across the Nordic countries. This work was initiated by the increasingly divergent legal situations regarding family law, inheritance law and child law in the Nordic countries. Many families who had moved from one Nordic country to another experienced legal uncertainty. To enhance harmonisation, the Nordic Council of Ministers commenced work within these three legal areas to clarify the similarities and differences among the five Nordic countries. The focus was on the wording of the existing acts in the areas mentioned, their interpretation and their purpose. Additionally, the project aimed to identify areas that could form the basis for Nordic legislative work in the short, medium and long term. In June 1998, the Nordic Council entrusted the project to three family law professors from Sweden, Norway and Denmark. During 2003–2004, the project resulted in the publication of four books, each around 500 pages, which were included in the Nordic Council of Ministers' publications.[15] The books described the legal positions of all five countries, with the same subtitle: 'A comparative study of Danish, Finnish, Icelandic, Norwegian, and Swedish law, discussing harmonisation possibilities and reform needs'. The Scandinavian authors wrote in their respective languages, and they had engaged in intense collaboration with each other. They had also assistance from colleagues in Finland and Iceland, so that the authors could describe the legal situation of the two countries correctly.[16] Before the publication of the books, Professors Anders Agell and Peter Lødrup wrote a summary on the possibilities and benefits of the legal harmonisation of marriage and inheritance law for a session at the 36th Nordic Lawyers' Meeting in 2001.[17] Again in 2005, Professors Anders Agell, Peter Lødrup and Svend Danielsen delivered a joint presentation for a family law session on Nordic law harmonisation in family law at the 37th Nordic Lawyers' Meeting.[18]

---

14 See K. Boele-Woelki and T. Sverdrup, above n. 1, p. 22.

15 P. Lødrup, *Nordisk arverett*, Nord 2003:3, Nordisk Ministerråd, Copenhagen 2002; A. Agell, *Nordisk äktenskapsrätt*, 2003:2, Nordiske Ministerråd, Copenhagen 2003; P. Lødrup, A. Agell and A. Singer, *Nordisk børneret I: Farskap, morskap og underhåll till barn*, Nord 2003:3, Nordisk Ministerråd, Copenhagen 2003; and S. Danielsen, *Nordisk børneret II: Forældreansvar*, Nord 2003:14, Nordisk Ministerråd, Copenhagen 2003.

16 19 meetings had been held over a total of 55 days.

17 Äktenskapsrätten och successionsrätten i de fem nordiska länderna. Om möjlighetema och nyttan av lagharmonisering. See *Förhandlingarna vid Det 36 nordiska juristmötet i Helsingfors 15–17 augusti 2002*, utgivna av lokalstyrelsen för Finland, Helsingfors, 2002, pp. 37–85, https://jura.ku.dk/jurabog/pdf/ nordiske-juristmoeder.

18 *Forhandlingerne ved det 37. nordiske Juristmøde i Reykjavik, 18.-20. august 2005*, vol. 1, udgivet af Den islandske Styrelse, Reykjavik 2005, pp. 7–36, https://jura.ku.dk/jurabog/pdf/ nordiske-juristmoeder.

The Nordic books have been important in several ways. Lawyers facing legal issues in other Nordic countries have benefited from the wealth of information in the books. Furthermore, the books have frequently been used for research in comparative Nordic law, and the legal policy considerations in the books have proven useful in this context. On the other hand, there has been limited interest at the ministerial level in utilising the harmonisation considerations of the Nordic family law books, even though the project was presented at two Nordic Lawyers' Meetings immediately after each other.

As the legal status of unmarried cohabitants was not included in the Nordic Council project of 1998, six professors from the Scandinavian region decided to write a book on Nordic cohabitation law based on the same model with consulting assistance from two professors from Finland and Iceland, respectively.[19] The authors were inspired to collaborate by a Nordic family law seminar on unmarried cohabitation at Uppsala University in 2009. In 2014, the book *Nordisk Samboerrett* was published, written in the Scandinavian languages.[20] The following year, an English version, *Nordic Cohabitation Law*, was published in the European Family Law Series.[21]

In Denmark, a committee undertook, from 2009 to 2015, a considerable revision of the legislation on the property relations of spouses. The committee had to address a number of issues of both a technical and principled nature. As family law reforms were no longer considered to be a political issue, politicians were not appointed as members. The members were nominated by several relevant organisations, and one member was personally appointed due to his specific expertise. The committee consisted of 11 expert members, all of whom were lawyers, including a professor of family law, a special expert in family law, two family law attorneys, representatives from the courts, and representatives of ministries and agencies. The chairman was a high court judge. The terms of reference stated: 'In light of the tradition of cooperation between the Nordic countries in the area of family law, the committee should include the development trends in other Nordic countries in its work.'[22] In the final report, each of chapters 5–17 included a description of the legal situation in Norway and Sweden. Additionally, in 2011, Professor Tone Sverdrup from the University of Oslo met with the committee. It is quite common for Nordic committees in their introductory phase to invite a law professor from another Nordic country to provide information about the legal situation in that country. Sverdrup thoroughly explained the Norwegian property regime of spouses, particularly

19 See on the authors' proposals for a Cohabitation Act below section 7.4.

20 J. Asland, M. Brattström, G. Lind, I. Lund-Andersen, A. Singer and T. Sverdrup, *Nordisk Samboerrett*, Gyldendal Norsk Forlag AS, Oslo 2014.

21 J. Asland, M. Brattström, G. Lind, I. Lund-Andersen, A. Singer and T. Sverdrup, *Nordic Cohabitation Law*, Intersentia, Cambridge/Antwerp/Portland 2015.

22 Report No. 1552:2015 p. 150.

regarding the division of property, debt and compensation claims. However, at this time, no other committees in the Nordic countries were addressing these topics. Therefore, the aim was not to achieve Nordic harmonisation, but to gain inspiration.

A majority in the Danish Marriage Committee proposed a new type of division rule, which involved a gradual division of the community property, so that spouses would only equally share the property after seven years of marriage.[23] The committee's minority found that a major argument against this model was that it does not exist in any other European countries, including other Nordic countries.[24] Two minority members proposed a division model that bore similarities to the German *Zugewinngemeinschaft* and to the Norwegian rule of unequal division, according to which, at the request of a spouse, there is no division of the value of the assets that a spouse possessed before marriage, or gifts and inheritances.[25] Such a legal regulation exists in many European countries. Another minority member proposed a discretionary unequal division rule, which corresponded to the proposal that a minority member had made in the Norwegian Marriage Committee's report from 1987.[26]

The Danish Ministry for Children and Social Affairs decided not to make any changes in the new act on the property regime between spouses, as the deferred community of property is simple, predictable and reasonable.[27] Spouses were instead encouraged to make use of the extensive freedom to agree on individual arrangements. In short-term marriages, a narrow unequal division rule was maintained.

7. NEW FAMILY FORMS

The legal framework surrounding the division of property for unmarried cohabitants illustrates the varied solutions the Nordic countries have adopted in the absence of cooperation, resulting in markedly different levels of protection for the weaker party. One important difference lies in whether a solution is based on the principles of property law or whether special family law rules have been introduced for unmarried cohabitants. Another key distinction is whether the

23 Ibid., pp. 249–252. Inspiration for this proposal was probably taken from the Finnish and Swedish proposals for a step-by-step increased division of spouses' property within the first ten years of marriage, see the Swedish Family Law Committee's considerations in report SOU 1981:85, pp. 170–173. These proposals were never implemented.

24 Ibid., p. 254.

25 Ibid., pp. 249, 252–257.

26 Ibid., pp. 262–264.

27 Explanatory notes to proposal no. L 178 of the Danish Parliament 2016–17 on the Act regarding Spouses' Economic Relations.

legal status of unmarried cohabitants corresponds, in whole or in part, to that of married couples, or if cohabitants are accorded a less extensive legal status.

Regarding the regulation of same-sex relationships within family law, all Nordic countries have, one by one, supported giving same-sex couples the same legal status as spouses. This progressive approach has quickly positioned the Nordic countries on the global map as particularly progressive.

The following section will provide a retrospective look at these developments.

7.1. PROPERTY RELATIONS BETWEEN COHABITANTS

As unmarried cohabitation became more common around 1970, the courts had to find a solution for how to divide the assets. The primary issue involved the division of the typically most valuable asset – the value of the family home – which was often solely owned by one party, generally the man, according to official documents. In these cases, judges had to base their decisions on property law principles interpreted within a family law context.

In Norway, Iceland and Sweden, the courts opted in these cases for a broader application of co-ownership than that provided for by general principles of the law of property. The Supreme Court of Norway reached the most favourable decision for the weaker party, determining in 1975 that the efforts of a housewife can be considered equivalent to making a financial contribution to acquiring co-ownership (a housewife judgment). To establish co-ownership in these situations, there must be substantial direct or indirect contributions, and the property must be purchased as a joint project for the couple's common use.[28] The same assessment applies to the relationship between spouses. In Iceland, since 1981 the courts have developed case law on co-ownership that resembles Norwegian law, although in recent years higher demands have been placed on financial contributions.

Since the early 1980s, Swedish case law has evolved to recognise a principle of concealed co-ownership.[29] The prerequisites for this principle are that the concealed owner must have made a financial contribution to the open owner's acquisition of the property intended for the couple's joint use, and that both parties must have operated under the assumption that the property would be co-owned. Today, this principle is primarily viewed within the context of family law, and it is equally applicable to both cohabitants and spouses.

In Denmark, the regional courts in the 1970s similarly established co-ownership based on a broader discretionary assessment, which included both financial contributions and household and care work from the party who

28 Ibid., pp. 71–75.
29 Ibid., pp. 66–67.

was not the registered owner. This practice, which only applied to cohabitants and not to spouses, bore similarities to the Swedish practice regarding the concealed rights of co-ownership. In 1980, the Danish Supreme Court rejected this specific co-ownership construction and instead awarded the non-owner a compensation amount based on the doctrine of unjust enrichment and the doctrine of reasonable expectations.[30] Contributions in the form of childcare and housework are only acknowledged to a limited extent.

Finnish legal practice largely alternates between the Swedish solution and the Danish equivalent, with a high standard of proof being required for the parties' intention before a departure from formal ownership is permitted.[31] In cases where co-ownership is not established, it is possible in Norway and Finland to award compensation – often in limited amounts – based on considerations similar to those in Denmark.[32] The Swedish courts have been reluctant to apply the doctrine of unjust enrichment,[33] while the state of the law in Iceland remains unclear.[34]

Sweden and Finland have introduced legislation regarding the division of property between cohabitants, which is why legal practice concerning co-ownership in the two countries is no longer so important, yet it remains applicable. In Sweden, the Cohabitants (Joint Homes) Act was introduced in 1987. According to this act the net value of the joint home and household goods shall be divided between cohabitants, provided the goods have been acquired during cohabitation.[35] As regards the joint home and household goods, this solution deals with cohabitants in the same way as married partners with deferred community property. Consequently, the division rule can be seen as the implementation of the principle of neutrality between different forms of family structures.

In 2010, an act was passed in Finland, the Act on Dissolution of the Household of Cohabiting Partners, which was based on principles of unjust enrichment.[36] A cohabitant may acquire a right to compensation, contingent upon an evaluation of contributions to the shared household, which in turn has facilitated the other cohabitant in increasing or preserving their property. Contributions for the benefit of the joint household include work for the household, paying for joint household expenses and the investment of money in the property that is owned by the other cohabitant.

Some of the solutions chosen in the Nordic countries differ significantly from each other, while others share certain similarities. From a democratic

---

30 Ibid., p. 65 and pp. 119–122.
31 Ibid., p. 65.
32 Ibid., pp. 124–128.
33 Ibid., pp. 129–130.
34 Ibid., pp. 128–129.
35 Ibid., pp. 114–117.
36 Ibid., pp. 117–119.

perspective, it may be concerning that a few judges at the Supreme Court determine a legal position in one country, while in other countries statutory laws are enacted on the basis of thorough preparation. In all countries, family law considerations have been incorporated to varying degrees, with the aim of protecting the weaker party. However, from a Nordic perspective, it seems unsustainable that in some situations an economically disadvantaged cohabitant in one country will not be awarded any amount, while in another country the same individual would be entitled to a larger sum.[37]

7.2. THE LEGAL SITUATION OF SAME-SEX COUPLES

In Sweden, a commission issued a report in 1984 on 'The Situation of Homosexuals in Society'.[38] The commission concluded that cohabiting homosexual couples should be granted legal protection equal to that applicable to heterosexual non-marital *de facto* cohabitation according to the 1973 Act on the Joint Home of Unmarried Cohabitees. The commission did not support the introduction of a solution allowing same-sex couples to register in order to obtain legal rights, as such a scheme could undesirably identify homosexual individuals, thereby risking the reinforcement of prejudices against them.

The solution proposed by the commission was subsequently followed, and the Cohabitants (Joint Homes) Act of 1987 was extended to also cover homosexual couples.

Denmark was the first country in the world, in 1989, to introduce an Act on Registered Partnership with nearly the same legal effects as marriage.[39] The main reason for introducing the act was to make a political statement favouring the visibility of homosexual people in society. Only by giving these couples almost the same legal status as married couples would it be possible to gain full social recognition. However, the road towards this goal was not without obstacles. The Danish HomoCommission published a report in 1988. The majority (six) of the members were against the introduction of this new legal institution. Among the six members were a judge, four officials from different ministries and the chairman, who was a Member of Parliament for the Socialist People's Party. The majority stated that there was no need for such a far-reaching act and that there could be negative reactions from other countries. The minority (five) of the members pointed out that specific amendments in certain laws were unable to achieve the same results as registration. Three minority members were representatives from the National Association of Lesbian and Gay People, who

37 Ibid., pp. 131–132.
38 Report SOU 1984:63.
39 The 1989 Act made exceptions regarding the legal status in relation to children and access to a church ceremony, which was later amended.

had for many years worked to obtain increased rights for same-sex couples, a representative from the Danish Women's Society, and a professor of sexology. The National Association of Lesbian and Gay People lobbied in favour of a registration scheme among the political parties, and a partnership bill was proposed by MPs from the Social Democratic Party and the Social Liberal Party. The MPs were given a free vote and the Registered Partnership Act was passed on 26 May 1989 by 71 votes to 47, with 5 abstentions.[40]

In Sweden, the question of formal registration was revisited after the Registered Partnership Act had been enacted in Denmark, and in 1991 the Swedish government set up a commission to consider the adoption of the Danish solution. The Commission published a report in 1993 proposing an Act on Registered Partnership.[41]

In the period from 1993 to 2001, the other Nordic countries introduced similar legislation on registered partnerships like the Danish solution: in 1993 (Norway), 1994 (Sweden), 1996 (Iceland), and 2001 (Finland). During these years, other European countries, such as the Netherlands and France, also introduced registration options with varying degrees of legal effects for same-sex couples.

The new acceptance of the regulation of same-sex couples' relationships led to increasing pressure on the governments in Europe to establish rules that allowed these couples to enter into marriage. The first two countries to allow couples of the same sex to marry were the Netherlands in 2001 and Belgium in 2003. Norway was the first of the Nordic countries where, after a lengthy debate in Parliament, a majority could agree in 2008 to introduce marriage for same-sex couples.[42]

Gender-neutral marriage was introduced in all the Nordic countries, albeit at different times: 2008 (Norway), 2009 (Sweden), 2010 (Iceland), 2012 (Denmark), and 2015 (Finland).[43] The reason why Denmark was late to introduce gender-neutral marriage was political. During the period from 2001 to 2011, the government was composed of centre and conservative parties, which did not

---

40 See more in detail I. Lund-Andersen, 'The Danish Registered Partnership Act' in K. Boele-Woelki and A. Fuchs (eds), *Legal Recognition of Same-Sex Couples in Europe*, Intersentia, Antwerp/Oxford/New York 2003, pp. 13–15. See also J.M. Lorenzo Villaverde, 'Legal Recognition of Same-Sex Couples in Denmark: From the First Debates to the Enactment off the Registered Partnership Act of 1989' in H. Petersen, J.M. Lorenzo Villaverde and I. Lund-Andersen (eds), *Contemporary Gender Relations and Changes in Legal Culture*, DJØF Publishing, Copenhagen 2013, pp. 147–164.

41 See more in detail M. Savolainen, 'The Finnish and the Swedish Partnerships Acts – Similarities and Divergencies' in K. Boele-Woelki and A. Fuchs (eds), *Legal Recognition of Same-Sex Couples in Europe*, Intersentia, Antwerp/Oxford/New York 2003, pp. 24–25.

42 See T. Eeg, 'Registered Partnerships in Norway' in J.M. Scherpe and A. Hayward (eds), *The Future of Registered Partnerships*, Intersentia Cambridge/Antwerp/Portland, 2017, p. 67.

43 See J. Asland, M. Brattström, G. Lind, I. Lund-Andersen, A. Singer and T. Sverdrup, above n. 21, pp. 267–268.

support such marriage. When the Social Democrats took office in 2011, there was then a parliamentary majority in favour of gender-neutral marriage.

This development demonstrates that the Nordic countries have moved in the same direction, although at different speeds, through inspiration and legal transplants but without closer cooperation.[44] The legal status in this area is nearly uniform. Both registered partnerships and same-sex marriage offer the advantage that once there is an acceptance of the two legal constructs, it is legally straightforward to implement them.

7.3. NORWEGIAN COMMITTEE ON COHABITATION

In February 2022, the Norwegian government established a committee to investigate whether there is a need for the financial relationship between unmarried cohabitants to be regulated, also allowing parties to opt out.[45] The deadline for the committee's work was set for 1 May 2025. The professor of family law Katrine Kjærheim Fredwall has been appointed as the head of the Cohabitation Law Committee. The remaining two members include another family law professor and a practising lawyer specialising in family law.

This committee works in a way that resembles the working method during the earlier Phase 1, see above section 6. It is a small committee, composed of only three members, with academia having a prominent role, and notably it includes no politicians. Moreover, the committee has engaged in dialogue with interest groups and with experts from other Nordic countries. In particular, it is worth noting that, in November 2022, the committee conducted a two-day working seminar in Oslo, where around ten family lawyers from across the Nordic region participated. This included several family law professors, among them four authors of the book *Nordic Cohabitation Law.*

Thus, great expectations are attached to the work being carried out by the Norwegian Committee on cohabitation.

7.4. NORDIC PRINCIPLES FOR THE REGULATION OF THE FINANCIAL CIRCUMSTANCES OF COHABITANTS

There is no political pressure group to advocate for the legal interests of unmarried cohabitants – similar to the organisations for homosexuals in the 1980s and 1990s. Therefore, the six authors of the book *Nordic Cohabitation Law* found it pertinent to outline certain principles – a concise draft law – that were rooted in the regulations established in Sweden and Finland, incorporating case law,

44 If a country adopts rules from another country, the terms 'reception' or 'transplants' are used.
45 https://nettsteder.regjeringen.no/samboerlovutvalget/.

and also demonstrating innovation in certain areas. The proposed principles deal with the financial circumstances of cohabiting couples (a Cohabitation Act).[46] These principles are intended as inspiration for future law reforms in the Nordic countries, and the principles recall the types of principles for European family law drawn up by the Commission on European Family Law.[47]

The best solutions from different Nordic countries were chosen and unified.[48] Furthermore, it was proposed to introduce two types of rules, as cohabitants with a child in common constitute a special group. These couples bear the responsibility to ensure that their child has the best possible upbringing conditions, even after the end of the cohabitation, and therefore the parents should be covered by extensive property rules.

When a cohabiting relationship is terminated, the principle of the division of property states that for cohabitants with a child in common, the division rules should be similar to the Swedish Cohabitation Act's division rule concerning the joint home and the household goods.[49] For other couples and as a supplement to the aforementioned rule, a discretionary compensation rule was proposed if a cohabitant has significantly contributed to the increase in the value of the other's property during the cohabiting relationship by contributing to the common expenses, by housework or care provision, or otherwise. This principle is based on the doctrine of unjust enrichment. This doctrine lies behind the Finnish rule on compensation and the awards of compensation in Finnish, Danish and Norwegian case law. This principle is supplemented by a broad discretionary assessment principle to ensure that a party is not placed in an unreasonable financial situation. Finally, the only restriction on the freedom of contract was that cohabitants with a child in common during cohabitation may not waive the rights derived from the discretionary assessment principle, which provides minimum protection.

The formulation of these principles was established through a couple of meetings, where the authors engaged in thorough discussions regarding the overarching concepts and the precise wording of the principles themselves. Consensus was achieved with relative ease, as all participants were experts in the field and had no vested interests to protect. The objective was to select the solution that would function optimally across the Nordic countries. Particularly noteworthy was the support for more extensive rules concerning cohabiting couples with a child in common, an innovative idea. Detailed comments were attached to the proposed principles.[50] This comprehensive proposal for legislative

---

46 J. Asland, M. Brattström, G. Lind, I. Lund-Andersen, A. Singer and T. Sverdrup, above n. 21, pp. 280–282.
47 Ibid., p. 269 n. 12.
48 Ibid., pp. 280–282.
49 See above section 7.1.
50 J. Asland, M. Brattström, G. Lind, I. Lund-Andersen, A. Singer and T. Sverdrup, above n. 21, pp. 269–280.

principles also included matters of succession, taking over a joint dwelling and household goods, as well as contracts.

The principles were presented at the 40th Nordic Lawyers' Meeting in August 2014 during the session entitled 'The Legal Status of Cohabitants in the Nordic Countries'. It was emphasised during the session meeting that the aim of the proposed principles is not to create common Nordic legislation, but rather for the principles to serve as a source of inspiration, so that legal development moves in the same direction, i.e. towards a greater degree of harmonisation. The discussion revealed that significantly more people were in favour of legislation inspired by the principles than were against it.[51]

8. CONCLUDING CONSIDERATIONS

The golden age of Nordic cooperation in family law was in the early 20th century, when the forward-looking marriage acts were crafted in the three Scandinavian countries. The efforts towards harmonisation were significant. Legal experts in family law served on the marriage committees. Through cooperation, they aimed to introduce new legislation reflecting the spirit of the times by granting rights to women, whose roles in society were undergoing substantial changes. Since then, reforms of national marriage acts have taken place at different times. However, harmonisation exists on an overarching level, as highlighted by Professor Peter Lødrup in 2008.[52] There is a Nordic model, even after the most recent major reforms in the area, the latest being in 2018, when a new act concerning the financial relations of spouses was introduced in Denmark. The most notable aspect of the new act was the retention of the deferred community of property as the default system.

The next legal reform, where societal groups demanded rights as a result of changes in social and moral conditions, was the regulation for same-sex couples. Once again, similar societal conditions in the Nordic countries paved the way for adopting the same approach. Uniform rules came into force in all of the countries in question, not through cooperation but through mutual inspiration.

The same degree of harmonised rules, unfortunately, has not been implemented concerning the division of property between unmarried cohabitants on the termination of cohabitation. The legal status has developed in a fragmentary way. Legal experts in the field believe that there is potential for a higher degree of harmonisation in the longer term, although not all rules need

---

51 *Forhandlingene ved det 40. nordiske juristmøte i Oslo, 21.–22. august 2014*, vol. 2, udgitt av det norske styret, Oslo 2015, pp. 141–143, https://jura.ku.dk/jurabog/pdf/nordiske-juristmoeder.

52 See K. Boele-Woelki and T. Sverdrup (eds), above n. 1, p. 25.

to be identical.[53] It is likely that the only way towards a more harmonised legal status for unmarried cohabitants is if the Nordic Council of Ministers reaches an agreement to initiate such work.

Among lawyers there is still great interest in the Nordic community, as evidenced by the overwhelming participation from all countries at the Nordic Lawyers' Meetings, with over 1,000 attendees from a wide range of legal disciplines. Although discussions at the meetings do not always lead to swift action, they often lay the groundwork for actions to be taken at a later stage. Furthermore, the current family law topics are discussed at Nordic family law seminars and the debate may lead to collaborations among university staff in the Nordic countries, including on articles or books to be jointly written.

Overall, the Nordic cooperation today is no longer as focused on harmonisation, but there is a strong desire for inspiration, which could result in the countries moving in the same direction.

53 See J. Asland, M. Brattström, G. Lind, I. Lund-Andersen, A. Singer and T. Sverdrup, above n. 21, pp. 268–269.

CHILD LAW IN THE NORDIC COUNTRIES

Principles and Present Challenges

Hrefna FRIÐRIKSDÓTTIR

1. WHAT IS CHILD LAW?

The title of this chapter begs the following question: what is child law? Historically, the focus in child law has been on the formal legal relationship between children and parents. This can be referred to as child law in a narrow sense, within the realm of family law, framing concepts such as mother, father, parent, parental responsibilities, contact and parental child support. In modern times, child law in a broad sense refers to the legal framework that governs all rights of children, a discipline in its own right but also intersecting with multiple other legal disciplines.[1] This is often discussed under the framework of children's rights with a reference to the broad scope of the Convention on the Rights of the Child (CRC).[2]

The aim of this chapter is to present the general principles underpinning child law in the narrow sense and to offer reflections on a few challenges within child law.

2. NORDIC CHILD LAW

The Nordic countries share a history, culture and common values, and in particular they have a long history of legislative cooperation with the aim of attaining the greatest possible uniformity.[3] Child law in the Nordic countries is firmly embedded in the developments of the Nordic welfare model. The Nordic model is moulded on principles of equal opportunity and social security

---

1 L.R.L. BENDIKSEN and T. HAUGLI, *Sentrale emner i barneretten* 5th ed., Universitetsforlaget, Oslo 2022, pp. 23–26.

2 W. VANDENHOLE et al., *Children's Rights: A Commentary on the Convention on the Rights of the Child and its Protocols*, Edward Elgar Publishing, Cheltenham 2019, p. xvii.

3 U. BERNITZ, 'What is Scandinavian Law?' (2007) 50(1) *Scandinavian Studies in Law* 28.

with an emphasis on social cohesion, pragmatic solutions, consultations and compromises.[4]

Historically, legal relationships between children and parents constituted links to property, power and obligations. In modern times, these relationships are strongly related to rights, care and commitments. This broad perspective requires a careful balancing of (often) contradictory notions of rights, responsibilities and empowerment, as well as protection, needs and wants.[5]

It is also important to realise that law is limited in dealing with the growing complexities of family life. It may be easy to identify general principles in child law but much more difficult to create a holistic, rational, unified system. This is evident in the Nordic countries.

3. GENERAL PRINCIPLES IN NORDIC CHILD LAW

The two general principles that overwhelmingly underpin child law in the Nordic countries (and beyond) are *gender equality* and *the best interests of the child*.[6] In recent times it has become increasingly challenging and complicated to define, integrate and balance these principles in law and practice.

Gender equality is a fundamental ideology in the Nordic countries. The Nordic countries have all ratified (and some have legalised) the United Nations Convention on the Elimination of All Forms of Discrimination Against Women (CEDAW) from 1979, which establishes common principles that the states are committed to respect. The Nordic countries were instrumental in shaping Article 5 CEDAW, which requires all appropriate measures to be taken to modify the social and cultural patterns of conduct with a view to achieving the elimination of prejudices and all practices based on stereotyped roles for men and women. The Nordic countries are thus committed to eliminating entrenched gendered roles in relation to child law. With changing social conceptions of gender and family formations and biotechnological advances, it becomes increasingly difficult to judge which differences actually warrant different treatment and in what context.

The best interests of the child has been the guiding compass for the development of all child law reforms for many decades. Since the early 20th century, the Nordic countries have strived to make children and their needs the axis

---

4 H. Friðriksdóttir, 'The Nordic Model: Same-Sex Families in Love and Law' in D. Gallo, L. Paladini and P. Pustorino (eds), *Same-Sex Couples before National, Supranational and International Jurisdictions*, Springer, Berlin/Heidelberg 2014.

5 H. Friðriksdóttir, 'Nordic Family Law: New Framework – New Fatherhoods'. in G.B. Eydal and T. Rorstgaard (eds), *Fatherhood in the Nordic Welfare States: Comparing Care Policies and Practice*, Policy Press, Bristol 2015, p. 55.

6 Ibid., p. 56.

of family law instead of the perspective of parents.[7] Some significant steps are obvious, such as abolishing differences between children born within and out of wedlock. In modern times, the fundamental values that guide child law reform are enshrined in the CRC from 1989, which the Nordic countries have all ratified (and many have legalised). One of the most significant articles thereof is Article 3, which requires that the best interests of the child shall be a primary consideration in all actions concerning children. But we are all aware of the ambiguities in best interests tests and how they provide more questions than answers.[8] The Nordic model has relied to a certain extent on social and psychological sciences, which can play an important role. Firstly, research can provide knowledge to support law reform, and secondly, such sciences provide important tools to determine individual cases. Alas, both uses are limited and are sensitive to historical and cultural biases and moral value judgements.[9]

Law reform in the Nordic countries within the area of child law has consistently been based on the above-mentioned abstract principles of justice, with their embedded ideas that children benefit from the common responsibilities of both parents to protect and care for them. But actual legal regulation is about more than just abstract principles; it also requires a much more detailed realisation of actual rights and responsibilities in different settings. The search for a balance between gender equality and the best interests principle has been a persistent challenge in the Nordic countries.[10] This is reflected in the fact that the laws on the relationship between parents and children in the Nordic countries have been under almost constant revision since the beginning of the 1980s. And solutions are becoming more and more diverse.

4. SOME CHALLENGES

The aim here is to reflect on some challenges that the Nordic countries face in balancing the above-mentioned principles when regulating different aspects of child law. This section will focus on some thought-provoking questions rather than providing an in-depth analysis or answers.

---

7 Ibid., p. 56–57.

8 Vandenhole argues that Article 3 remains one of the most controversial and debated provisions of the CRC, W. Vandenhole et al., above n. 2, p. 60.

9 See e.g. M. Garrison, 'Integrating Facts and Values in Family Law' in J. Scherpe and S. Gilmore (eds), *Family Matters: Essays in Honour of John Eekelaar*, Intersentia, Cambridge/Antwerp 2022, pp. 181–196.

10 Ibid., pp. 70–72. Sverdrup has argued that 'child law has become a battlefield for gender policy', T. Sverdrup, 'Norway: equal rights at any cost?' in E.E. Sutherland (ed.), *Future of Child and Family Law: International Predictions*, Cambridge University Press, Cambridge 2012, pp. 296–329. See also T. Sverdrup, 'The changing concept of "family" and challenges for family law in the Nordic countries' in J. Scherpe (ed.), *European Family Law: Volume II*, Edward Elgar Publishing, Cheltenham 2016, p. 202.

The regulation of child law in the narrow sense can be broadly divided into two parts: on the one hand, rules on *becoming a parent* and, on the other, rules on *being a parent.*

4.1. BECOMING A PARENT

Medical advances in assisted reproductive technologies (ART) have brought numerous challenges with them. A fundamental question is what should be the defining factors in allocating parenthood. To what extent should it be biology, to what extent should it be a contract between or the consent of persons wishing to be parents and persons willing to donate gametes, and how should we recognise and value social relationships?

With regard to biology, medical advances today and in the future will give rise to extremely complicated questions about what building blocks of life or the origins of a child actually are.[11] How does the right of a child to know its origins tie in with different rules on the allocation of parenthood?

And what does it mean to prioritise biology in allocating parenthood? Do we see *pater est/parens est* rules as mainly upholding marriage as the preferred status and providing practical solutions – or do we see *pater est* as a strong presumption of a biological truth? On the one hand, relying on the former set of justifications can be framed as discriminatory if this results in not applying *pater est/parens est* to lesbian marriages. On the other hand, relying on the latter set of justifications makes it rational to only apply *pater est/parens est* where a biological link is possible (and is considered overwhelmingly likely).

Another question is whether there is a fundamental difference between the person giving birth and the other parent. Can we justify allocating parenthood differently to a person providing an egg and a person providing sperm? In this area, the acceptance and regulation of surrogacy plays an important part, as rejecting surrogacy arrangements makes it difficult to accept an egg donor as a parent. This also raises the question of what the intentions and outcomes are for banning or allowing surrogacy arrangements.

What does it mean to prioritise contract or consent? Should one be able to contract in and out of parenthood? And if so, subject to what conditions? This ties in with the question of whether the same rules should apply to informal and formal ART or whether there are fundamental differences that justify different treatment.

---

11 See further e.g. H. Willekens, 'What (If Anything) Can Justify the Use of Biological Criteria for Allocating Parental Rights and Obligations?' in J. Scherpe and S. Gilmore (eds), *Family Matters: Essays in Honour of John Eekelaar*, Intersentia, Cambridge/Antwerp 2022, pp. 567–580.

4.2. BEING A PARENT: EXERCISING PARENTAL RESPONSIBILITIES

As mentioned above, legislative reforms in recent decades have increasingly centred on co-parenting ideals. Special measures have been designed to strengthen these ideals and to modify gendered behaviour in this respect.

This works well when parents are together. When parents are not together, co-parenting ideals have created extensive tensions between competing ideas of active/involved parents and equal parents.

I will go so far as to say that legal reforms and practices on equal shared parenting have in fact instigated – in a relatively short period of time – an enormous, far-reaching social experiment in how children perceive concepts such as the home, family, relationships, stability and care.

The greatest challenges in this area relate to how general principles have become political slogans and tools for competing interest groups and how general principles are thus defined and interpreted too broadly as legal presumptions.[12]

Carefully crafted policies on *shared parenting* can encourage understanding, acceptance and parental co-operation – both in relation to law reform and also to inform best interest tests for each and every child. Broad presumptions of *equal shared parenting* are prone to simplifications, thus disregarding the best interests of each child involved, and can provide avenues for ongoing power imbalances, harassment, intimidation and violence. A growing concern is, for example, a disregard for the complexities of contact disputes – the persistent ideas of punishing the 'bad' parent seen as alienating the child from the 'good' parent and ignoring the effects that such measures can have on the child involved.

5. REFLECTIONS

There is no definitive, scientific solution for how to balance gender equality and the best interests of the child. Excessive dependence on abstract principles is misleading and can end up being harmful. In the search for a satisfactory balance it may be helpful to keep in mind that:

- the implementation of the general principles in child law has to be multidimensional;[13]

---

12 See similar criticism of legal reform in Australia, R. Chisholm, 'Reforming Children's Law: Learning from the Australian Experience' in J. Scherpe and S. Gilmore (eds), *Family Matters: Essays in Honour of John Eekelaar*, Intersentia, Cambridge/Antwerp 2022, pp. 835–852.

13 See further e.g. M. Maclean, 'Family Law and Social Policy: Justice and Welfare' in J. Scherpe and S. Gilmore (eds), *Family Matters: Essays in Honour of John Eekelaar*, Intersentia, Cambridge/Antwerp 2022, pp. 41–56.

- we have to balance, on the one hand, parentage and, on the other, parenthood – carefully looking at who contributes to the making of a child and who should subsequently become a parent and why – and then look at what it means to be a parent;
- as far as possible we need to balance intentions with actual outcomes, for all children and for each and every child;
- importantly, we need to restrict the use of presumptions in imposing parenting or contact regimes;
- specifically, we need to be mindful of lived gendered realities, and the extra burdens that rules may place on actual primary carers; and
- we need to carefully create and balance substantive rules and interdisciplinary procedural provisions – with a view to reducing parental conflicts, both in the short term and in the long run if at all possible.

FUTURE NORDIC COOPERATION IN SUBSTANTIVE FAMILY LAW

What? Why? How?

Tone Sverdrup

A new party constellation has emerged in family law over the past 50 years: two parties that both participate in the market and at the same time live together in an economic union with a shared residence and consumption. This party constellation came to life in the 1970s when married women entered the paid workforce on a large scale. Since then, we have seen a rising number of divorces, a sharp increase in the number of cohabitants and an increase in wealth, which together have led to many disputes over financial assets both in the Nordic countries and other countries in the Western world.

Two parties that act independently in the market and at the same time form a unit of work, consumption and investment – does any similar party relationship exist in private law? The closest would be two participants in a company – but the economic mechanisms are quite different: the more capital that is injected into a company, the greater the expected profits. The more capital that is injected at the start of a marriage, the less value will usually be created during the relationship.

This phenomenon can be illustrated with an example where Peter owns a house before he meets Mary. They have two children and enter into a marriage a few years later. The spouses have average incomes and do not need to save much, because the home is already mostly paid off. Twenty years later they divorce. Peter keeps the value of the house undivided, as only assets created during the marriage are divided equally upon divorce in their jurisdiction.[1] Mary is left with nothing.

---

1 Premarital assets, gifts and inheritances are exempted from division in many countries in Southern and Eastern Europe, as well as in countries like Germany, Switzerland, Norway and the Netherlands, see K. Boele-Woelki, F. Ferrand, C. González Beilfuss, M. Jänterä-Jareborg, N. Lowe, D. Martiny and V. Todorova, *The Principles of European Family Law Revisited*, Intersentia, Cambridge 2024, pp. 133–177. See also K. Boele-Woelki, F. Ferrand, C. González Beilfuss, M. Jänterä-Jareborg, Nigel Lowe, D. Martiny and W. Pintens, *Principles of European Family Law Regarding Property Relations Between Spouses*, Intersentia, Cambridge 2013.

What should Mary have done differently? She should have set aside part of her income during the relationship in the event of a possible future divorce. However, it is hard for the non-owning partner to make such provisions, as they form a joint consumption unit. The two spouses share the same meals, go on the same holidays together, and – last but not least – both are responsible for their children's expenses. In practice, they must agree on reducing consumer expenditure in the family. For the majority of spouses with average income levels, most expenses appear to be necessary. For couples in higher income brackets, it is easier, as it is a matter of reducing more luxury-oriented consumption.

Therefore, a home owned by one of the partners before marriage or cohabitation is often an impediment to capital accumulation during the relationship. The partners adjust their level of consumption to the fact that the basic investment in a home is already available. The outcomes are particularly noticeable in the Nordic countries where the majority own (rather than rent) their homes.[2] The majority of couples will use their income for the family's ongoing consumption expenses and the spouse without property will be hard hit when nothing is saved for equal distribution when they part company.

Premarital assets, gifts and inheritances are exempted from equal division upon divorce in many countries. The rationale is likely to be that such assets are not the result of joint efforts by the spouses during their marriage. The other spouse has not contributed to the accumulation of these assets; therefore, they should not be divided equally at the end of the relationship. One might ask what kind of justice underlies this rationale. If we consider the two Aristotelian conceptions of justice – corrective and distributive justice – we can conclude that this is a form of corrective justice: one transfer is the reason for the other transfer between two parties. It is not distributive justice, where benefits are allocated equitably between the parties based on their relative merits.[3]

Corrective justice is the DNA of private law – a loss or gain that one party has inflicted on the other justifies a transfer in the opposite direction, and the status quo will then be restored.[4] Reciprocity is the fundamental principle underlying not only contract law but torts and unjust enrichment as well. The parties' performances are compared with the aim of achieving the highest possible correlation between performance and return.

---

2 About 80% of the population live in an owner occupied home in Norway: https://www.ssb.no/bygg-bolig-og-eiendom/bolig-og-boforhold/statistikk/boforhold-registerbasert. In Finland about 70%, in Sweden around 65% and in Denmark about 60%: https://ec.europa.eu/eurostat/databrowser/view/ILC_LVHO02__custom_3553007/bookmark/table?lang=en&bookmarkId=2457e44e-df35-4995-aacc-e79684402691.

3 T. Sverdrup, 'Contractual thinking in couple relationships' in S. Millns and S. Wong (eds), *Wealth and Poverty in Close Personal Relationships: Money Matters*, Routledge, Abingdon/New York 2017, chapter 6.

4 E.J. Weinrib, *The Idea of Private Law*, Harvard University Press, Cambridge, MA 1995.

In market relationships, it would be unthinkable to claim compensation from a homeowner on the grounds that one had been living in the owner's home and was therefore impeded from investing in a home oneself. In intimate relationships, however, the logic is different, as demonstrated by the example above. The family home holds a unique position and cannot be compared with any other item of property.

Over time, it has become increasingly evident that the principles of corrective justice do not always align well when applied to economic settlements following the breakdown of intimate relationships. Let us illustrate the issue with another example, this time from a *de facto* relationship. The cohabiting couple, Anna and George, share domestic work and childcare equally, but George's income is significantly higher than Anna's. She earns €25,000 a year (after tax) while George earns €40,000 (after tax). Corrective justice implies that cohabitants should pay for their own consumption – in this case, they should each cover half of the family's consumption expenses. The yearly consumption expenditure for this family is €50,000; therefore, they should each cover €25,000. This means that Anna's entire income goes towards covering the family's consumption expenses, while George invests or saves €15,000 per year. Over the next ten years, George saves €150,000, while Anna still has no wealth. How could Anna manage to save money to avoid being left without assets after the breakdown of the relationship? The two cohabitants eat the same food, live in the same house, use the same household goods, and are both responsible for the children's day-to-day and other items, etc. Since they are locked into consuming equally, it seems unfair that half of the family's total consumption expenses are debited against Anna, even though this is her actual consumption. Instead of deducting half of the expenses, each party could be charged according to their ability to pay, that is, in proportion to the size of each cohabitant's respective income (adjusted for the facilitation effect of care provision, etc.). One could argue that such a calculation based on ability better reflects the economic behaviour in couple relationships.[5] However, this is not in line with corrective justice, as the cohabitants have, in fact, consumed half of the material goods each.

Corrective justice does not always fit well into marriage and cohabitation, as this concept of equality emphasises the interaction between two independent parties but overlooks that they form a collective unit. Legal professionals are bound to view couple relationships through the lens of private law, and the mindset and use of private law terminology could sometimes conceal reality. There is an interrelationship between the parties' services in marriages and cohabitation, but it is not contractual in nature. As a starting point, both parties are responsible for providing childcare and financial support, and if one

---

5 T. Sverdrup, 'Family solidarity and the mind-set of private law' (2015) 3 *Child and Family Law Quarterly* 237, 244.

undertakes either of these efforts, it proportionally affects the effort required from the other. And as we have seen, the investments of spouses (or cohabitants) are also interdependent. If one owns a house before the relationship begins, the other does not need to invest in housing, and when one of the cohabitants earns significantly more than the other, it is difficult for the latter to save money when each cover half of the family's expenses. In other words, spouses and cohabitants form both a work unit and a consumption and investment unit, and, consequently, the financial position of one party can hardly avoid being influenced by the other's. Economically, this adaptation is fundamental to living together as a unit, especially when they have children together.

This new party constellation that has emerged in the last 50 years has no parallel in the market where service and counter-service have originated independently of each other. The Nordic countries are well suited for research projects aimed at examining how different principles for the division of assets work in practice – both in marriage and in *de facto* relationships. The countries are similar in terms of their demography, culture and legal system, but have different legal regulations regarding the financial settlements after a break-up. In this way, the five countries can serve as 'control groups' for each other in studies focused on the practical workings of different financial settlements upon the breakdown of a relationship.

In marriage, all assets are divided equally upon divorce in Denmark, Finland, Iceland and Sweden. In contrast, only assets accumulated during the marriage are divided equally in Norway, where spouses keep premarital assets, gifts and inheritances undivided.[6]

In *de facto* relationships, no division of assets takes place upon a relationship breakdown in Denmark, Finland, Iceland, and Norway, as cohabitants retain their separate property and liability for debts. However, compensation for unjust or unfounded enrichment can be granted in exceptional cases.[7] Sweden stands out among the Nordic countries, as the net value of the family home and household goods is divided equally, provided these items were acquired for

---

6 See CEFL Property Relations reports by jurisdiction (https://ceflonline.net/property-relations-reports-by-jurisdiction/) and CEFL update reports 2021 (https://ceflonline.net/update-reports-by-jurisdiction/). See also K. Boele-Woelki, F. Ferrand, C. González Beilfuss, M. Jänterä-Jareborg, N. Lowe, D. Martiny and V. Todorova, above n. 1, pp. 242–253.

7 CEFL Informal Relationships reports by jurisdiction (https://ceflonline.net/informal-relationships-reports-by-jurisdiction/) and CEFL update reports 2021 (https://ceflonline.net/update-reports-by-jurisdiction/), see K. Boele-Woelki, F. Ferrand, C. González Beilfuss, M. Jänterä-Jareborg, N. Lowe, D. Martiny and V. Todorova (eds), *Principles of European Family Law Regarding Property, Maintenance and Succession Rights of Couples in de facto Unions*, Intersentia, Cambridge 2019 and K. Boele-Woelki, F. Ferrand, C. González Beilfuss, M. Jänterä-Jareborg, N. Lowe, D. Martiny and V. Todorova, above n. 1, pp. 178–223. See also T. Sverdrup, 'Regulation of cohabitation in the Nordic countries' in R. Probert and S. Thompson (eds), *Research Handbook on Marriage, Cohabitation and the Law*, Edward Elgar Publishing, Cheltenham 2024, pp. 313–321.

joint use.[8] If this settlement would result in an unreasonable outcome for the cohabitant owning most of the divisible assets, the settlement can be adjusted to result in a smaller share or no division of assets.[9]

The main question is how these different financial settlements operate in marriages and cohabitations where the partners have average incomes – in other words, for the majority of spouses and cohabitants. Equally important is how various settlements work for the children in these families – which rules create the least conflict? Several other questions may also be raised, including the sharing of pension rights and inheritance for cohabitants with joint children.

Such cross-border research where the effects of the various rules in the Nordic countries are compared requires extensive collaboration between legal academics and social scientists. Experience has shown that these kinds of interdisciplinary research projects can be difficult to implement – as social scientists do not wish to be an 'assistant science' for the legal profession, and vice versa. It might be best if these research initiatives could occur in collaboration between the Nordic countries at the governmental level.[10]

---

8 Swedish Cohabitation Act 2003, s. 3, cf. s. 4.

9 Swedish Cohabitation Act 2003, s. 15. Such an adjustment is typically seen in shorter-term relationships where gifts and inheritances are invested in the home, see M. Brattström, 'Property Issues in Cohabitation Relationships' in J. Asland, M. Brattström, G. Lind, I. Lund-Andersen, A. Singer and T. Sverdrup, *Nordic Cohabitation Law*, Intersentia, Cambridge 2015, section 2.2.3.

10 Several concrete proposals for Nordic legal cooperation – among others regarding cohabitation – are described in I. Lorange Backer, *Styrket nordisk lovsamarbeid. Muligheter og utfordringer*, Nordic Council of Ministers, 2018. This report was commissioned by the Ministers for Nordic co-operation and the Secretary General, see https://norden.diva-portal.org/smash/record.jsf?pid=diva2%3A1183811&dswid=-4557 and https://www.norden.org/en/news/review-co-operation-legislative-affairs.

PART III

REVISITING THE CEFL PRINCIPLES OF EUROPEAN FAMILY LAW AND REQUESTS FOR REFORM IN EUROPEAN JURISDICTIONS

COMPARISON AS A METHOD IN THE WORK OF THE CEFL

Dieter MARTINY

1. INTRODUCTION

This contribution will concentrate on the methods employed in the work of the Commission on European Family Law (CEFL). Three major issues will be addressed. After some brief remarks on the CEFL as such, the main aspects of comparison in the work of the CEFL are described more generally. At the end there is a look at the recently revisited Principles.

2. THE COMMISSION ON EUROPEAN FAMILY LAW

The CEFL is an independent group of family law scholars whose main goal is the creation of Principles of European Family Law that are thought to be the most suitable for harmonisation. Teamwork is a basic element of the Commission's activities. The group is made up of experienced national experts drawn from, at present, 29 jurisdictions throughout Europe;[1] they work under the guidance of CEFL's President, Professor Katharina Boele-Woelki, and an Organising Committee of seven persons. Over the years the CEFL has published more than 58 titles in its European Family Law Series, including conference reports and studies, also covering methodological issues.[2]

The harmonisation of law is a main goal of the CEFL. One of the activities of the CEFL is therefore the creation of Principles of European Family Law. Over a period of almost two decades, the CEFL has developed and published four trilingual sets of Principles covering several fields of family law:

- Divorce and Maintenance Between Former Spouses (2002);
- Parental Responsibilities (2004);

---

1 See K. BOELE-WOELKI, F. FERRAND, C. GONZÁLEZ BEILFUSS, M. JÄNTERÄ-JAREBORG, N. LOWE, D. MARTINY and V. TODOROVA, *The Principles of European Family Law Revisited*, Intersentia, Cambridge 2024, pp. 3–6. See also https://ceflonline.net/experts/.

2 See https://ceflonline.net/efl-series/.

- Property Relations Between Spouses (2008); and
- Property, Maintenance and Succession Rights of Couples in *de facto* Unions (2015).[3]

These Principles are complemented by the recently revisited Principles.

3. COMPARATIVE METHOD OF THE CEFL

3.1. GENERAL APPROACH

Comparison is one of the main elements of the work of the CEFL. It allows for the crossing of national boundaries and opens the door to harmonisation proposals. The CEFL basically follows the techniques of traditional comparative studies. However, the objective of its work is intended unification. Nevertheless, this contribution will concentrate as far as possible on the comparative process as such.

However, using comparative techniques means that not only the advantages of these methods but also their limits and weaknesses become relevant. From its very beginning, the CEFL has therefore dealt with and discussed methodological problems of comparative work in the field of family law.[4]

3.2. FIELDS THAT ARE SUITABLE FOR HARMONISATION

The CEFL concentrates mainly on single fields of family law, often in the context of outstanding or pending law reforms. However, general aspects of family law are also taken into account.

One of the first challenges is to find a field that is suitable for harmonisation. Selecting important and limitable fields involves not only existing national law but also new tendencies and developments, for example the diversity of family relationships and the growing contractualisation thereof.

3.3. LAW IN ACTION

A constant problem is to take into account the law in action. The goal is not only to capture the law in books but also to draw up national reports that reflect living

3 See https://ceflonline.net/principles/. The English text of all Principles can be found in K. Boele-Woelki, F. Ferrand, C. González Beilfuss, M. Jänterä-Jareborg, N. Lowe, D. Martiny and V. Todorova, above n. 1, pp. 229–259.

4 For the methodological aspects see K. Boele-Woelki, F. Ferrand, C. González Beilfuss, M. Jänterä-Jareborg, N. Lowe, D. Martiny and V. Todorova, above n. 1, pp. 1 et seq.

law. All relevant aspects – including, as far as possible, empirical data – should be covered. Thus far, however, the CEFL has to a large extent been dependent on the various results of the national reports.

3.4. FUNCTIONAL APPROACH

The research concentrates on specific problems. As far as possible, formulating the objects of research is independent of a single national legal system. This functional approach is followed when elaborating the underlying questions.[5]

The CEFL concentrates on substantive family law. In its work, however, it is aware that family law is only one part of the legal system. Divergences due to differences in social security, the administration of justice, and the law of procedure also have to be taken into account. A specific distinction between different legal families is not made. However, in particular where additional general private law rules have to be applied, the national background and also the civil law/common law divide have to be taken into account.

4. QUESTIONNAIRES AND PRINCIPLES

4.1. DRAFTING A QUESTIONNAIRE AND DRAWING UP NATIONAL REPORTS

For the creation of its Principles, the CEFL has developed a multistep approach.[6] Initially, a detailed questionnaire for the respective field of study is drafted. The CEFL has in general not only described trends but has also attempted to look for precise answers to specific issues. The questionnaire identifies and systematises the main problems and must be sufficiently detailed to encompass different approaches and the avenues followed when finding solutions. However, the substantive questions are posed – as far as possible – in purely functional terms

---

5 Cf. K. Boele-Woelki, 'The Commission on European Family Law: Taking Stock after Almost 20 years' in K. Boele-Woelki and D. Martiny (eds), *Plurality and Diversity of Family Relations in Europe*, Intersentia, Cambridge 2019, pp. 3, 6.

6 K. Boele-Woelki, 'The Working Method of the Commission on European Family Law' in K. Boele-Woelki (ed.), *Common Core and Better Law in European Family Law*, Intersentia, Antwerp 2005, pp. 15, 17 et seq.; K. Boele-Woelki, 'Zwischen Konvergenz und Divergenz – Die CEFL-Prinzipien zum europäischen Familienrecht' (2009) 73 *Rabels Zeitschrift für ausländisches und internationales Privatrecht (RabelsZ)* 241, 253 et seq.; K. Boele-Woelki, 'The impact of the Commission on European Family Law (CEFL) on European family law' in J. Scherpe (ed.), *European Family Law: Volume I*, Edward Elgar Publishing, Cheltenham 2016, pp. 209, 210 et seq.

and without any reference to the concepts of a specific legal system.[7] Drawing up the national reports is the task of the national experts. Their reports are then published and accessible on the CEFL website.

4.2. DRAFTING THE PRINCIPLES

The next important step consists of drafting Principles drawn from the responses to the questionnaire. This is done by the members of the Organising Committee. In an introduction to the respective Principle, figures and estimations are reported concerning, for example, the frequency and various structures of *de facto* relationships. The accompanying comment on each Principle starts with the existing statements thereon by international instruments. This is followed by a comparative overview of the approaches based on the national reports.

A final step is to complete and disseminate the final version of the Principles following a discussion with the wider group of experts. The Principles consist of rules which are as specific and detailed as possible. However, in some cases the Principles use hardship clauses which allow for a departure from their results in extraordinary cases.[8]

4.3. ESTABLISHING A COMMON CORE

In drafting the Principles, the CEFL has applied both the common core method as well as a better law approach. In its broadest sense, a 'common core' is an almost universally used solution that is found in all of the jurisdictions surveyed.[9] When a certain solution is found to be applied in a majority of the jurisdictions, it has generally been followed by the CEFL, but only after a critical evaluation. If no common core has been identified, the CEFL nevertheless attempts to establish a Principle.

---

7 A certain exception is the Principles on Property Relations Between Spouses. Here, already in the questionnaire different specific questions were asked for different systems, mainly community property and separate property with participation.

8 See Divorce Principle 1:9, Maintenance Principle 2:6 and Matrimonial Property Principle 4:15. In more detail, see K. Boele-Woelki, 'Ziel- und Wertvorstellungen der CEFL in ihren Prinzipien zum europäischen Familienrecht' in A.-L. Verbeke, J.M. Scherpe, C. Declerck, T. Helms and P. Senaeve (eds), *Confronting the Frontiers of Family and Succession Law: Liber Amicorum Walter Pintens*, Intersentia, Cambridge 2012, pp. 167, 184 et seq.

9 See for more detail on the common core, D. Martiny, 'Diverse Legal Cultures, Common Core? The CEFL Principles of European Family Law' in N. Dethloff and K. Kaesling (eds), *Between Sexuality, Gender and Reproduction*, Intersentia, Cambridge 2023, pp. 51 et seq.

4.4. BETTER LAW

Sometimes a 'better solution' has been preferred. Identifying that solution requires – as with the final evaluation in classical comparative law – a careful consideration of the individual issue, and it is a determination that is rarely completely unassailable.[10] In rare cases, the better law approach has been adopted even in the face of a clear common core, for example in the case of the death of a parent. If a parent having sole parental responsibilities dies, responsibilities should be attributed to the surviving parent. However, contrary to the common core, this does not automatically occur under the CEFL Principles. In the interests of the child, a decision by the competent authority is necessary.[11]

It is not only national law that serves as a basis for the common core. Some fundamental values, such as the equality of the sexes and a certain respect for party autonomy, are already stated to be the basis in the preambles to the CEFL Principles.[12]

5. THE REVISITED PRINCIPLES

5.1. THE NEED FOR REVISITING

Time does not stand still, including not in family law. There are changes in the legal landscape, and even the most progressive principles are becoming older. Legislative reforms, case law and legal literature have to be considered. A fresh look at the effectiveness and appropriateness of the CEFL Principles therefore seemed to be useful.

5.2. CREATING THE REVISITED VERSION

A revision of all the existing Principles did not seem to be feasible. However, one of the peculiarities of the Principles is their broad comparative basis. A look at the changes and the content of the Principles from today's perspective was therefore inevitable.[13] A practical problem was to bring different perspectives

10 Cf. for the problems in contract law, R. Zimmermann, 'The Significance of the Principles of European Contract Law' (2020) 28 *European Review of Private Law* 487.

11 See Principles on Parental Responsibilities, Principle 3:31(2), comment 3.

12 For values see K. Boele-Woelki, above n. 8, pp. 167, 178 et seq.

13 See for the method K. Boele-Woelki, F. Ferrand, C. González Beilfuss, M. Jänterä-Jareborg, N. Lowe, D. Martiny and V. Todorova, above n. 1, p. 8.

together. With the help of the CEFL experts – in general the authors of the former reports – several steps have been taken:

- national update reports from 2021 dealing with national reforms and European and international developments;
- a CEFL online expert meeting in January 2023; and
- the creation of update memorandums and comparative charts.

By means of a questionnaire, the national experts were asked which important new developments (legislation, national case law and discussions in legal literature) had taken place in their respective jurisdictions. The case law of the European Court of Human Rights and the European Court of Justice was also a subject of inquiry. The questionnaire encompassed the field of divorce since 2002; maintenance between former spouses, also since 2002; parental responsibilities since 2004; property relations between spouses since 2008; and *de facto* unions since 2015.

These national reports allowed for an assessment of the jurisdictions surveyed at the same moment in time.

The update reports from 2021 were published on the CEFL website.[14]

Then, in January 2023, there was an online expert meeting dealing with the different fields of the Principles. Not only were traditional questions dealt with but also new trends, such as the growing diversity and plurality of family forms.[15] A questionnaire asked about several crucial aspects in the different fields, for example the trend of non-judicial divorce and the principle of self-sufficiency for granting maintenance after divorce. Other aspects were the position of the child in respect of agreements on parental responsibilities, the protection mechanisms for matrimonial property agreements, and the restriction of compensation rights after the termination of *de facto* unions.[16]

The information gathered in the process of revisiting allowed for a final assessment to be made. The published version in the resulting book contains for each field an update memorandum and a comparative chart. Both were prepared by the members of the Organising Committee and are based on the reports of the experts and the discussion with them.

---

14 See update reports by jurisdiction at https://ceflonline.net/update-reports-by-jurisdiction/.

15 See in more detail K. Boele-Woelki, F. Ferrand, C. González Beilfuss, M. Jänterä-Jareborg, N. Lowe, D. Martiny and V. Todorova, above n. 1, pp. 7 et seq.; J. Heaton and A. Kemelmajer, 'General Report: Family Forms and Family's Function – A Comparative Report' in J. Heaton and A. Kemelmajer (eds), *Diversity and Plurality in the Law: Family Forms and Family's Functions*, Intersentia, Cambridge 2023 pp. 1, 4 et seq.

16 See in more detail N. Lowe and C. Gonzalez Beilfuss, 'Revisiting the Principles of European Family Law: an Evaluation' in this volume, pp.__ et seq.

The respective memorandums explain the trends of legal developments and compare recent case law and reform laws with the existing CEFL Principles.[17] The charts indicate for the different subjects, and on a country-by-country basis, the national sources and the content of the numerous reforms.[18] The developments in the different jurisdictions are also accompanied by a comparison with the respective CEFL Principles, with which they are often, but not always, in line. This allows for a topic-related evaluation for research purposes and legislative reform projects.

6. CONCLUSION

As a result, the use of comparative techniques has created a solid basis for the harmonisation efforts. A wealth of comparative information is also accessible in the book revisiting the Principles. New trends are revealed and a comparison with the existing CEFL Principles is made possible. A multistep approach, such as the one employed by the CEFL, is certainly time consuming. However, it avoids hasty results without sufficient reflection. All in all, the revisited Principles form a bridge between current law, new developments and the future.

17 See in general K. Boele-Woelki, F. Ferrand, C. González Beilfuss, M. Jänterä-Jareborg, N. Lowe, D. Martiny and V. Todorova, above n. 1, p. 8; Divorce (pp. 11–19), Maintenance Between Former Spouses (pp. 45–58), Parental Responsibilities (pp. 77–89), Property Relations Between Spouses (pp. 133–144), *De facto* Unions (pp. 179–199).

18 See K. Boele-Woelki, F. Ferrand, C. González Beilfuss, M. Jänterä-Jareborg, N. Lowe, D. Martiny and V. Todorova, above n. 1, Divorce (pp. 21–43), Maintenance Between Former Spouses (pp. 59–75), Parental Responsibilities (pp. 91–132), Property Relations Between Spouses (pp. 145–177), *De facto* Unions (pp. 201–223).

REVISITING THE CEFL'S PRINCIPLES OF EUROPEAN FAMILY LAW

An Evaluation

Nigel LOWE and Cristina GONZÁLEZ BEILFUSS

1. INTRODUCTION

Established in 2001, the Commission on European Family Law (CEFL)'s main objective was to launch a pioneering theoretical and practical exercise relating to the harmonisation of substantive family law in Europe with the ambitious goal of creating a set of Principles of European Family Law. Over the next 20 years the CEFL produced five sets of Principles: Divorce, Maintenance Between Former Spouses (published together in 2004), Parental Responsibilities (2007), Property Relations Between Spouses (2013), and Property, Maintenance and Succession Rights of Couples in *de facto* Unions (2019). The methodology underpinning the drafting of the Principles has been explained in the previous chapter. Suffice to say that integral to the methodology was the commission and analysis of national reports.

In 2020, the CEFL commissioned updating national reports across all five of the above-mentioned fields,[1] so as to provide the opportunity to reflect upon, but *not* to redraft, all the Principles in the light of subsequent developments. That review in turn led to the publication, in 2024, of *The Principles of European Family Law Revisited*. Here we provide a core summary of the five sets of Principles, together with an evaluation of them in the light of the recent developments recorded in the update reports.

2. DIVORCE

Taking its cue from the clear overall trend that was evident in 2004, the underlying strategy of the Divorce Principles (the CEFL's first set of Principles)

1 These update reports can be found on the CEFL's website: http://ceflonline.net/country-reports-by-jurisdiction.

is to provide a simplified non-fault basis upon which divorce can be obtained. A distinction is made between divorce by mutual consent and divorce without the consent of one of the spouses, divorce being easier in the former case than in the latter and immediately available if the parties have been factually separated for six months. In the latter case, divorce is available simply upon the basis of factual separation for one year. Various safeguards are in place to protect the interests of children under the age of 16 and to give some protection to the economic needs of spouses. An important innovation of the Principles was the removal of any reference to the 'irretrievable breakdown of the marriage'. The underlying thinking is that, apart from safeguarding the interests of the children involved and giving some protection to economically vulnerable adults, the state has little interest in preventing a divorce, more especially so where that is the mutual wish of the spouses, and on the contrary, should provide a straightforward means of doing so.

Overall, given their advocacy for simpler and easier divorce and for the removal of fault, the Divorce Principles have stood the test of time. Indeed, many of the suggestions contained in the Principles have been adopted in several jurisdictions and expressly informed and shaped the 2008 Portuguese divorce law reforms[2] and were referred to during the parliamentary debate on the reform of Belgian divorce law.[3] As anticipated, the grounds/conditions for divorce have generally continued to ease, with fault largely being abandoned as a ground (see e.g. Belgium, Bulgaria, England and Wales, France, Ireland, Italy and Portugal). Accompanying this easing has been a general reduction of the required periods of separation before being able to apply for divorce (as in France, Ireland, Italy and Scotland) and the simplification of proceedings (as in e.g. Belgium, England and Wales, France, Greece and Scotland). Of course, post-2002 developments have not been uniform and some have bucked the trend with the creation of new fault grounds (as in Denmark and Greece) or have been individualistic as, for example, in England and Wales, where no distinction is made between consensual and non-consensual divorce such that in *all* cases all that is required is for the applicant, or both spouses in the case of a joint application, to make a statement that the marriage has broken down irretrievably and, after 20 weeks, repeat that statement.[4]

Not all developments have been anticipated and three in particular give pause for thought.[5] The first is the introduction in some jurisdictions of *non-judicial*

---

2 See G. De Olivera, 'Changes Going on in Portuguese Family Law' (2008) *Zeitschrift für das gesamte Familienrecht* 1712.

3 See the Belgian update report.

4 Matrimonial Causes Act 1973, s. 1(2) and (5), as substituted by the Divorce, Dissolution and Separation Act 2020, s. 1(2) and (5). The divorce only becomes final after a further period of six weeks.

5 It is worth noting that since 2004 the right to marry has been extended to same-sex couples in a significant number of jurisdictions (14 of those originally surveyed), meaning that divorce

or *extra-judicial divorce*. Although note was taken of the few jurisdictions (Denmark, Norway, Portugal and Russia)[6] that provided for 'administrative divorces', the Principles do not, at any rate expressly, permit non-judicial divorces. Indeed, Comment 1 to Principle 1:2 says that the Principle 'emphasises that a divorce is a secular matter, and, reflecting the position in all jurisdictions surveyed, is governed by a legal process.' It was intended to exclude purely private or purely religious divorces. However, Estonia,[7] France,[8] Greece,[9] Italy[10] and Spain[11] now permit non-judicial divorce, that is, by notarial agreement, by a private agreement countersigned by two lawyers and filed in a notary public's records or by a private agreement approved by the public prosecutor. Under French and Greek law, the non-judicial process is mandatory for consensual divorces. Distinctively, France does not require any scrutiny of the agreement in respect of parental responsibilities; it only states that even if the spouses wanted to make use of non-judicial divorce, judicial proceedings must be instituted if a minor child capable of expressing his or her views requests to be heard by the judge. In England and Wales, a new quasi-administrative divorce procedure has been introduced, albeit one that requires the final orders to be granted by a court. As the CJEU has held,[12] there is a clear distinction between agreed mutual divorces which have been registered by a public authority and those that are purely private or purely religious. Following that decision it seems clear[13] that the non-judicial divorces currently provided by EU Member States are all recognisable under Brussels IIb. Were Principle 1:2(2) to be revisited, account

has consequentially been extended to same-sex married couples. But this development does not substantially affect the Divorce Principles, albeit that they were drafted on the assumption that divorce concerned different sex couples, as they are expressed to apply to 'spouses', which is not defined. But were those Principles being drafted anew, that point would have expressly been made clear.

6 It is also clear from the Estonian update report (this jurisdiction was not included in the national reports originally relied upon when drafting the Divorce Principles) that divorces have long been granted by the Vital Statistics Office.

7 Estonian Family Law Act.

8 Law Act no. 2016-154 of 18 November 2016, as extended by Law Act no. 2019-222 of 23 March 2019.

9 Law Act no. 3500/2006.

10 Law 10 November 2014 no. 162.

11 Law Act no. 15/2015 of 2 July 2015.

12 Case C-646/20, *Senatsverwaltung für Inneres und Sport, Standesamtsaufsicht v TB*, ECLI:EU:C:2022:879 (*TB*) – a ruling on the application of Council Regulation (EC) No 2201/2003 of 27 November 2003 (Brussels IIa). Brussels IIa has, from 1 August 2022, been replaced by Council Regulation (EU) No 2019/1111 of 25 June 2019 (Brussels IIb).

13 Though the basis upon which recognition may be based will depend upon whether or not the public authority empowered by national law to grant divorce retains control over its granting. If it does, then on the basis of *TB* the divorce should be recognised as a 'judgment' within the meaning of Article 2(4). If it does not, as arguably is the position under the French system, such divorces are still recognisable by reason of Article 65, provided the Member State which empowered the public authority or other authority to register the agreement had jurisdiction under Chapter II of the Regulation.

would clearly need to be taken of these developments, albeit that it cannot yet be said that non-judicial divorce between consenting spouses is 'common core'.

A second issue is whether there is or should be a *right* to divorce. Notwithstanding the ECtHR ruling in *Johnson v Ireland*,[14] that the Convention confers no such right, the trend is clearly moving in that direction. Not only are the grounds easing overall, but in most jurisdictions even non-consensual divorce is, subject to periods of separation (or, in the case of England and Wales, subject to a 26-week period between the divorce application and the final order), effectively available as of right. This has become more clearly the position in Belgium, England and Wales, France, Italy, Portugal and Spain as a result of post-2004 reforms.

Principle 1:1(1) states that '[t]he law should permit divorce', by which was meant that the state should provide a legal mechanism to obtain a divorce rather than there should be a right to divorce. But the last sentence of Comment 1 is not as clear as it might be in this regard when it says that Principle 1:1(1) 'in theory goes beyond' the ECtHR rulings. Perhaps that Comment would now be drafted differently.

A third development relates to spousal agreements on the consequences of divorce. This has been the focus in a number of jurisdictions, for example in Austria, Bulgaria, Catalonia, France, Italy, Poland, Portugal and Spain. These agreements should be taken into account by the authority that grants divorce, unless they are not in accordance with the child's best interests. Attention is also paid to facilitating mediation or other forms of ADR, as in for example Belgium, Bulgaria, Catalonia, France, Ireland and Spain. Although it is implicit in the Principles that it is preferable for the spouses to agree both on the divorce and on its consequences, they do not directly deal with mechanisms, such as mediation, for helping the spouses to reach an agreement.[15] Were the Divorce Principles to be revisited, provision would now expressly be made for ADR. What the Divorce Principles do provide for is a period of reflection. Principle 1:5(1) makes it mandatory to have a period of reflection in the case of divorce by consent if the spouses have children under the age of 16 (three months if the spouses have agreed upon all the consequences, six months if they have not agreed upon all the consequences unless (see Principle 1:5(3)) they have already been separated for six months at the commencement of the proceedings). Where the spouses have no children under the age of 16, a three-month period of reflection is required (see Principle 1:5(2)), again unless (see Principle 1:5(3)) they have already been separated for six months at the commencement of the proceedings. Whether Principle 1:5 is over-elaborate can be debated.

---

[14] (1986) 9 EHRR 203, ECtHR.

[15] Cf. Principle 5:27 in the Principles of European Family Law Regarding Property, Maintenance and Succession Rights of Couples in *de facto* Unions – the CEFL's final Principle.

3. MAINTENANCE BETWEEN FORMER SPOUSES

The aim of the Maintenance Principles (the CEFL's second set of Principles, but published together with Divorce) is to provide a common set of principles covering spousal support after divorce, regardless of whether the divorce is consensual or not. The broad underlying strategy is to limit post-divorce claims to where the creditor spouse has insufficient resources to meet his or her needs and the debtor spouse has the ability to satisfy those needs. But an exception to this position is provided by Principle 2:6, which allows a competent authority, in cases of exceptional hardship to the debtor spouse, to 'deny, limit or terminate maintenance because of the creditor spouse's conduct'. For the most part, post-divorce spousal maintenance is envisaged to be short-term, but Principle 2:8 also provides that a competent authority can, in exceptional cases, grant maintenance 'without time limit'. In all cases, Principle 2:9 provides that the maintenance obligation terminates upon the creditor spouse's remarriage or entry into a long-term relationship[16] and ceases upon either spouse's death. Allowance is made for the spouses to make their own maintenance agreement, but it has to be in writing and is subject to scrutiny by the competent authority.

Overall, bearing in mind they only establish a framework, the Maintenance Principles have stood the test of time well. There is a clear trend for claims being restricted because former spouses are expected to be self-sufficient, which is in line with Principle 2:2. Indeed, both Belgium and Portugal have codified the self-sufficiency principle, while reform in Germany has brought German law more in line with it. Lump-sum payments have become easier, which is in line with Principle 2:5(2). Similarly, in line with Principle 2:8, there has been a trend towards maintenance being time-limited. Finally, and consistent with Principle 2:9, post-2004 reform statutes (see, for example, Austria, Belgium, Estonia (remarriage) and Hungary) generally provide for the cessation of the maintenance obligation upon the claimant spouse entering into another marriage, registered partnership or cohabitation (in Portugal it is expressly stated that the obligation ends upon the claimant 'entering into a *de facto* union').

As with the Divorce Principles, the Maintenance Principles were drafted on the assumption that divorce concerned different-sex couples, but they nevertheless equally apply to divorcing same-sex couples, there being no definition of 'spouses'. Nevertheless, had those Principles been drafted now, this point would have been expressly made clear.

Although, in line with Principle 2:10, maintenance agreements are generally permitted, the spouses' freedom to waive maintenance varies. In Belgium, for example, rights to maintenance cannot be waived before the dissolution

[16] In the light of the subsequent Principles on *de facto* unions, reference might now be made to 'enduring relationships' instead.

of the marriage. In Estonia, unreasonable restrictions are not accepted. In Germany, waivers of maintenance claims are only effective if both spouses are fully informed about the consequences. Waiver of maintenance claims is not mentioned in Principle 2:10, though the issue is adverted to in Comment 2 to the extent of saying that the spouses 'should be free to decide that no maintenance will be paid'. Whether more attention should have been paid to this question can be debated, though it should not be overlooked that the need for agreements to be in writing and the overall power of the competent authority to scrutinise the validity of agreements (Principle 2:10(2) and (3)) provide some broad-brush safeguards.

One development not anticipated by the Principles is that posed by agreements being made in the context of non-judicial divorce when there could be less opportunity for scrutiny by a competent authority. This issue has been specifically addressed in separate legislation, but in different ways, for example in France and Greece. No doubt, were the Principles to be reconsidered, attention would be paid to this development, but it may be that, in any event, the already mentioned general safeguards, under Principle 2:10, might be thought to be as far as one could go in the absence of any widespread trend or experience.

But one issue that could profitably have been expressly addressed in the Maintenance Principles is family mediation. That issue has been addressed in, for example, Catalonia, France and Ireland, though, interestingly, in the Netherlands the number of cases referred to a mediator by a court has reportedly decreased.[17]

4. PARENTAL RESPONSIBILITIES

The overall aim of the Principles on parental responsibilities is to strengthen the rights of children and to bring this area of the law in line with the UN Convention on the Rights of the Child and other international instruments. This third set of Principles was, in fact, the first to comprehensively consider the relevance of international instruments and, in particular, Recommendations adopted by the Council of Europe. A reference to international instruments was included by the CEFL in all the subsequent sets of Principles.

One of the challenges was to find an adequate conceptual framework that would overcome the divergence of concepts and terminology across Europe. The term 'parental responsibilities' and the distinction between attribution and exercise, which was not easily understood at the period of drafting, has gained acceptance and has been adopted in jurisdictions such as Portugal.[18] The update

17 See the Dutch update report, Part B.
18 See Law No. 61/2008.

reports, however, show that a variety of terminology continues to subsist under national law. This is sometimes a challenge when trying to understand foreign law and is likely to create difficulty in cross-border scenarios.

The Parental Responsibilities Principles' strong focus on the rights of children has stood the test of time; it has been reinforced in recent national reforms that have in some cases been driven by Recommendations from the UN Committee on the Rights of the Child. The best interests of the child are the overarching criterion to assess the suitability of measures in this area of the law. One development not anticipated by the Principles is, however, the formulation of checklists or factors to provide guidance to authorities when determining the child's best interests. Were the Principles to be redrafted, it would be worth considering whether such checklists are feasible and useful. The CEFL used lists of factors in connection with specific matters, such as alternate residence and relocation, but did not develop this methodology in connection with the general principle of the best interests of the child (Principle 3:3).

The right of the child to non-discrimination that was formulated in Principle 3:5 has been given further prominence in the law of several European jurisdictions. A development that is fully in line with the Principles is the strengthening of the position of unmarried fathers and the elimination of discrimination as regards children of same-sex partners. The Principles themselves did not mention same-sex parents explicitly but the use of gender-neutral language like 'parent' or 'parental responsibility holder' and the reference to sex and sexual orientation in Principle 3:5 was clearly intended to cover them.[19]

The Principles put great emphasis on the right of the child to be heard. Principle 3:37 deals with the right to be heard in judicial proceedings. New provisions on this have been introduced in several European jurisdictions.[20] An interesting development is the clarification made by Belgian law that the child also has a right to refuse to be heard.[21] Under Principle 3:6, the right of the child to be heard applies generally and not only in judicial proceedings. The update reports, however, show that the law very rarely deals with this right in connection with agreements between parental responsibility holders. Should the Principles be revisited, this aspect would most probably be further developed since the exercise of private autonomy in connection with parental responsibilities needs to include the child, who cannot be viewed as a mere object of such agreements. The need to further develop the child's right to participation in the context of agreements also seems pertinent since there might be a conflict of interest between children and parents, a matter dealt with under Principle 3:7, which provides that 'the interests of the child should be protected whenever they may be in conflict with the interests of the holders of parental responsibilities'.

19 See the Comment on Principle 3:5.
20 It is also a core principle in Brussels IIb, see Article 21.
21 Articles 1004/1 paras 2 and 3 and 1004/2 Judiciary Code.

Principle 3:19(2) explicitly bans corporal punishment and any other humiliating treatment. The update reports show that legal reforms undertaken since 2004 have enlarged the number of European jurisdictions that expressly prohibit corporal punishment when regulating parental responsibilities.

The Principles' emphasis on agreements between holders of parental responsibilities has stood the test of time. Many reforms in European jurisdictions seek to favour agreements by reinforcing the recourse to mediation, as already anticipated in Principle 3:36, which provides that 'in all disputes regarding parental responsibilities alternative dispute resolution mechanisms should be available.' Some jurisdictions have made institutional arrangements in the area of procedural law that, while being outside the scope of the Principles, reinforce the focus on non-adversary dispute resolution that inspired them.

The Parental Responsibilities Principles were mostly based on the common core and international instruments. Where the CEFL used the better law method, it seems to have correctly identified the contentious issues. The Principles contain specific rules concerning the child's residence after the separation of parental responsibility holders that were innovative when they were drafted.

Principle 3:20 deals with alternate residence. It establishes that parental responsibility holders who jointly exercise parental responsibilities and live apart should agree upon with whom the child resides. Alternate residence is possible upon either an agreement approved by a competent authority or a decision by the competent authority. After 2004, the alternate residence model was introduced through statutory reform in several jurisdictions. Contrary to Principle 3:20(2), many jurisdictions continue to provide that alternate custody orders cannot be decreed by a court in the absence of agreement. Were the Principles to be redrafted, it would be interesting to empirically[22] assess the alternate residence scheme in order to gain further insight as to how it works out for the child both when there is agreement and in the absence of agreement between parental responsibility holders. Twenty years after the adoption of the Parental Responsibilities Principles, it would certainly be pertinent to evaluate whether this possibility is often used in practice, how it is experienced by children and parents, and the factors considered by courts when taking the decision or approving the agreement. Principle 3:20 mentions: (a) the age and opinion of the child; (b) the ability and willingness of the holders of parental responsibilities to cooperate with each other in matters concerning the child, as well as their personal situation; and (c) the distance between the residences of the holders of parental responsibilities and the child's school.

Principle 3:21 deals with relocation disputes. It provides rules in order to solve the conflict that arises when parental responsibilities are exercised jointly

22 An increased attention to empirical data was developed by the CEFL during the course of its work and was an important matter in the national reports leading to the last set of Principles dealing with *de facto* unions.

and one of the holders of parental responsibilities wishes to change the child's habitual residence. As rightly anticipated by the CEFL, this topic has become one of the most difficult type of family law disputes in Europe. Reforms have been undertaken on the matter in a number of European jurisdictions and the rules developed by the CEFL have been highly influential. The Council of Europe Recommendation on preventing and resolving disputes on child relocation explicitly refer to them.[23] Relocation continues to be relevant for the Hague Conference on private international law, which convened an international conference on the matter in April 2025.

A development not fully foreseen by the CEFL is the trend towards enlarging the circle of adults who, because of their close connection with the child, can be legally empowered to exercise parental responsibilities. The two-parent principle is implicit in many of the rules developed. Yet the Principles provide under 3:9 that parental responsibilities can be attributed to third persons in whole or in part. The Principles did not deal with parenthood, which is one of the most contentious topics at present, except to provide that parents should have parental responsibilities for the child (Principle 3:8), unless discharged by the competent authority where their behaviour causes a serious risk to the person or the property of the child (Principle 3:32).

All in all, it can be said that the Parental Responsibilities Principles have stood the test of time. Many of the issues that are presently discussed are outside their scope and relate to procedural law or to the area of parenthood. This is not to say that they would not be amended should they be redrafted. Recent developments take matters one step further, by providing, as mentioned, the right of the child to refuse to be heard or imposing an obligation, not only a right, on parents to maintain a personal relationship with the child. A special focus at present are high-conflict cases, particularly in connection with domestic violence, which did probably not receive enough attention when the Principles were drafted.

5. PROPERTY RELATIONS BETWEEN SPOUSES

The Principles on Property Relations Between Spouses were published in 2013. The basic aim is to provide a common set of principles on property relations between spouses that strike a proper balance between solidarity and protection and private autonomy.

23 See Recommendation CM/Rec(2015)4 of the Committee of Ministers to member States on preventing and resolving disputes on child relocation and Evaluation of Recommendation CM/Rec(2015)4 on Preventing and Resolving Disputes on Child Relocation (CDCJ(2021)27E (report prepared by Cristina González Beilfuss).

These Principles were probably the most challenging and difficult set to draft. They refer to a very traditional subject matter where there has been very little convergence in the law of the different jurisdictions and the impact of international instruments has been limited. The CEFL did however refer to a number of international instruments, including the UN Convention on the Elimination of all forms of Discrimination against Women (CEDAW).[24] A further source of difficulty was the very technical character of the law in this area and its many connections to property law. Particularly challenging was the inclusion of England and Wales and Ireland, where the concept of matrimonial property as such is unknown.

The CEFL overcame difficulties by taking a functional approach and focusing on practical needs and contemporary views as regards the relationship between spouses. Interestingly, the update reports show that there have been far-reaching legislative reforms since the adoption of the Principles. Such reforms have sought to modernise the law and are fully in line with the Principles in that they seek to promote values such as equality, self-sufficiency and independence

Several trends are evident. The first is to extend matrimonial property law to cover registered partnerships or civil unions in jurisdictions that have introduced such institutions. This was not expressly addressed when drafting the Principles since they are limited in scope and only referred to relations between spouses. This does not, however, prevent the Principles from being a useful source of inspiration when regulating the property relations between registered partners. Self-evidently, in jurisdictions that have opened marriage to same-sex partners, the rules on spousal property relations apply to all married couples regardless of sex and sexual orientation. This applies likewise to the Principles.

The Principles contain a chapter on general rights and duties that applies irrespective of the matrimonial property regime.[25] The most relevant provisions in practice are probably those in connection to the family home and household goods. Some recent reforms adopt the same approach. Under Belgian law, the provisions on the allocation of the family home, household goods and professional assets apply to all matrimonial property regimes.[26] The general duty of information contained in Principle 4:8 has also been reinforced in recent reforms as a means to ensure fairness.

Marital property agreements are prominent in the Principles. Principle 4:9 states that spouses should be free to enter into agreements determining their marital property relationship and Chapter II includes six Principles dealing with private autonomy. The update reports indicate an increased scope and variety for permitted agreements across the jurisdictions surveyed. A remarkable

24 See the extensive analysis in the Introduction of the Principles.

25 See Principle 4:1.

26 Articles 1389/1 and 1389/2 of the old Civil Code.

development is that of Bulgaria; instead of a single imperative regime, three matrimonial property regimes are now available.[27]

Increased freedom goes hand-in-hand with control mechanisms. In line with Principle 4:11, the intervention of a competent authority is commonly required. A duty of disclosure as established in Principle 4:12 has also become common. A major trend in the national reforms is to facilitate agreements before and during marriage, which is also permissible under Principle 4:10.

The Principles include an exceptional hardship clause permitting the competent authority to set aside or adjust a marital property agreement having regard to the circumstances when the agreement was concluded or those subsequently arising. Some of these ideas have found their way into national law. Austrian law now provides under section 97(3) Marriage Act that the court has powers to adjust agreements on usage rights of the matrimonial home that are detrimental to the living conditions of a spouse or a common child. Other agreements can also be adjusted if they would disadvantage one spouse inequitably, thus going further than the Principles, which require exceptional hardship.

The Principles propose two different default property regimes – participation in acquisitions and community of acquisitions – from which the national lawmaker can draw inspiration. This was a difficult choice for the CEFL, but has proved to be the correct way forward since national reforms very rarely substitute one regime for the other. These are also the two prevalent default regimes across Europe. The Netherlands moved away from universal community of goods towards a community of acquisitions in 2018, which is largely or even fully in line with the CEFL model.

All in all, it can be said that the Principles have stood the test of time well and that the CEFL rightly identified the pressing matters. When striking the balance between autonomy and solidarity, perhaps the CEFL leaned more towards protecting the weaker spouse than many national lawmakers. This is particularly evident in the context of agreements. With hindsight one might also question whether the Principles went too far into the technicalities of the proposed matrimonial property regimes. On the one hand, a certain level of detail is necessary in order to make the proposed model understandable; on the other, however, national lawmakers need to go further in their regulation.

6. PROPERTY, MAINTENANCE AND SUCCESSION RIGHTS OF COUPLES IN *DE FACTO* UNIONS

The overall aim of the Principles on Property, Maintenance and Succession Rights of Couples in *de facto* Unions (the CEFL's fifth set of Principles) is to provide

---

[27] Articles 18–43 Bulgarian Family Code.

a common set of principles governing, safeguarding and, in some instances, improving the legal situation of *de facto* couples. These Principles cover an area of contemporary concern and debate and over which there is often no common consensus and against a background of declining numbers of marriages and an increasing number of enduring relationships. The basic standpoint of the Principles is to respect individuals' choices to live their family lives as they wish and to promote that family's well-being, but at the same time to take into account and endorse traditional family relationships by focusing protection on partners with joint children and/or on relationships of a reasonably long duration. It is a delicate balance and terminology and scope had to be carefully considered.

An immediate issue is what these relationships should be called. The term 'informal relationships' was rejected, as that could suggest that such relationships lack commitment. 'Non-formalised relationships' might have been used, but that still has a negative connotation. '*De facto* unions' was concluded to be suitably gender neutral and more universally understood. Account has also to be taken of the nature of the relationship to distinguish, for example, simple house/flat-sharing arrangements from those of an intimate nature, and of the duration of the relationship, especially as the relationships covered by the Principles give rise to rights and obligations. We could all agree that a 'one-night stand' should not be sufficient to confer property or inheritance rights and could hardly be considered 'cohabitation' in any real sense. In the general absence of an overall legal definition among the states surveyed, the CEFL defined *de facto* unions as 'two persons living together as a couple in an enduring relationship' (Principle 5:1(1)), but applied the Principles to 'qualified' *de facto* unions, that is (with some exceptions) to cases where 'the partners are in an enduring relationship for at least five years or have a common child' (Principle 5:1(2)). The long duration is to be seen as an indicator of a more intensive relationship, which justifies more protection. The same can be said if there is a common child (a term that includes an adopted child). Among the surveyed jurisdictions, it is common to provide that for mutual rights and duties to arise, the relationship must have lasted for between two and five years. The existence of a common child is often of relevance. The Principles, however, are more nuanced by providing for slightly different qualifications in the case of protecting the family home and household goods both during the union and upon separation, inasmuch as the common child must either be a minor or be dependent upon the partners (Principles 5:6 and 5:18). Different qualifications also apply where the union ends because of death.

The position of *de facto* couples, as defined by the Principles, is governed by separate chapters dealing with general rights and duties, making agreements, rules on the partners' property and debts, the position following separation, the position following a partner's death, and dispute resolution.

The most challenging are the two Chapters (V and VI) dealing with the position upon separation *and* upon death. With few exceptions, the surveyed jurisdictions adopt a more fragmentary approach such that, roughly speaking, a dividing line exists between the choice of a 'separation model' and a 'death model' and in respect of the rights and protection conferred in each situation.

In the case of separation, the Principles contain three stand-out provisions. First, under Principle 5:18, in the absence of agreement between the partners and provided there has been an enduring relationship for at least five years or where the couple have a common child who is either a minor or is dependent on them, the competent authority can grant one of the partners continued use of the home and goods. While the reported trends in the surveyed jurisdictions are in line with this Principle, they do not go quite as far.

Secondly, Principles 5:17 and 5:18 give a qualifying partner a *right of compensation* in respect of contributions made to the other partner's property, business or profession, and/or the household. This is not the common core. Indeed, national courts are generally reluctant to grant compensation claims, primarily with reference to the close personal and economic relationship that usually prevails between cohabiting partners, and the partners' duty to contribute to the joint living expenses.[28]

Thirdly, although Principle 5:19 espouses the principle of the partners' self-sufficiency after their separation, Principle 5:20 provides that after separation in a relationship of at least five years' duration or where there is a common child, an ex-partner who has insufficient resources to meet his or her needs has a claim for maintenance from the other ex-partner subject to various specified conditions. The majority of the surveyed jurisdictions apply the principle of self-sufficiency but do not give *de facto* partners a right to post-separation maintenance. Whether states will move towards the position taken by the Principles remains to be seen.

The Principles on the position following the *death of one of the partners* are equally challenging. Principle 5:22 provides for two separate rights: (a) occupancy rights and the continued use of household goods; and (b) the right to take over the tenancy of the family home where it was in the name of the deceased partner. The former right is time-limited – it lasts for six months after the deceased partner's death – but the latter is not, although any right will depend upon the terms of the tenancy. The rationale for this distinction is that the former impinges upon the right of third parties, whereas the latter does not. The occupancy rights conferred by Principle 5:22(1) only arise in relation to the 'family home', which must have been 'owned' by the deceased. The overarching limitation is that the survivor must have been a 'partner' of the deceased at the time of death, meaning that he or she must have been sharing a household with

28 See e.g. in France, Cass. civ. 1, 13 January 2016, No. 14-29.746; Cass. civ. 1, 8 July 2020, No. 19-12.250; and Cass. civ. 1, 2 September 2020, No. 10-10.477; in Germany, see 26 BGH 11 July 2018, NJW-RR (Rechtsprechungs-Report Zivilrecht) 2018, 1217; in the Netherlands, see ECLI:NL:HR:2019:707A; and in Sweden, see Judgment NJA 2019 p. 23.

the deceased as a couple in an enduring relationship. Limited though these rights are, they do not reflect the common core, which is generally against giving surviving partners rights of occupation of the family home. Even where such protection is afforded, there is no clear consensus on what that protection should be. The CEFL's position is based upon general principles of equality and prohibition of discrimination espoused by the Universal Declaration of Human Rights 1948 and the International Covenant on Civil and Political Rights 1966 and the need to protect partners, particularly women, upon the ending of *de facto* relationships as highlighted in the General Recommendations of the CEDAW Committee. In fact, since the publication of the *de facto* Union Principles, jurisdictions such as those of Austria and Italy now grant the right to occupancy of the family home in the event of a partner's death.

Under Principle 5:23, a partner enjoys a general freedom of testation, which means they can make wills in favour of their surviving partner. This was the position in all of the surveyed jurisdictions. Indeed, international and national bodies in Europe commonly recommend unmarried couples to make use of testamentary dispositions, where appropriate, in order to protect the surviving partner and the couple's common children in case of death. A point not addressed by the Principles is the effect, if any, of the ending of the *de facto* relationship during the lifetime of both partners on a testamentary disposition in favour of the former partner. In this respect there seems evident attraction in the Austrian position that upon the ending the relationship, there is a presumption that any testamentary disposition in favour of the former partner expires.[29]

Absent a will in their favour, in the surveyed jurisdictions the surviving partner's situation remains generally weak, in comparison with that of a spouse. Principle 5:24 seeks to redress this weakness by granting qualified surviving partners (see below) the same rights as enjoyed by a spouse to succeed to the deceased partner's estate. In going against the common core, the CEFL bore in mind the increasing cohabitation rates throughout Europe, and based on general principles of equality and the need for protection, considered it right and fair to provide for succession rights for certain surviving partners to a *de facto* union. However, given the overwhelming common core, it was felt to be going too far to base such rights solely on even lengthy *de facto* relationships. Similarly, it was felt inappropriate to ground such rights solely on the existence of a common child. The compromise under Principle 5:24 is to limit those qualifying for succession rights to survivors of a *de facto* union which, at the time of death, had existed for at least five years *and* where there is a common child. This latter requirement means that couples who begin their *de facto* unions later in life will

[29] Austrian Civil Code, §725(1).

not acquire succession rights under Principle 5:24. Such couples, it was thought, are more likely to be better informed and more focused, particularly if they have children by previous relationships, on the implications of death. They should be encouraged to make appropriate wills.

Principle 5:25 gives a surviving partner without rights of succession according to Principle 5:24, or under the deceased partner's will, a right to make a lump-sum claim against the deceased partner's estate or, where appropriate, the heirs. This claim is limited to providing basic short-term economic protection having regard to the survivor's means (Principle 5:25(3)). It is conditional on the surviving partner having been in an enduring relationship with the deceased at the time of death, so for at least two years, or having a common child with him or her. The claim under Principle 5:25 is *not* one for maintenance; rather, it is designed to afford limited short-term economic protection in the immediate aftermath of the partner's death to enable a surviving partner who is in need to adjust to the new circumstances.

This extra form of protection does not reflect the common core, which is generally (though not so overwhelmingly as in the case of not giving succession rights) against giving surviving partners rights to make claims upon the deceased partner's estate. But again, the CEFL felt that notions of equality and fairness justified giving this limited right to make a single lump-sum claim against the deceased partner's estate. Nevertheless, given the common core, this limited claim is only open to qualified surviving partners. However, in this respect, the qualifying period of the enduring relationship is less than that required to confer rights of succession under Principle 5:24 to reflect the fact that the right to make a claim is a more limited one. On the other hand, the alternative qualifying condition, that there is a common child, reflects the nature of the right conferred, namely short-term economic protection.

The *de facto* Union Principles are relatively new, so there has been less time for there to have been developments. It may be that in time surviving *de facto* partners will generally enjoy similar protection to those of surviving spouses or civil partners. We anticipate that they will. In that case there will be less need to provide different qualifying conditions, which some may think makes the Principles complicated.

7. CONCLUDING REMARKS

When the CEFL first embarked upon its project, the question of whether one could or should seek to harmonise European family law was a live issue. One argument against harmonisation in general, and family law in particular, is that because laws are culturally specific, harmonisation would lead to a loss of an important aspect of one's culture. Meulders-Klein argued that family law is so deeply 'embedded' in each nation's history that it is totally inappropriate to consider it an appropriate field to harmonise.[30] Advocates for harmonisation, on the other hand, pointed out that national laws are not fixed and not resistant to the reception of foreign family law. Pintens, for example, forcibly argued that '[c]ultural embeddedment does not mean that we are embedded in a culture to such an extent that we give up our identity when culture changes occur'.[31] Others, such as Dethloff,[32] argue that in any event for family law the often differing political values and morals are on the decline and, rather than being shaped predominantly by certain basic convictions, most European countries increasingly take social realities into consideration, such that family law is now primarily concerned with solving comparable social problems.

At the outset, the CEFL was committed to the view that family law is not so special that it cannot or should not be harmonised. However, while there may be no principled objection to the harmonisation of family law, there is the practical issue of inevitably having to squeeze out the extremes. For example, had Malta been included in the jurisdictions surveyed for divorce (as it was for matrimonial property), it would have been impossible to harmonise its law since, alone of the European jurisdictions, it did not then permit divorce (it does now). Equally, there could be no real harmonisation between the Irish law of divorce, under which, at the time of drafting the Principles, the parties had to have been separated for at least four of the previous five years (these periods have now been reduced to separation for two of the previous three years), and, say, Finnish law, which had no grounds for divorce but was (and still is) based on the principle of divorce on demand – that is, one or both spouses may apply for a divorce and, after a mandatory period of six months' reflection, the divorce must be granted upon a renewed application. That said, it was surprising just how much seemingly spontaneous convergence there has been in family law throughout Europe, both within and without the EU, from north to south, east to west, and between civil law and common law jurisdictions.[33] Indeed, one of the enduring contributions made by the CEFL has been, through its commission and publication of national reports, to promote comparative law study and

---

30 M.T. Meulders-Klein, 'Towards a Uniform European Family Law? A Political Approach' in M. Antokolskaia (ed.), *Convergence and Divergence of Family Law in Europe*, Intersentia, Antwerp 2007, pp. 272–273.

31 W. Pintens, 'Europeanisation of Family Law' in K. Boele-Woelki (ed.), *Perspectives for the Unification and Harmonisation of Family Law in Europe*, Intersentia, Antwerp 2003, p. 8. See also J.M. Scherpe, 'The Gametes of a European Family Law' [2008] *International Family Law* 98.

32 N. Dethloff, 'Arguments for the Unification and Harmonisation of Family Law in Europe' in K. Boele-Woelki (ed.), *Perspectives for the Unification and Harmonisation of Family Law in Europe*, Intersentia, Antwerp 2003, p. 61.

33 See further M. Antokolskaia (ed.), above n. 30.

enhance knowledge of a wide range of European jurisdictions in the five fields covered by its Principles.

Notwithstanding the obvious limitations, the CEFL has surely demonstrated that a form of harmonisation of core principles of at least parts of European family law is possible. Of course, producing Principles has been nothing more than an academic exercise (albeit a challenging and exciting one). We have no mandate over individual legislators, nor did we have to juggle the often competing views of interest groups, a problem that, of course, confronts all legislators. Even among ourselves, we had long debates about what our Principles should cover, let alone how they should be worded. We rejoice that the Principles have had and will probably continue to have some influence on legislators in Europe and, above all, that they have contributed to an enhanced use of comparative law in family law.

THE WAY AHEAD

Parent–Child Relationships, New Forms of Adult Relationships and Protection from Domestic Violence

Nina DETHLOFF, Barbara NOVAK and Felix LEVEN*

1. INTRODUCTION

After a quarter of a century, it is now time not only to take stock of the successful work of the Commission on European Family Law (CEFL) but also to look ahead. Since its foundation in 2001, the CEFL has drafted and published five highly recognised sets of Principles of European Family Law – starting in 2004, with the latest Principles being published in 2019 – which provide national legislators with model laws to serve as guidance for the reform of their own family law systems.[1] However, the Commission's work did not stop there, but kept on incorporating more recent developments in family law in Europe into its analysis and revisiting its Principles.[2] The CEFL Principles have been dealing with both marriage and *de facto* unions, i.e. with the relationships on the horizontal level in family law, as well as with parent–child relationships, the vertical level. This contribution will address 'The Way Ahead' with regard to topics as well as perspectives and take up where the Principles left off on both levels: Which are the relationships

---

* This contribution is based on Nina Dethloff's presentation 'The Way Ahead: Parent-Child Relationships. New Forms of Adult Relationships' and Barbara Novak's presentation 'The Way Ahead: Protection from Domestic Violence' at the conference *What Family Law for Europe?*, organised by the Royal Swedish Academy of Letters, History and Antiquities and the Commission on European Family Law (CEFL), Stockholm, 10–11 October 2024, and was written in collaboration with Felix Leven.

1 On the work of the CEFL see K. BOELE-WOELKI, 'The Commission on European Family Law: Taking Stock after Almost 20 Years' in K. BOELE-WOELKI and D. MARTINY (eds), *Plurality and Diversity of Family Relations in Europe*, Intersentia, Cambridge 2019, pp. 3 et seqq.; D. MARTINY, 'Diverse Legal Cultures, Common Core? The CEFL Principles of European Family Law' in N. DETHLOFF and K. KAESLING (eds), *Between Sexuality, Gender and Reproduction: On the Pluralisation of Family Forms*, Intersentia, Cambridge 2023, pp. 51 et seqq.

2 See K. BOELE-WOELKI et al., *The Principles of European Family Law Revisited*, Intersentia, Cambridge 2024. In 2021, national update reports on important new developments regarding the five CEFL working areas were published on the CEFL website: https://ceflonline.net/update-reports-by-jurisdiction/ (last accessed 28.11.2024).

that we should address in the future? Where is reform in European jurisdictions currently being called for? And where can we thus enrich the debate on 'what family law for Europe?' from a comparative perspective?

The main focus of the Principles so far has been on the horizontal level. Here, the 2004 Principles Regarding Divorce and Maintenance Between Former Spouses and the 2013 Principles Regarding Property Relations Between Spouses dealt extensively with the legal effects and consequences of marriage.[3] Moreover, the 2019 Principles Regarding Couples in *de facto* Unions[4] have tackled the novel field of *de facto* relationships, and have once again provided invaluable advice in this field of research. To date, however, only the 2007 Principles Regarding Parental Responsibilities[5] have distinctly addressed the vertical level. There still remains important work to be done regarding the parent–child relationship which will be dealt with first (section 2). However, on the horizontal level, too, promising ideas and perspectives have emerged with regard to the recognition and protection of new forms of adult relationships (section 3). From an overarching perspective, we will finally address the increasingly urgent topic of domestic violence, both on the horizontal level between adults, and on the vertical one in parent–child relationships (section 4).

2. PARENT–CHILD RELATIONSHIPS

A future focus of Europe-wide research should be on parent–child relationships, that is, on the vertical level.

Over the last few decades, fundamental changes in society as well as in law have led to an increasing pluralisation of family forms.[6] The ostensible ideal of 'natural parents' in a nuclear family, that is, two parents who are genetically and

---

3 K. Boele-Woelki et al., *Principles of European Family Law Regarding Divorce and Maintenance Between Former Spouses*, Intersentia, Cambridge 2004; K. Boele-Woelki et al., *Principles of European Family Law Regarding Property Relations Between Spouses*, Intersentia, Cambridge 2013.

4 K. Boele-Woelki et al., *Principles of European Family Law Regarding Property, Maintenance and Succession Rights of Couples in de facto Unions*, Intersentia, Cambridge 2019.

5 K. Boele-Woelki et al., *Principles of European Family Law Regarding Parental Responsibilities*, Intersentia, Cambridge 2007.

6 See N. Dethloff, K. Kaesling and F. Leven, 'From Marriage to Family: Pluralisation of Family Forms from a Comparative Perspective' in N. Dethloff and K. Kaesling (eds), *Between Sexuality, Gender and Reproduction: On the Pluralisation of Family Forms*, Intersentia, Cambridge 2023, pp. 1 et seqq.; see also A.-M. Jensen, 'Pluralization of Family Forms' in J. Qvortrup, W.A. Corsaro and M.-S. Honig (eds), *The Palgrave Handbook of Childhood Studies*, Palgrave Macmillan, London 2009, pp. 140, 153, referring to 'the changing role of marriage' followed by 'extramarital births, consensual unions and stepfamilies' but also mentioning 'same-sex partnerships' and 'self-chosen single parenthood'. Other family forms could be added, such as, in particular, families using assisted reproductive technologies (ART) and families of gender minorities, cf. F.F. Furstenberg et al., 'Kinship Practices

biologically related to the children in their shared household, is eroding. It is a fact that there have always been families in which children have been brought up by adults who are not their genetic and biological parents – be it in step-families, in foster care or in the case of childcare by distant relatives or godparents. In more than a few cases, not only do such adults actually take on the parental role – and thus the corresponding responsibility – but an emotional bond also develops between the child and the 'parental' figures. Social parenthood is therefore not a new phenomenon. As a result of major social, technological and legal shifts, however, the social aspect of being a parent has gained increasing attention and importance in recent years.

In particular, the rise of assisted reproductive technologies (ART) has led to an increasing number of cases in which the different facets of parenthood – the genetic, biological, social and legal relations between an adult and a child – are being disentangled and even severed.[7] Hence, not only is there an increasing diversity of family forms, but also a *pluralisation of parenthood.* For example, while the focus of procreative techniques was initially on homologous conceptions using the husband's or partner's sperm, in the case of male infertility or subfertility the use of donor sperm has become more frequent. Nowadays, donor conception is widely accepted where male gametes are concerned and existing restrictions have been abolished.[8] As a result of gamete donation, however, three or more individuals may now play a parental role for the child. In some cases, it may be agreed that the donor will be more than a mere donor of gametes but will be more or less actively involved in the child's life or even take on the role of a parent from birth, in addition to the intended mother and father. In other situations, the child will have a mother, a loving social father and an additional relation to an uninvolved donor. The importance of knowing the latter for the development of the child's identity (but also, for example, for certain health issues) should not be underestimated, even if the donor does not want to be responsible for the child's care and upbringing.[9] Thus, the increasing

---

Among Alternative Family Forms in Western Industrialized Societies' (2020) 82(5) *Journal of Marriage and Family* 1403, 1405 et seq.

7 See N. Dethloff, K. Kaesling and F. Leven, above n. 6, pp. 3 et seqq.

8 An overview is provided by T. Glennon, 'Legal Regulation of Family Creation Through Gamete Donation – Access, Identity and Parentage' in S. Golombok et al. (eds), *Regulating Reproductive Donation*, Cambridge University Press, Cambridge 2016, pp. 60, 63 et seqq.; consistent with the regulations of some Muslim-majority countries, Turkey still bans the use of donor gametes, cf. C. Kooli, 'Review of Assisted Reproduction Techniques, Laws, and Regulations in Muslim Countries' (2019) 24 *Middle East Fertility Society Journal* Article No. 8; Z.B. Gürtin, 'Banning reproductive travel: Turkey's ART legislation and third-party assisted reproduction' (2011) 23(5) *Reproductive BioMedicine Online* 555.

9 See, for example, E. Decorte, 'The Right to Access Information about One's Genetic Origins in the Context of Medically Assisted Reproduction: Time Changes Everything?' in I. Boone and M. Vonk (eds), *The Right to Identity and Access to Information on Genetic Origin and Parentage*, Intersentia, Cambridge 2024, pp. 33, 36. On the corresponding legal situation in Europe in the context of gamete donation, J.-R. Binet and European Committee on

use of ART[10] has brought about fundamental changes, major challenges and a shift from nature to nurturing.

From a legal standpoint, the different facets of parenthood are increasingly to be considered independently of each other. With respect to certain legal issues, genetic and biological parenthood may be essential, particularly in the context of the right to know one's genetic parentage and the circumstances of one's origin. In other matters, however – for example, with regard to parental authority and child maintenance – increasing weight is given to the intention to become a parent and the responsibility for conceiving the child, but also to the subsequent assumption of a 'parental role' only after the birth of the child.

The growing recognition of same-sex partnerships and parents has had a significant impact on the changing concepts of family and parenthood.[11] The desire of many same-sex partners to start a family is evidently strong.[12] Gradually, same-sex couples have been allowed to adopt children, often at first just the partner's child through second-parent adoptions and later also in the form of joint adoptions.[13] Moreover, same-sex couples are increasingly being granted access to assisted reproduction.[14] Despite the opposition that – unfortunately – still exists to some extent, it is therefore clear that the European trend is towards the legal recognition of same-sex parenthood. In many jurisdictions, for example, lesbian couples' co-motherhood is being progressively recognised.[15] Among queer families, however, there is also a rising number of shared parenthood projects.[16] Lesbian couples often use private sperm donation and sometimes would like the genetic father not only to be in regular contact with the child but also to be involved in raising and caring for the child. Gay

---

LEGAL CO-OPERATION, *Comparative study on access of persons conceived by gamete donation to information on their origins*, Council of Europe Publishing, Strasbourg 2022.

10 On the usage of assisted reproductive technologies in European countries see, for example, P. PRÄG and M.C. MILLS, 'Assisted Reproductive Technology in Europe: Usage and Regulation in the Context of Cross-Border Reproductive Care' in M. KREYENFELD and D. KONIETZKA (eds), *Childlessness in Europe: Contexts, Causes, and Consequences*, Springer, Cham 2017, pp. 289, 291 et seqq.

11 See N. DETHLOFF, K. KAESLING and F. LEVEN, above n. 6, pp. 9 et seqq.

12 According to a survey on the situation in Germany, three-quarters of all homosexual people would like to have children and 64% even wish for two or more, see L. DE VRIES, *Regenbogenfamilien in Deutschland*, DJI Verlag, Munich 2021, pp. 17 et seq.

13 Cf. N. DETHLOFF, *Familienrecht*, 33rd ed., C.H. Beck, Munich 2022, §15 mn. 87; N. DETHLOFF, K. KAESLING and F. LEVEN, above n. 6, p. 12.

14 See N. DETHLOFF, K. KAESLING and F. LEVEN, above n. 6, pp. 12 et seq.

15 See, for example, Belgium: Art. 325/1 et seqq. Code civil; the Netherlands: Art. 1:198 Burgerlijk Wetboek; the United Kingdom: ss. 42, 44 Human Fertilisation and Embryology Act 2008; N. DETHLOFF, K. KAESLING and F. LEVEN, above n. 6, pp. 1, 13. Legal co-motherhood is furthermore possible in Austria, Denmark, Finland, France, Iceland, Ireland, Norway, Portugal, Slovenia, Spain, Sweden and Switzerland.

16 According to a survey, 31% of lesbian women and 26% of gay men would consider raising a child together with a homosexual couple with whom they are friends, cf. C. HAAG, *Emergence of a new type of family?*, University of Bamberg Press, Bamberg 2016, p. 173.

couples are also increasingly starting a family with a woman – or a female couple. In such families, two children might grow up who have neither the same genetic mother nor the same genetic father, but in fact the same four parents. All these multi-parent families are characterised by the fact that the assumption of parental responsibilities by several people is consensually intended from the start, even before conception.

Finally, the existing paradigms are questioned by the increasing acceptance of trans, non-binary and intersex persons.[17] New concepts of legal gender are challenging traditional terms of fatherhood and motherhood. Thus, it appears more urgent than ever to focus joint efforts on parent–child relationships.

Future pan-Europe research is therefore called for to address the law of parenthood in a comprehensive way, thereby covering both 'becoming parents' and 'being parents'.

It would thus be essential to deal with which methods of ART are allowed under what preconditions – from the donation of sperm, eggs and embryos to surrogacy or post-mortem insemination, including 'brand new ways to make babies',[18] like ectogenesis, in-vitro gametogenesis or mitochondrial donation. Egg as well as embryo donation are increasingly accepted, though not yet as widely as sperm donation.[19] The much more controversial reproductive technique of surrogacy is prohibited in many countries and legal in others.[20] While most European jurisdictions do not allow any form of surrogacy, altruistic surrogacy is permitted in some.[21] Elsewhere, both commercial surrogacy as well as different forms of altruistic surrogacy may be found.[22] In recent years, a growing number

---

17 See N. Dethloff, K. Kaesling and F. Leven, above n. 6, pp. 14 et seqq.

18 Nils-Eric Sahlin drew attention to these 'brand new ways' with his presentation 'Synthetic Human Embryos, Artificial Wombs, in vitro Gametogenesis (IVG), and Other (Reproduction) Technologies. Brand New Ways to Make Babies. Do We Have the Laws and Regulations We Need?' at the conference *What Family Law for Europe?*, Stockholm, 10–11 October 2024.

19 An overview of legal permissibility is provided by T. Glennon, above n. 8, pp. 63 et seqq.; see also S.J. Ory and International Federation of Fertility Societies, *IFFS Surveillance 2016*, pp. 32 et seqq.

20 A legal comparative overview is provided by A. Büchler and A. Schmucki, 'Das Abstammungsrecht in rechtsvergleichender Sicht' (2020) (1) FamPra.ch 1, 16 et seqq.; N. Dethloff, 'Leihmutterschaft als Herausforderung für Rechtsprechung und Gesetzgebung – Altruistische Leihmutterschaft aus rechtsvergleichender Perspektive' in A. Dutta et al. (eds), *Das Familienrecht in seiner großen Vielfalt: Festschrift Hans-Joachim Dose*, Gieseking, Bielefeld 2022, pp. 77, 80 et seqq.; N. Dethloff, 'Leihmutterschaft in rechtsvergleichender Perspektive' in B. Ditzen and M.-P. Weller (eds), *Regulierung der Leihmutterschaft*, Mohr Siebeck, Tübingen 2018, pp. 55 et seqq.; see also the country reports in J.M. Scherpe, C. Fenton-Glynn and T. Kaan (eds), *Eastern and Western Perspectives on Surrogacy*, Intersentia, Cambridge 2019.

21 A prominent example of the permissibility of surrogacy in Europe is the United Kingdom: Surrogacy Arrangements Act 1985; further EU Member States allowing for altruistic surrogacy are Belgium, Denmark, Greece, Ireland, the Netherlands and Portugal.

22 Commercial surrogacy is, for example, permitted in Ukraine: G. Druzenko, 'Ukraine' in K. Trimmings and P. Beaumont (eds), *International Surrogacy Arrangements*, Hart Publishing,

of European countries have also introduced legislation to allow post-mortem fertilisation.[23] However, even if more and more such methods of ART are being permitted in many countries, the preconditions for using these options differ widely. Common questions are whether only married people should be granted access, or also unmarried or even single people,[24] and whether this also applies to homosexual couples. Furthermore, it may be made dependent on other circumstances, for example medical conditions, on the age of the intended parents or parent,[25] or on necessary consent from certain persons.

In addition, the focus should be on the consequences of the usage of different methods of ART and how they challenge traditional concepts of parentage. With the different facets of parenthood split across several persons, their roles, rights and duties need to be redefined. Urgent questions arise: Who are and should be the legal parents? With regard to different forms of multi-parenting, what rights and obligations should they as well as other persons have?[26] And importantly, how can the children's right to know their genetic origin be realised?[27]

A vision would be to ultimately bring together these subjects in a large European project on 'The Law of Parenthood' that includes both a broad comparative perspective with many participating jurisdictions as well as an interdisciplinary approach, and that covers parentage, parental responsibilities and the right to know one's origin and have access to information thereon. This would allow us to establish the current common ground and assess the existing diversity. A great deal of work has already been done on many of these aspects, by many of those who participated in the conference. But all of this needs to be brought together – and much more work needs to be done!

Taking into consideration the increasing mobility as well as cross-border relationships and the vast diversity that exists in some areas, it would be desirable to

London 2013, pp. 357, 358 et seq.; for the complex legal situation in the USA, see A. Büchler and A. Schmucki, above n. 20, pp. 16 et seqq.; see also N. Dethloff, 'Leihmutterschaft als Herausforderung für Rechtsprechung und Gesetzgebung' above n. 20, pp. 80 et seqq.

23 For example, post-mortem fertilisation is legal in Belgium, England and Wales, Greece, the Netherlands, Portugal and Spain.

24 In Slovenia, for instance, single women have access to ART, as established by the Constitutional Court of the RS in decisions U-I-418/20-20 and U-I-847/21-21, dated 16 October 2024, published in the Official Gazette of the RS, No. 100/2024.

25 The Slovenian Constitutional Court, however, annulled a regulation that set an age limit of 43 years for women undergoing ART procedures, see decision Up-459/17, U-I-307/19, dated 21 January 2021, published in the Official Gazette of the RS, No. 42/2021. Therefore, as demonstrated in this example, in some jurisdictions the focus may be more on the individual's ability (physical and psychological) to care for a child.

26 The concept of two holders of parental responsibilities is challenged; see already K. Boele-Woelki et al., *The Principles of European Family Law Revisited*, Intersentia, Cambridge 2024, pp. 7, 89.

27 These and other important issues have already been raised in the context of the two panels on 'Assisted Reproduction Techniques, Ethics and the Right to Know One's Origins' and 'Legal Genders and Identities in a European Perspective' at the conference *What Family Law for Europe?*, Stockholm, 10–11 October 2024.

include a genuinely European law perspective. The Court of Justice of the European Union (CJEU) has accepted the challenging task of safeguarding the established rights of EU citizens to protect their freedom of movement, while leaving the autonomy of states in matters of domestic substantive family law untouched.[28] Corresponding rulings of the Court, in turn, have provided impetus to the proposal of the so-called 'Parenthood Regulation',[29] which could lead to a substantial harmonisation and unification of conflict-of-law rules in the area of family law. While such an undertaking is a true challenge in itself,[30] it most certainly requires an in-depth knowledge of the substantive law of the various European countries. Comparative research in this area is therefore urgently needed. One important goal would be to ultimately prevent diversity from resulting in the creation of barriers to the freedom of movement and the separation of children from their parents.

3. NEW FORMS OF ADULT RELATIONSHIPS: BEYOND LOVE AND KINSHIP

3.1. *DE FACTO* UNIONS

Let us now turn to the horizontal level. Here the bulk of work has already been done by the CEFL, with profound principles on marriage as well as the latest ones on couples in *de facto* unions. With regard to the latter, however, there still remains a considerable need for reform at the national level. The Principles of European Family Law Regarding Couples in *de facto* Unions advocate strongly in favour of a legal regime for such relationships.[31] In this regard, the CEFL recommends a model which links regulations on the dissolution of a partnership in particular to joint parenthood. In many Western countries, specific legal rules have already been created for *de facto* unions.[32] In particular, for cohabiting

---

28 Cf. Case C-490/20, *Stolichna obshtina, rayon 'Pancharevo'*, ECLI:EU:C:2021:1008; Case C-673/16, *Coman and Others*, ECLI:EU:C:2018:385; N. Dethloff, K. Kaesling and F. Leven, above n. 6, p. 14.

29 Cf. Proposal for a Council Regulation on jurisdiction, applicable law, recognition of decisions and acceptance of authentic instruments in matters of parenthood and on the creation of a European Certificate of Parenthood, 7 December 2022, COM(2022) 695 final.

30 See for a critical appraisal and suggestions for improvement The Marburg Group, *Comments on the European Commission's Proposal for a Council Regulation on jurisdiction, applicable law, recognition of decisions and acceptance of authentic instruments in matters of parenthood and on the creation of a European Certificate of Parenthood*, 2023; see also the European Law Institute's project *Enhancing Child Protection: Private International Law on Filiation and the European Commission's Proposal COM/2022/695*.

31 See K. Boele-Woelki et al., *Principles of European Family Law Regarding Property, Maintenance and Succession Rights of Couples in de facto Unions*, Intersentia, Cambridge 2019.

32 See N. Dethloff, *Familienrecht*, above n. 13, §8 mn. 42 et seqq.; A. Dutta, 'Paarbeziehungsregime jenseits der Ehe: Rechtsvergleichende und rechtspolitische Perspektiven', *AcP* 216 (2016), 609, 638 et seqq.; E. Goossens, 'One Trend, a Patchwork of

couples with children or in long-lasting relationships, there are more and more legal regimes or provisions in Europe today that do not require formalisation, for example through registration. However, this is a step that the German legislator, for example, has yet to take![33] The truly impressive work of the CEFL therefore deserves to be promoted even more in order to further implement the groundbreaking and visionary concepts contained therein.

3.2. BEYOND LOVE AND KINSHIP

In addition, there is one topic that appears to be worth exploring: in many societies, adults are increasingly taking on responsibility for one another in a variety of situations – not only in relationships of love and kinship, but beyond.[34] With the number of single-person households rising, this may be the case when close friends take care of one another in times of sickness or old age. Other examples include situations where individuals who are not in a romantic relationship decide to raise a child together, for example in the context of postmodern co-parenting, or in families in which a child has been conceived by means of gamete donation and where the donor is equally involved in the care of the child. In these situations, the adults bear responsibility not only for the children, but might at the same time take on responsibility for each other. This is the case, for example, when one is forgoing employment in order to care for the children. Here, as in many other areas, we can see how protection on the vertical level also depends on appropriate regulation on the horizontal level. The two levels are thus intertwined.

In many jurisdictions, such relationships are recognised by law in one form or another in different areas – be it in social security law, where cohabitants are partly treated in the same way as spouses; in insolvency law, where special consideration is given to the closeness to the debtor; or in adult protection law, where close relationships of various kinds are legally recognised while attempting to establish appropriate support. However, a more comprehensive

Laws. An Exploration of Why Cohabitation Law is so Different throughout the Western World' (2021) 35(1) *International Journal of Law, Policy and The Family* 1, 3 et seqq.

33 With a critical view Sachverständigenkommission des Neunten Familienberichts, *Neunter Familienbericht: Eltern sein in Deutschland – Ansprüche, Anforderungen und Angebote bei wachsender Vielfalt: Empfehlungen für eine wirksame Politik für Familien*, BT-Drs. 19/27200, pp. 68 et seqq., 506 et seq.; see also N. Dethloff, A. Timmermann and F. Leven, 'Verantwortungsgemeinschaften im Recht', *NJW* 2022, 3056, 3061; N. Dethloff and F. Leven, 'Adult relations of love and beyond: what legal recognition and protection do they need?' in F. Swennen, E. Goossens and T. Van Hof (eds), *Rethinking Law's Families and Family Law*, Edward Elgar Publishing, Cheltenham 2024, pp. 139, 142 et seq.

34 In detail N. Dethloff and F. Leven, above n. 33, pp. 139 et seqq.; N. Dethloff, A. Timmermann and F. Leven, above n. 33, pp. 3056 et seqq.

legal recognition also of non-intimate adult relationships in family law is still very rare.[35] It is also almost always limited to two persons.[36]

The German government had proposed to introduce a so-called 'community of responsibility' as a new legal institution.[37] This community could have been established on the basis of a 'multilateral community of responsibility contract'. Two to six adults would have been able to conclude such a contract, with a choice between two levels – a so-called 'basic level' and an 'advanced level'. The 'advanced level' would have contained four selectable modules, labelled 'information and representation in health matters', 'living together', 'care and support', and 'community of accrued gains'. Due to the collapse of the German coalition government in November 2024, however, this proposal is currently no longer being pursued.

Considering the latest development of the proposal and the related discussion, this might not be a cause for significant regret, as one could have serious doubts about its potential. But the basic idea of a 'community of responsibility' has drawn attention to quite a novel issue: it raises the question of how the law does and should protect such adult relations in Europe. In different areas of the law? Do other forms of responsibility and care relationships also need legal recognition in family law? As a standard contract or status?

At first glance, one might find this to be superfluous. However, a new legal institution could provide more legal certainty for the parties involved. Beyond couple relationships and kinship, the assumption of responsibility by adults for each other has so far hardly been adequately addressed by the law. In Germany, for example, a number of provisions in a variety of legal areas cover such relations.[38] However, there is no comprehensive and differentiated concept of protection. Instead, various isolated mechanisms for the legal recognition of closeness and relationships of responsibility can be found. For responsibility relationships beyond kinship and legally recognised – romantic – partnerships, this ultimately means in many cases an overwhelming variety of piecemeal regulations. This

35 See, however, Art. 1475 Code civil (Belgium; *cohabitation légale*); s. 3(2) Adult Interdependent Relationships Act (Province of Alberta, Canada; the status of *adult interdependent partners*); and the *caring relationships* according to s. 5 Relationships Act 2003 (Tasmania, Australia) and s. 5 Relationships Act 2008 (Victoria, Australia).

36 See N. Dethloff and F. Leven, above n. 33, pp. 140 et seqq. However, a legal institution called *las relaciones convivenciales de ayuda mutua*, found in Art. 240-1 to 240-7 of the Catalan Civil Code, is open to up to four unrelated adults or any number of adults related in the collateral line.

37 *Mehr Fortschritt wagen* (Coalition Agreement 2021–2025 between SPD, BÜNDNIS 90/DIE GRÜNEN and FDP, 2021), p. 101; the announcement in the coalition agreement is loosely based on a motion from 2020, see BT-Drs. 19/16454; see also the first assessment by N. Dethloff, A. Timmermann and F. Leven, above n. 33, pp. 3056 et seqq. Since February 2024, key points for a possible design of the *community of responsibility*, as envisaged by the German government, can be found in the position paper of the German Federal Ministry of Justice: 'Eckpunkte des Bundesministeriums der Justiz für die Verantwortungsgemeinschaft', 2 February 2024.

38 In detail N. Dethloff, A. Timmermann and F. Leven, above n. 33, pp. 3057 et seq.

results in considerable legal uncertainty and gaps in protection.[39] Such gaps exist even in cases of *de facto* unions.[40] Many people who take on responsibility for each other or would like to do so in the future are therefore largely dependent on making private agreements. However, they often abstain from making any such agreements at all due to a widespread status quo bias and/or optimism bias.[41]

A new comprehensive legal framework could render complicated and expensive private arrangements dispensable. A clever design could remove or at least reduce potential hurdles to private ordering. It could thus allow for the protection of the weaker party or parties in case of dissolution, be it due to separation or death. It would be another fascinating project to discuss this with experts from all over Europe – and beyond!

4. DOMESTIC VIOLENCE

4.1. OVERVIEW OF EMERGING CHALLENGES

The CEFL Principles have made significant contributions to key areas such as marriage,[42] *de facto* unions[43] and parent–child relationships.[44] However, domestic violence was not a primary focus during their initial formulation. In recent years, domestic violence is becoming an increasingly pressing issue. According to findings from the European Union Agency for Fundamental Rights (FRA), women in Europe face widespread violence. In most cases, the perpetrator is a family member or relative of the victim (30%), and very often, it is the partner. The majority of victims are attacked in their own homes (35%).[45] A significant number suffer physical and psychological consequences of the violence, such as panic attacks, depression and difficulties in forming new relationships.[46]

---

39 With a critical view N. Dethloff and F. Leven, above n. 33, pp. 144 et seqq.; N. Dethloff, A. Timmermann and F. Leven, above n. 33, pp. 3057 et seq.

40 See above section 3.1.

41 See N. Dethloff and F. Leven, above n. 33, p. 148; N. Dethloff, A. Timmermann and F. Leven, above n. 33, p. 3059.

42 K. Boele-Woelki et al., *Principles of European Family Law Regarding Divorce and Maintenance Between Former Spouses*, Intersentia, Cambridge 2004; K. Boele-Woelki et al., *Principles of European Family Law Regarding Property Relations Between Spouses*, Intersentia, Cambridge 2013.

43 K. Boele-Woelki et al., *Principles of European Family Law Regarding Property, Maintenance and Succession Rights of Couples in de facto Unions*, Intersentia, Cambridge 2019.

44 K. Boele-Woelki et al., *Principles of European Family Law Regarding Parental Responsibilities*, Intersentia, Cambridge 2007.

45 See FRA, 'Persistent challenge: violence against women', 8 March 2021, https://fra.europa.eu/en/news/2021/persistent-challenge-violence-against-women (last accessed 07.01.2025).

46 FRA, 'Violence Against Women: an EU-wide survey', 5 March 2014, https://fra.europa.eu/en/publication/2014/violence-against-women-eu-wide-survey-main-results-report (last accessed 07.01.2025).

To improve the situation of women, the Council of Europe Convention on Preventing and Combating Violence Against Women and Domestic Violence (commonly known as the 'Istanbul Convention', IC) was adopted in 2011. The IC entered into force on 1 August 2014, and by 2023 38 countries had ratified it.[47] On 1 October 2023, the IC also came into effect in the EU. This development ensures that the EU will uphold international standards, propose its own comprehensive legislation and integrate the obligations of the IC across all areas of EU policy. Together with Directive (EU) 2024/1385 of the European Parliament and of the Council of 14 May 2024 on combating violence against women and domestic violence,[48] the IC establishes a robust legal framework. This framework sets out common minimum standards for EU member states in preventing violence, protecting and supporting victims, ensuring access to justice, and fostering cooperation and coordination among relevant services.[49] A crucial step toward achieving these objectives will undoubtedly be the implementation of Directive (EU) 2024/1385 into national legal systems by 2027. Among other requirements, the Directive mandates that countries introduce appropriate criminal offences for violent behaviour involving new technologies, as some states have yet to criminalise such acts.[50] These European efforts highlight the importance of a unified and comprehensive legal approach to addressing violence against women and domestic violence. Effectively addressing this issue in family law also demands the support of criminal law and other legal disciplines. An interdisciplinary approach is essential and should be a central focus in any future revision of the CEFL Principles.

Reports from national human rights ombudsmen[51] and evaluation assessments by the Group of Experts on Action against Violence against Women and Domestic Violence (GREVIO) emphasise the growing prevalence of violence against women and the significant challenges states face in addressing this issue.[52] Recommendations from GREVIO, an independent body monitoring the implementation of the IC, reveal widespread non-compliance among states, including the absence of legislative measures to operationalise its principles.[53]

---

47 Turkey was the first to sign the IC on 12 March 2012, but it withdrew from it in 2021.

48 OJ L 2024/1385, 24 May 2024.

49 Statement by Helena Dalli, European Commissioner for Equality, dated 7 March 2023, https://www.dnevnik.si/1043018418/mnenja/odprta-stran/nasilje-nad-zenskami-potrebujemo-revolucijo (last accessed 09.08.2023).

50 *Buturugă v Romania*, no. 56867/15, 11 February 2020.

51 See, for example, the Annual Report of the Human Rights Ombudsman of the Republic of Slovenia for 2022, pp. 68, 81, 85, https://www.varuh-rs.si/porocila-projekti/publikacije-gradiva/letna-porocila-priporocila-dz-odzivna-porocila-vlade/ (last accessed 07.01.2025).

52 Timetable baseline evaluation procedure, https://rm.coe.int/provisional-timetable-for-the-baseline-evaluation-procedure-2016–2028/1680a9d977 (last accessed 07.01.2025).

53 See the GREVIO report for Slovenia, https://rm.coe.int/first-baseline-report-on-slovenia/1680a4208b, the GREVIO report for Germany, https://rm.coe.int/report-on-germany-for-publication/1680a86937, and the GREVIO report for Italy, https://rm.coe.int/grevio-report-

In response, several countries are initiating legislative reforms to address these shortcomings.[54] In early December 2024, for example, the German Federal Ministry of Justice presented a draft amendment to the Protection Against Violence Act (*Gewaltschutzgesetz*, GewSchG).[55] The proposed changes aim to enable family courts to impose electronic tagging on the perpetrators of violence and to improve the monitoring and enforcement of court-ordered protective measures.

In family environments where violence against women occurs, children are often present as well. A family environment marked by violence poses a serious threat to a child's healthy development and demands decisive measures to safeguard the child's best interests. The nature of these measures and their legal foundations raise numerous questions in the judicial practices of European countries. As part of the ongoing revision of the CEFL Principles, it is crucial to identify and analyse these challenges, exploring how national legislations, judicial practices and the jurisprudence of the European Court of Human Rights (ECtHR)[56] address them.

4.2. EMERGING CHALLENGES AT THE HORIZONTAL LEVEL

The horizontal scope of this section examines intimate partner violence. Marriage remains the most widely adopted legal framework for regulating partnerships across Europe. Consequently, any revision of the CEFL Principles must prioritise an analysis of the mechanisms states use to protect individuals from intimate partner violence within marriage. A key focus should be on

italy-first-baseline-evaluation/168099724e (last accessed 08.01.2025). GREVIO also calls on the French authorities to take the necessary steps to ensure that decisions regarding custody and visitation rights consider the violence to which children are exposed, as well as the risk of ongoing violence following separation – the GREVIO report on France, p. 54, https://rm.coe.int/grevio-inf-2019-16/168098c61a (last accessed 08.01.2025).

54 In January 2024, the German Federal Ministry of Justice (Bundesministerium der Justiz, BMJ) published a position paper with key points for a reform of parental responsibilities, contact and adoption which also addressed the implementation of the IC, see 'Eckpunkte des Bundesministeriums der Justiz für eine Reform des Kindschaftsrechts: Modernisierung von Sorgerecht, Umgangsrecht und Adoptionsrecht', 16 January 2024, https://www.bmj.de/SharedDocs/Downloads/DE/Themen/Nav_Themen/240115_Eckpunkte_Kindschaftsrecht.html (last accessed 08.01.2025). However, as a result of the collapse of the German government in November 2024, many of the previous government's plans – including the aforementioned reform – will no longer be implemented.

55 German Federal Ministry of Justice (Bundesministerium der Justiz, BMJ), 'Referentenentwurf des Bundesministeriums der Justiz: Entwurf eines Ersten Gesetzes zur Änderung des Gewaltschutzgesetzes', 2 December 2024. See also *Verantwortung für Deutschland* (Coalition Agreement between CDU, CSU and SPD, 2025), p. 91. In mid-2025, this reform is still pending.

56 For the practice of the ECtHR, see P. Volke, 'Die Rechtsprechung des EuGHMR zum Thema „Häusliche Gewalt gegen Frauen"', *FamRZ* 2023, 333, 339.

whether existing family law protections – particularly those concerning the preservation of the family home and temporary measures – are adequate. It is also crucial to determine whether these protections only apply during the marriage or extend to its dissolution and beyond. Research consistently shows that domestic violence often persists beyond the end of a partnership and may escalate when a victim chooses to leave an abusive partner. In extreme cases, such violence can become life-threatening for women and children.[57]

When revising the CEFL principles, it is crucial to understand how states interpret the widely accepted comparative legal prohibition of mediation in cases of domestic violence. If mediation is excluded in instances of domestic violence, the court should not suspend proceedings for mediation purposes,[58] although such suspensions still occur in practice.[59] The prohibition of mediation in cases of violence raises the question of whether the ban only prevents the consideration of agreements reached through mediation or also applies to agreements that spouses did not reach during the mediation process.[60] If the prohibition of mediation is understood as an obstacle to concluding all types of agreements, then, in cases of domestic violence between spouses, the possibility of a court settlement or the creation of an enforceable notarial protocol – such as agreements on mutual support between spouses or the division of joint property – is excluded. The inadmissibility of reaching agreements also calls into question the possibility of a consensual divorce before a court or notary (i.e. a private divorce). This implies that, in cases of violence, only a judicial divorce upon request from one spouse is available. However, how should a divorce procedure be structured to ensure adequate protection for the victim? The issues that arise include, in particular, the speed of the procedure, establishing facts ex officio, cooperation between the court and other authorities, separate hearings of participants,[61] and the prohibition of disclosing the victim's whereabouts.[62] An additional dilemma concerns how states should manage potential counselling

57 According to a British study highlighted in GREVIO's report on Germany, mental or physical violence often continues even after partners separate, https://rm.coe.int/report-on-germany-for-publication/1680a86937 (last accessed 11.01.2025).

58 On this, B. Novak, *Family Code in light of the Istanbul Convention* (*Družinski zakonik v luči Istanbulske konvencije*), Litteralis, Ljubljana 2023, p. 20.

59 In its report on Slovenia, GREVIO notes that, according to information provided by women's rights non-governmental organisations in the country, courts often encourage parties involved in cases of severe violence to reach an agreement, https://rm.coe.int/first-baseline-report-on-slovenia/1680a4208b (last accessed 07.01.2025).

60 See Mid-term Horizontal Review of GREVIO baseline evaluation reports, February 2022, https://rm.coe.int/prems-010522-gbr-grevio-mid-term-horizontal-review-rev-february-2022/1680a58499 (last accessed 09.01.2025).

61 OLG Zweibrücken, decision no. 6UF 18/22, dated 30 June 2022, *FamRZ* 2022, 1938.

62 See G. Schirrmacher and T. Meysen, 'Häusliche Gewalt: Perspektiven für einem Kindeswohlorientierten, effektiven Schutz vor Gewalt in Kindschafts- und Familienverfahrensrecht', *FamRZ* 2021, 1933, 1939.

procedures before divorce, which are intended to encourage spouses to reach an agreement on mutual matters and child-related issues.[63]

Although victims of violence are most often women in heterosexual relationships, all partners must receive comprehensive protection regardless of their gender, sexual orientation or the type of partnership in which they live. In this context, it is essential to analyse the situation across different countries and to determine whether the protection provided to spouses can serve as a model for other types of partnerships. This includes, for example, specific legal regulations for same-sex couples in countries where such laws are still in place, as well as the legal frameworks governing *de facto* unions.

From the perspective of equality in protection against violence, the question arises whether the legal recognition of a specific type of relationship should matter at all when it comes to ensuring such protection. This issue is particularly supported by the reflections presented under the heading 'New Forms of Adult Relationships' in section 3 of this contribution. These considerations raise the dilemma of whether family law protection should be extended to all adults living together, regardless of whether they are connected by love, kinship, guardianship or some other bond. In the spirit of equality, the question arises whether protection should also be extended to partners who have never cohabited, as well as to individuals who are co-parents but were never in a romantic relationship.

4.3. EMERGING CHALLENGES AT THE VERTICAL LEVEL

The vertical focus of this section examines domestic violence against children. The children may witness violence in the family, experience direct abuse, or endure both. Each form of violence leaves lasting impacts on a child. Domestic violence, even when directed solely at a parent or another child in the family, significantly affects the emotional, economic and social well-being of the entire family.[64] The IC specifically addresses the issue of violence in decision-making processes concerning measures to protect the child's best interests, such as decisions regarding custody, care and contact. States parties are obligated to adopt the necessary legislative or other measures to ensure that incidents of domestic violence are considered when determining custody, care and visitation rights.

---

63 In Slovenia, a preliminary counselling process is conducted at the social work centre before any court proceedings concerning child-related matters. During this process, the social work centre is required to inform parents about the benefits of reaching an amicable agreement and to present mediation as an option. However, these provisions are entirely inappropriate and ineffective in cases involving domestic violence.

64 Point F of the European Parliament Resolution of 6 October 2021, on the impact of domestic violence and custody rights on women and children (2019/2166(INI)), OJ C 123/27, 24 March 2022.

These arrangements must be implemented in a way that does not jeopardise the rights or safety of the victim or the children (Article 31 IC). However, most states still lack specific provisions to concretely implement the IC in decisions related to custody, care and contact. In Germany, as part of the intended reform of the law on parental responsibilities, contact and adoption, it was planned to implement Article 31 IC, one of the key provisions of the IC on protection against gender-based violence.[65] However, at the beginning of November 2024, the German government collapsed. As a consequence, the reform mentioned will no longer be implemented – at least not in its original form.[66]

Due to the absence of specific legal provisions, the application of general rules often fails to interpret cases in light of the principles set out in the IC. As a result, a parent who is a victim of violence is frequently not granted independent protection but only protection tied to the best interests of the child. This concept is often misunderstood when decision-making authorities fail to recognise the harm that witnessing violence can cause to a child. Such a misinterpretation of the child's best interests may lead courts to decide that both parents, even in cases where domestic violence against a parent or a child has occurred, can share custody and care, despite their inability to cooperate equitably and effectively. This misunderstanding can also result in visitation arrangements that harm the child or perpetuate domestic violence. In practice, mothers are often victims of violence during child handovers. Fathers may subject children to emotional abuse during visitation, threaten physical violence, intimidate, speak derogatorily about the mother,[67] or instruct the child to convey insulting messages to her.[68] A child whose father has threatened their mother's (or sibling's) life is typically afraid of the father and suffers distress during visitations, partly due to witnessing the ongoing emotional anguish of the mother (or sibling) caused by these visits.

The dilemmas surrounding decisions on custody, care and visitation must be addressed in the future, and solutions must be found to prevent courts from prioritising the perpetrator's visitation rights over the child's needs and the

65 In January 2024, the German Federal Ministry of Justice (Bundesministerium der Justiz, BMJ) published a position paper with key points for a reform of parental responsibilities, contact and adoption, see 'Eckpunkte des Bundesministeriums der Justiz für eine Reform des Kindschaftsrechts: Modernisierung von Sorgerecht, Umgangsrecht und Adoptionsrecht', 16 January 2024.

66 In early 2025, however, at least a future legal entitlement to protection and counselling for (female) victims of domestic violence was established, including the provision of safe and appropriate accommodation, cf. *Gesetz für ein verlässliches Hilfesystem bei geschlechtsspezifischer und häuslicher Gewalt*, BGBl. I 2025 no. 57; see also BT-Drs. 20/14025. Apart from this, the German government is now focusing primarily on criminal law instruments and the electronic tagging of perpetrators of violence, see *Verantwortung für Deutschland* (Coalition Agreement between CDU, CSU and SPD, 2025), p. 91.

67 Decision of the Higher Court in Ljubljana, no. IV Cp 211/2023, 17 February 2023 – SOVS database.

68 Compare the *I.M. and Others v Italy*, no. 25426/20, 10 November 2022.

victim's right to safety. Additionally, there is a lack of clear guidelines on when supervised visitations are genuinely in the child's best interests. Current practices indicate that courts often indiscriminately order supervised visitations in cases of violence,[69] creating the impression of an unwritten rule that supervised visits are preferred over the complete removal of visitation rights. This assumption is harmful, as it is not based on a general assessment of cases suitable for supervised visits or on a thorough evaluation of risks and their management.[70] As highlighted in GREVIO's report on Slovenia,[71] supervised visitations do not eliminate the risk of the perpetrator using visits as an opportunity to harm the victim and/or the child. If there is any threat of violence during visitations, the visits are not in the child's best interests and should not be allowed by the court. Judicial decisions must ensure that perpetrators cannot exploit visitations to replace the former relationship, exert control or wield power over the former partner.[72]

When developing general criteria for determining visitation in cases of domestic violence, it is important to consider whether the legislator should automatically prohibit joint custody, care and visitation in such cases, or whether legal provisions should allow courts some degree of discretion. This issue was recently addressed by the German legislator, which announced plans to clarify that violence against one parent is explicitly a reason to deny the other contact with the child. According to the key issue paper, in contact proceedings, the family court was required to comprehensively and systematically identify any indications of domestic violence against the child and/or the other parent, assess its effects and conduct a risk analysis. The court could restrict or exclude contact if this was necessary to prevent a specific risk to the parent affected by violence. This provision also explicitly took Article 31 IC into account.[73] Joint custody should not only be excluded in cases of violence against the child but also in cases of partner violence. As an additional protective measure, the family court should also have the authority to order contact guardianship (*Umgangspflegschaft*) to mitigate risks to the safety of the parent affected by violence.[74] However, following the fall of the government in November 2024, it remains uncertain whether such a provision will be introduced in the future.

---

69 See *I.M. and Others v Italy*, no. 25426/20, 10 November 2022.

70 See the decision of the Higher Court in Ljubljana, no. IV Cp 858/2022, 5 July 2022 – SOVS database.

71 See the GREVIO report for Slovenia, https://rm.coe.int/first-baseline-report-on-slovenia/1680a4208b (last accessed 07.01.2025).

72 See the GREVIO report for Germany, https://rm.coe.int/report-on-germany-for-publication/1680a86937 (last accessed 08.01.2025).

73 The family court should also examine, in accordance with the applicable law, whether the specific circumstances of the case require a restriction or exclusion of contact in order to protect the best interests of the child (Section 1684(4) sentences 1 and 2 BGB).

74 See German Federal Ministry of Justice (Bundesministerium der Justiz, BMJ), 'Eckpunkte des Bundesministeriums der Justiz für eine Reform des Kindschaftsrechts: Modernisierung von Sorgerecht, Umgangsrecht und Adoptionsrecht', 16 January 2024, p. 11.

It is also necessary to analyse judicial practices when a parent raises concerns about visitation rights, as well as custody and care rights for a violent parent. It is crucial that courts do not automatically label such a parent as uncooperative or unsuitable, or accuse them of alienating the child, without investigating whether these concerns stem from a violent family situation.[75] Furthermore, it is essential to examine whether courts continue to rely on the concept of parental alienation syndrome (PAS).[76] GREVIO has highlighted that PAS lacks any scientific basis.[77] No professional association has recognised parental alienation syndrome as a valid medical condition or mental disorder. PAS is not listed in the International Statistical Classification of Diseases and Related Health Problems by the WHO, nor is it recognised by the American Medical Association or the American Psychiatric Association,[78] both of which the European Parliament considers to be leading institutions in the field of mental health.[79] The use of PAS has also been rejected by the Court of Appeal of England and Wales, and the Canadian Ministry of Justice advises against its application.[80] Moreover, the European Parliament Resolution of 6 October 2021, on the impact of domestic violence and custody rights on women and children (2019/2166(INI)) explicitly opposes the use of PAS and similar concepts.[81]

Another important issue to explore is how to consider the child's opinion during proceedings, particularly when it aligns with the mother's refusal of contact with the father.[82] Additionally, it is critical to determine how to protect the child who has expressed their opinion, especially in relation to the violent parent.

5. CONCLUSION

For two decades, the CEFL with its Principles has invaluably contributed to advancing the research in comparative family law in a rapidly changing world, thereby providing input for important law reforms in a number of countries.

75 *I.M. and Others v Italy*, no. 25426/20, 10 November 2022.

76 P. Volke, 'Die Empfehlungen des Expertenausschusses zur Umsetzung der Istanbul-Konvention im Hinblick auf familiengerichtliche Verfahren', *FamRZ* 2022, 1908, 1910.

77 The GREVIO group first became aware of this in its report on France, https://rm.coe.int/grevio-inf-2019-16/168098c61a, and also highlights it in its report on Germany, https://rm.coe.int/report-on-germany-for-publication/1680a86937 (last accessed 11.01.2025).

78 P. Volke, above n. 76, p. 1910.

79 The European Parliament Resolution of 6 October 2021, on the impact of domestic violence and custody rights on women and children (2019/2166(INI)), OJ C 123/27, 24 March 2022.

80 Compare https://en.wikipedia.org/wiki/Parental_alienation_syndrome (last accessed 17.08.2023).

81 OJ C 123/27, 24 March 2022.

82 P. Volke, OLG Köln, 'Beschluss v. 22.7.2022 – II-14 UF66/22 (Istanbul-Konvention)', *FamRZ* 2022, 134, 136; T. Meysen, 'EuGHMR: Berücksichtigung von häuslicher Gewalt bei gerichtlichen Umgangs- und Sorgerechtskonflikten', *FamRZ* 2023, 280, 283; OLG Frankfurt/Main, decision no. 1UF 205/21, dated 22 September 2022, *FamRZ* 2022, 1940; G. Walther, 'OLG Frankfurt/M., Beschluss v. 13. 7. 2020', *FamRZ* 2020, 2010, 2013.

Looking at the way ahead, our conference has clearly demonstrated that joint efforts are necessary to tackle future challenges. Topics and perspectives both on the vertical level of family relationships and on the horizontal level need to be explored with family law researchers from all European jurisdictions, including the perspectives of practitioners. Moreover, it appears important to include viewpoints from other fields of the law, for example social and tax law, but also constitutional and criminal law. Finally, these endeavours call for an interdisciplinary approach and close cooperation with scholars from other disciplines, in particular social sciences, psychology and ethics, but increasingly also, for example, medical or technological sciences. The overarching objective must be to create a legal framework for all families in their increasing diversity.

PART IV

A CHALLENGE OF OUR TIME

Balancing between Autonomy and Protection of Vulnerable Adults at International, European and National Level

COMPARATIVE FAMILY LAW BY FL-EUR

First Results and Working Method on Vulnerable Adults

Masha ANTOKOLSKAIA, Wendy SCHRAMA and Tim WUYTS*

1. INTRODUCTION

In February 2019, FL-EUR – Family Law in Europe: An Academic Network – was established in Amsterdam.[1] FL-EUR is a relatively recent newcomer to the heterogeneous club of academic initiatives launched around the turn of the millennium, which aim to undertake various comparative law projects focusing on the harmonisation and/or unification of private law in Europe. FL-EUR comprises experts from 31 European jurisdictions and is dedicated to the collection, systematisation and analysis of comparative legal knowledge in the field of family law and the law of persons.

After some delays due to the COVID-19 pandemic, FL-EUR has now harvested its first flowers. By 2023, national reports had been produced on its first subject: the empowerment and protection of vulnerable adults.[2] In many respects, FL-EUR can be regarded as a younger sibling of the Commission on European Family Law (CEFL), which was founded in 2001. However, while the remarkable achievements of CEFL served as an inspiration for the founders of FL-EUR, the latter does not directly follow in the footsteps of CEFL.

The issue of harmonisation began to garner increasing attention within European academic circles starting in the 1980s. Initially, EU institutions showed little interest in the topic. However, by the turn of the millennium the situation had changed and it started to look like the European Commission had almost assumed a leading role. The Commission's engagement further stimulated academic interest in harmonisation projects.

During the second decade of the 21st century, however, the political climate gradually became less favourable. The timing of FL-EUR's establishment might even raise some eyebrows, as it coincided with a period when enthusiasm for the

* This work is based on prior work by the authors and is partially the result of funding by the Dutch Research Council (NWO).

1 https://fl-eur.eu/.

2 https://fl-eur.eu/working_field_1__empowerment_and_protection/country-reports.

harmonisation of private law in Europe had dwindled significantly. This makes it particularly interesting to consider this new comparative law project within the broader context of the development of similar initiatives.

2. POSITION OF FL-EUR WITHIN THE CONTEXT OF EUROPEAN PRIVATE LAW

As has just been mentioned, comparative law projects aimed at the spontaneous harmonisation (convergence) or deliberate harmonisation, and later even unification, of private law in Europe, emerged as early as the 1980s.[3] All of these projects were academic initiatives, founded by high-profile law comparison groups that managed to build up broad international networks of leading academics from different countries. Clarity about the concepts of 'harmonisation' and 'unification' and concerning the different forms thereof is important in order to understand the differences between the goals and methods of these initiatives. Harmonisation and unification can be imposed by a higher authority (the top-down method) or on a voluntary basis (the bottom-up method).[4] Harmonisation can be the result of deliberate human efforts aimed at achieving greater similarity between laws, but it can also arise from a natural evolutionary process.[5] Top-down harmonisation is always the result of deliberate efforts by a central authority. In the context of European private law, these can be EU bodies. In contrast to top-down harmonisation, bottom-up harmonisation can be both the result of deliberate efforts, for example academic initiatives such as national or international bodies, and the result of spontaneous convergent legal systems.[6] From the outset, there was a clear difference between the objectives and methods of the initiatives aimed at the harmonisation and/or unification of private law in Europe.

A first group of initiatives goes no further than promoting and facilitating spontaneous harmonisation (convergence) and deliberately refrains from drawing up non-binding Principles in the form of articles of law, which can serve as models for future (harmonised) legislation. The most prominent projects

---

3 For a brief overview, see E. Hondius, 'Towards a European Civil Code' in A. Hartkamp et al. (eds), *Towards a European Civil Code*, 4th ed., Kluwer, Deventer 2011, pp. 15–18; A. Janssen, M. Lehmann and R. Schulze, 'The Future of European Private Law – An Introduction' in A. Janssen, M. Lehmann and R. Schulze, *The Future of European Private Law*, Nomos, Baden-Baden 2023, pp. 18–24.

4 J. Smits, *The Making of European Private Law: Towards a Ius Commune Europaeum as a Mixed Legal System*, Intersentia, Antwerp 2002, p. 6.

5 B. Trompenaars, *Pluriform unification and uniform interpretation: in particular the contribution of UNCITRAL to the international unification of private law*, Kluwer, Devener 1989, p. 12.

6 M. Antokolskaia, *Harmonisation of Family Law in Europe: A Historical Perspective*, Intersentia, Antwerp 2006, pp. 15–27.

in this group are the Common Core of European Private Law, which started in 1993, and the Ius Commune Casebook Project, initiated in 1994. FL-EUR joined this group of projects in 2019. The initiatives within this group aim to facilitate the convergence of legal systems by developing a common European legal science.[7] Thus, the aim of the *Ius Commune Casebooks for the Common Law of Europe* is described as an attempt to 'uncover the common roots of the different legal systems' and to promote the unification of European private law through natural 'bottom-up' growth by means of a 'gradual convergence of legal systems'.[8] In the description of the purpose of the Common Core of European Private Law, an even more cautious choice of words is used. The stated goals of the project are to map out Europe's private law,[9] to 'promote a common culture', and to 'develop a common legal education' through the creation of a 'model European legal school'.[10]

The aim of FL-EUR is to promote spontaneous bottom-up harmonisation of the law of persons and family law in Europe by collecting, systematising, analysing and making available knowledge on the relevant national law of the covered jurisdictions to academics, practitioners, national and supranational governments, and international organisations. The FL-EUR project focuses on substantive law but it also deals with *law in action* and *law in context*. FL-EUR is committed to applying a problem-solving, multidisciplinary approach, with a combination of the functional comparative law method and multidisciplinary methods. Legal solutions are described and analysed in their political and socio-economic context. The national experts are asked to also describe the underlying policy considerations and political and academic debates behind the legal instruments. Where available, existing empirical evaluations of relevant legislation are incorporated into the work to shed light on which national legal solutions work well and which do not. One deliberately limits oneself to looking for similarities, including functional equivalents, and differences, including functional disequivalents; learning from each other's experiences by identifying best practices and pitfalls; and looking at what works and what does not, and at the question of to what extent these outcomes are context-specific. Deliberate harmonisation and the design of Principles or any other models are explicitly not part of FL-EUR's ambitions.

A second group of initiatives goes a step further and focuses on the drafting of non-binding Principles for certain areas of private law, which can serve as inspiration and/or a model for future harmonised private law in Europe.

---

7 J. Gordley, 'Comparative Legal Research: Its Function in the Development of Harmonised Law' (1995) 43 *The American Journal of Comparative Law* 555.

8 W. van Gerven et al., *Torts. Scope of Protection*, Hart Publishing, Oxford 1998.

9 M. Bussani and U. Mattei, 'The Common Core Approach to European Private Law' (1997–1998) 3 *Columbia Journal of European Private Law* 340.

10 Ibid., p. 341.

The most well-known initiatives from this group are the UNIDROIT Commission on the Principles for International Commercial Contracts, founded in 1980, the Lando Commission on European Contract Law, founded in 1982, and the European Group on Tort Law, founded in 1992. The Commission on European Family Law (CEFL), founded in 2001, also belongs to this group. The aim of the CEFL is to establish non-binding Principles[11] that can serve as a point of reference for national legislators that are considering the renewal of their family law; for spouses and their advisers who draw up prenuptial agreements for international marriages; and for the EU legislator when drafting secondary legislation.[12]

A third group goes even further and aspires towards the top-down harmonisation or even unification of private law in Europe as the ultimate goal. The idea of top-down harmonisation, long seen as controversial,[13] was accompanied by the idea of a new codification of private law in Europe. In 1998, the German legal comparatist Christian von Bar launched the Study Group on a European Civil Code, which aimed to pave the way for a binding European Civil Code, preferably in the form of an EU Regulation.[14] Later this group moderated its ambitions.[15]

Because the option of the top-down harmonisation/unification of private law in Europe clearly cannot leave the realm of academic endeavour and reverie without active support from the EU, it only really became popular in 2001, when the attitude of the EU bodies changed from wait-and-see detachment to enthusiastic involvement.[16] At its peak, a mega-conglomerate of hundreds of European legislators worked for many years on a gigantic project sponsored by

11 K. Boele-Woelki, 'Objectives and Values of the CEFL in its Principles of European Family Law' in A.-L. Verbeke et al. (eds), *Confronting the Frontiers of Family and Succession Law. Liber Amicorum Walter Pintens*, Intersentia, Antwerp 2012, pp. 167–186.

12 Boele-Woelki explains that 'some of the Principles, but not all, have been drafted so that they could be implemented in a national system. Following this approach the Principles may serve two purposes: firstly, they could be considered as recommendations and, secondly, they may be used as a model for the applicable law'. K. Boele-Woelki, 'The principles of European family law: aims and prospects' (2005) 1(2) *Utrecht Law Review* 167,available at: https://doi.org/10.18352/ulr.13.

13 See for instance B. Markesinis, 'Why a Code is not the Best Way to Advance the Cause of European Legal Unity?' (1997) *European Review of Private Law* 520.

14 The intended output of the group was initially unequivocally described as 'an annotated professorial draft of a European Civil Code', accompanied by a comparative law commentary (C. von Bar, 'The Study Group on a European Civil Code' (2000) *Juridka Föreningen i Finland* 326) and preferably in the form of a Regulation (ibid., p. 326). Later, this objective was somewhat watered down.

15 C. von Bar, 'Paving the Way Forward with Principles of European Private Law' in S. Grundmann (ed.), *An Academic Green Paper on European Contract Law*, Kluwer, The Hague 2002, pp. 142–145.

16 In 2001 the EU Commission issued a groundbreaking Communication from the Commission to the Council and the European Parliament on European Contract Law, Brussels 11 July 2001, COM(2001) 398 final – C-0471/2001, OJ C 255, 13 September 2001. In 2003 the 'Action Plan

the EU and carried out by the Study Group on a European Civil Code and the Research Group on Existing EU Private Law (Acquis Group), founded in 2002.[17] In 2009, they produced a final academic Draft of a Common Frame of Reference (DCFR).[18] The designers hoped that this academic DCFR would become the blueprint for a 'political' Common Frame of Reference (CFR).[19] However, this never came about. The Zeitgeist began to change. The DCFR was received with caution by the European Commission.[20] In 2016, the Commission even withdrew the Proposal for a Regulation on a Common European Sales Law (CESL),[21] which included the relevant parts of the DCFR.[22] As a result of these vicissitudes, 'the euphoric codification of EU private law' disappeared from the political agenda,[23] and the idea of top-down harmonisation/unification was again shelved. Whether that is temporary or permanent only the future can tell.

3. WHAT IS FL-EUR?

As mentioned, FL-EUR belongs to the first group of initiatives described above. Like the other networks, FL-EUR is a purely academic initiative, not linked to government agencies or international organisations. All participants join the network in their personal capacity and enjoy full academic independence. Currently, the network unites 34 leading experts, including academics, judges and public officials, from 31 European jurisdictions, both within and outside the EU, and this number is growing.

At their first meeting, the members of FL-EUR selected their first topic, adult protection, from a shortlist that included two other topics: high-conflict divorces/separations and new forms of parentage. This choice is illustrative of the globally growing interest in adult protection. Two major global developments are responsible for the transformation of adult protection from a somewhat undervalued subject between private and family law into a hot topic. The first one is the development of the new global set of high human rights standards

---

on a More Coherent European Contract Law' COM (2003)68 final, OJ C 2003/63/1, followed on from this.

17 For an overview of the participants, see C. von Bar et al. (eds), *Principles, Definitions and Model Rules of European Private Law Draft Common Frame of Reference (DCFR)*, Outline Publication, 2009, pp. 47–54.

18 Ibid.

19 Ibid., Introduction, p. 8.

20 U. Magnus, 'EU Private Law – A Zeitgeist Idea from the Past?' in A. Janssen, M. Lehmann and R. Schulze (eds), *The Future of European Private Law*, Nomos, Baden-Baden 2023, p. 100.

21 Proposal for a Regulation of the European Parliament and of the Council on a Common European Sales Law COM/2011/0635 final – 2011/0284 (COD).

22 COM(2014) 910 final, Annex, pp. 2, 13. See also A. Janssen, M. Lehmann and R. Schulze, above n. 3, pp. 23–24.

23 U. Magnus, above n. 20, p. 100.

for the legal support and protection of adults. The successful proliferation of the UN Convention on the Rights of Persons with Disabilities (UNCRPD)[24] became a turning point in the important paradigm shift: from the traditional paternalistic approach, based on protection and substitute decision-making, to a modern, human rights-based approach, based on empowerment and supported decision-making.[25] Ratification of the UNCRPD obliges the countries in question to reshape their existing systems of legal adult protection so that they can meet the new high standards set by human rights instruments.[26] The problem is that human rights instruments set high standards without relating them to the available human and material resources, and the countries that implement these standards in their legal systems are constrained by the means that they have at their disposal. The second global development that made the legal protection of adults highly relevant is global ageing. The UNCRPD is applicable to adults of any age with impaired decision-making capacity. However, it is the rapidly increasing ageing of both the world's and the European population that has transformed the legal protection of older adults from the bridesmaid to the bride of private law. According to Eurostat, in 2021 people aged 65 and above represented 21% of the EU population; by 2050, around 30% of the European population will be over 65.[27] That results in an alarming increase in old age dependency, also known as 'grey pressure'. In 2021, there were around three Europeans of working age for every European aged 65 or over, representing an old age dependency ratio of 32%. By 2050, it is expected that there will be fewer than two working age adults for each elderly person, and the old age dependency ratio will rise to 56%.[28] This second global development places a constant strain on the human and financial recourses that are available for accommodating the needs of older adults, including their need for legal adult protection. The combination of these two trends means that countries are facing a demanding challenge of developing systems of measures for the legal protection of adults

[24] The 2006 UN CPRD has now been ratified by 186 countries, including all European countries and the EU.

[25] N. Devi, 'Supported Decision Making and Personal Autonomy for Persons with Intellectual Disabilities: Article 12 of the UN Convention on the Rights of Persons with Disabilities' (2013) 41(4) *Journal of Law, Medicine & Ethics* 792; C. Blankman, 'Bekwaamheid en bescherming van meerderjarigen' (2019) *NJB* 193.

[26] H.N. Stelma-Roorda, C. Blankman and M. Antokolskaia, 'A changing paradigm of protection of vulnerable adults and its implications for the Netherlands' (2019) *Family & Law*, http://www.familyandlaw.eu/tijdschrift/fenr/2019/02/FENR D 18 00006; W. Martin et al., *The Essex Autonomy Project. Three Jurisdictions Report. Towards Compliance with CRPD Art. 12 in Capacity/Incapacity legislation across the UK*, University of Essex, Essex 2016; N. Devi, above n. 25; C. Blankman, above n. 25.

[27] EU Commission Staff Working Document *The impact of demographic change – in a changing environment*, Brussels, 17 January 2023, SWD(2023) 21 final, p. 10, https://commission.europa.eu/system/files/2023-01/the_impact_of_demographic_change_in_a_changing_environment_2023.PDF.

[28] Ibid.

that, at the same time, meet the new high human rights standards and are also affordable and workable.

Solving this problem is already a huge challenge, but even this is only a part of the problem. There is no clarity on how far the requirements of the UNCRPD really go because of the difference between the text of the Convention itself and its interpretation in the General Comments of the Committee on the Rights of Persons with Disabilities.[29] Moreover, Article 12 UNCRPD states that empowerment should not come at the expense of protection. Therefore, finding an appropriate balance between protection and empowerment is currently one of the most important endeavours in the field of adult protection law worldwide.[30] This discussion is ongoing in many countries, and the outcome will determine the degree of modernisation of national systems of legal protection for adults. The FL-EUR project contributes to this discussion by bringing into the picture the European jurisdictions' approaches to and interpretation of the requirements of the UNCRPD and the stances adopted by the Committee.

Since all European countries have ratified the UNCRPD, there is a basic consensus about the direction in which reforms should proceed. In practice, however, the extent to which national systems have already adapted to the Convention's requirements varies considerably. The initial results of the FL-EUR project and other sources demonstrate significant diversity in this regard across European jurisdictions. Broadly speaking, three groups can be distinguished. Countries in the 'vanguard', including Germany, Ireland, Austria, Portugal, Norway, Spain, Belgium and Switzerland, have already aligned their systems with the requirements of the Convention. Some countries, such as Serbia, Bulgaria, and Greece, have done little to nothing. Other countries, including the Netherlands, belong to the group that has made only ad hoc changes to their systems thus far but still need to do much more. Given the consensus on the direction of the reforms, and the similarity of the problems they face, European jurisdictions can learn a great deal from each other and benefit from each other's practical experience.

4. METHODOLOGY OF FL-EUR

The FL-EUR methodology is in many ways similar to the methodology of the other networks, and in particular to that of the CEFL. The main difference between FL-EUR and the CEFL in this respect is that FL-EUR does not design Principles.

---

29 W. Martin et al., above n. 26; H.N. Stelma-Roorda, C. Blankman, M. Antokolskaia, above n. 26.

30 F. Schuthof, 'Forget me not: The human right to legal capacity of persons with dementia' (2024) 6 *European Human Rights Law Review* 525.

The CEFL has designed five sets of Principles during the more than 20 years of its existence.[31] These Principles are designed according to a comparative law method that is more or less standard for this type of harmonisation project, and which has been refined over the years.[32] Firstly, an extensive questionnaire is drawn up on the basis of comparative law. National reports are then produced by national experts. Based on the data in these reports, Principles are drawn up. The Principles are designed using the so-called 'common core' and 'better law' method.[33] The 'common core' method means that the designers can find a rule which is present in all or most of the systems studied.[34] That rule is then incorporated into the Principles. In many cases, however, the 'common core' method cannot offer a solution. Sometimes the diversity of national rules is so great that no common rule can be found at all. In other cases, sometimes a common rule can be found, but the quality and modernity of that rule do not meet the ambitions of the designers. In those two cases, it is necessary to use the 'better law' method. The CEFL then uses its academic freedom to choose a more modern, persuasive or permissive rule as 'better law' for the Principles,[35] even though this rule only exists in a minority of the jurisdictions examined. It is also possible that the designers do not think that any existing rule is good enough and instead they themselves create a 'better' rule.[36] The use of the 'better law' method is more demanding than that of the 'common core'. The choices behind the national rules have been made at the national level by governments and elected representatives. In the case of highly politicised divorce law, for example, these choices have been determined mainly by compromises reached at a national level between the political supporters and opponents of the modernisation and liberalisation of divorce law. By designating[37] one of these national rules, or even a rule of its own creation as the 'better law', and elevating it above the other national rules, the CEFL participates, as it were, in this political debate and makes an indirect value judgement on national choices made in this context. Even though this is not

[31] For an overview, K. Boele-Woelki, 'The Commission on European Family Law: Taking Stock after almost 20 Years' in K. Boele-Woelki and D. Martiny (eds), *Plurality and Diversity of Family Relations in Europe*, Intersentia, Cambridge 2019), pp. 3–16.

[32] K. Boele-Woelki, 'The Working Method of the Commission on European Family Law' in K. Boele-Woelki (ed.), *Common Core and Better Law in European Family Law*, Intersentia, Antwerp/Oxford 2005, pp. 15–41 and K. Boele-Woelki, above n. 31, pp. 3–16.

[33] K. Boele-Woelki, above n. 32, pp. 31–37.

[34] K. Boele-Woelki, 'Building on Convergence and Coping with Divergence In the CEFL Principles of European Family Law' in M. Antokolskaia (ed.), *Convergence and Divergence of Family Law in Europe*, Intersentia, Antwerp 2007, p. 256.

[35] Ibid., p. 257.

[36] See M. Antokolskaia, 'The "Better Law" Approach and the Harmonisation of Family Law' in K. Boele-Woelki (ed.), *Perspectives for the Unification and Harmonisation of Family Law in Europe*, Intersentia, Antwerp/Oxford 2003, p. 162.

[37] D. Bradley, 'A Family Law For Europe? Sovereignty, Political Economy and Legitimation' in K. Boele-Woelki (ed.), *Perspectives for the Unification and Harmonisation of Family Law in Europe*, Intersentia, Antwerp/Oxford 2003, p. 81.

an easy position for a group of academics that cannot rely on any authority, one could argue that it is exactly their independent large-scale comparative work that results in persuasive arguments. In many cases, it is the most permissive modern rules that the CEFL and other groups designate as the 'better law'.[38]

FL-EUR also bases its results on large-scale comparative research. Since little comparative law research exists in the field of the protection and support of vulnerable adults, the Coordinating Group of FL-EUR first developed short, quick scans to be filled in by the affiliated members for their own jurisdiction. These quick scans revealed significant variations in the use of terminology and required the Coordinating Committee to address the issue of unifying its use. Based on these quick scans, an extensive questionnaire was drawn up with the aid of the functional comparative law method. The FL-EUR members and the country rapporteurs (national experts in the relevant fields) then draw up country reports by answering the questionnaire. From this point onwards, the methods of FL-EUR and CEFL diverge, because FL-EUR deliberately refrains from designing Principles. FL-EUR also uses the 'common core' and 'better law' method, but in a different way. As with the Common Core project, FL-EUR only uses the 'common core' method to uncover what solutions are common to all or most of the covered jurisdictions. The 'better law' method is used by FL-EUR to discover the best national solutions and pitfalls and to assess them on their merits. The use of the 'better law' method in relation to FL-EUR's first field is considerably less demanding than for initiatives that design Principles. FL-EUR does not go any further than using the 'better law' method to map out which solutions meet the requirements of the UNCRPD and at the same time are feasible and practicable. Then, the available empirical data and evaluations are used in order to find which solutions seem to work best. Because there is no need to choose which of these solutions should be included in Principles, FL-EUR does not have to choose just one 'very best' solution itself. It is sufficient to describe all of the 'best solutions' found, including their advantages and disadvantages. The final choice between these solutions is left to those who wish to work with the results of the FL-EUR comparative law study, in particular the national legislators. They do have a political mandate to make further choices. FL-EUR's comparative law work can provide national decision-making processes with comprehensive, specialised comparative and empirical information that would have been difficult to obtain by other means. This will prevent national jurisdictions from having to reinvent the wheel over and over again.

---

38 K. Boele-Woelki, above n. 34, p. 257. The other groups also do this. For example, the founders of the Lando Commission wrote that their 'Principles of European Contract Law are intended to be "progressive"' (O. Lando and H. Beale, *Principles of European Contract Law*, Kluwer, Deventer 2000, p. xxii). The members of the European Group on Tort Law openly admit that they equate 'modern' with 'best' (J. Spier and O. Haazen, 'The European Group on Tort Law ("Tilburg Group") and the European Principles of Tort Law' (1999) *Zeitschrift für Europäisches Privatrecht* 480). For more on the current discussion, see R. Schulze and F. Zoll, *European Contract Law*, 3rd ed., Nomos, Baden-Baden 2021.

5. LOST IN TRANSLATION: CHALLENGES IN THE DESIGN AND INTERPRETATION OF THE QUESTIONNAIRE

As in any large-scale comparative law project, FL-EUR has encountered a range of complex challenges. These challenges arise not only from the intrinsic differences between legal systems but also from the practical difficulties that scholars meet when trying to systematise and compare various legal norms. In our working process so far, one of the most significant hurdles has been issues concerning terminology and translation.[39] These problems not only impede the clarity of legal analysis but also undermine the accuracy and efficacy of the results. We provide two examples to explain this, as well as our approaches to dealing with it.

5.1. EXAMPLE 1: LEGAL CAPACITY

The first example shows a comparative law project facing difficulty using legal terms in its questionnaire. For example, what is legal capacity?

The FL-EUR questionnaire refers to legal capacity in many questions. For instance, it is used to determine whether a legal system allows for the limitation of legal capacity (questions 8–15) and how a (state-ordered or voluntary) measure affects the legal capacity of the adult (questions 24 and 41). The questionnaire also refers to the notion of legal capacity when assessing a legal system regarding protection and empowerment (questions 67–68).

The FL-EUR questionnaire defines legal capacity as the ability to hold rights and duties (passive legal capacity or legal standing) and to exercise those rights and duties (active legal capacity or legal agency).[40] This definition is in line with the definition used by the Committee on the Rights of Persons with Disabilities in General Comment No. 1 (2014).[41]

However, while studying the country reports, it became clear that although the notion is essential in the assessment of compatibility with the UNCRPD, the country reporters used different interpretations.

As mentioned in the Swedish report,[42] the concept of 'legal capacity' is complicated and in many legal systems, not just under Swedish law, is reflected

39 See for various perspectives, A. Parise and O. Moréteau (eds), *Comparative Perspectives on Law and Language*, Eleven, The Hague 2022.

40 FL-EUR, *Questionnaire Legal Protection and Empowerment of Vulnerable Adults: definitions*, https://fl-eur.eu/working_field_1__empowerment_and_protection/country-reports.

41 Committee on the Rights of Persons with Disabilities, 'General Comment No. 1. Article 12: Equal recognition before the law', UN Doc. CRPD/C/GC/1, 19 May 2014, §13.

42 M. Brattström and T. Fridström Montoya, 'Country report Sweden', *Family & Law*, https://www.boomportaal.nl/tijdschrift/FenR/Country%20Reports (for all reports mentioned hereafter), p. 2, answer to question 1.

in such a way that it has different meanings in different contexts – sometimes referring to legal power, to legal competence or to legal capability – which could explain the difficulties.

According to the England and Wales report, in that jurisdiction there is no way to remove an individual's legal capacity prospectively.[43] However, following the same report, the inherent jurisdiction of the High Court could be used to prevent a person lacking relevant capacity from entering into a marriage.[44] It is unclear how the authority of the Court to prevent someone from entering into a marriage because of a lack of relevant capacity should be interpreted. In the reporter's opinion, England and Wales adopt a functional approach to capacity that is time- and decision-specific. Mental capacity is not a legal status that can be relied upon to deny the rights of persons to make decisions in all circumstances. However, it can be used to deny legal capacity in a time- and decision-specific way. Moreover, the Mental Capacity Act 2005 does recognise that the decisions of an adult may be limited to specific matters where they lack the ability to make the decision. The inherent jurisdiction is applicable where a vulnerable adult has been disabled from making a free choice and their autonomy is compromised by reason of something other than mental impairment.[45] A vulnerable adult, according to the case law, is someone who, whether or not mentally incapacitated and whether or not suffering from any mental illness or mental disorder, is or may be unable to take care of him- or herself or unable to protect him- or herself against significant harm or exploitation, or who is deaf, blind or dumb, or who is substantially handicapped by illness, injury or a congenital deformity. The High Court has the residual authority to make orders to protect vulnerable adults. In some cases these orders are directed towards the vulnerable adults themselves, which entails imposing an outcome or decision on them to ensure their protection (the so-called 'dictatorial approach'). A clear example mentioned in the report is the *Southend-on-Sea Borough Council v Meyers* case, where the High Court issued an order directed at the vulnerable adult which prevented him from living with his abusive son.[46] How should this limitation be interpreted?

Slovenia's rapporteurs answered question 8 on the state's limitation of the legal capacity of an adult by stating that it was not applicable ('N/A') in their legal system.[47] Should we conclude that it is not possible to limit this legal capacity? However, in answer to question 14, the rapporteurs mentioned that legal transactions entered into by a person without the necessary consent of

43 D. Bedford and B. Sloan, 'Country report England and Wales', *Family & Law*, p. 10, answer to question 8.

44 Ibid., p. 17, answer to question 9 b).

45 Ibid., pp. 10–11, answer to question 8.

46 Ibid., p. 32, answer to question 16.

47 B. Novak, 'Country report Slovenia', *Family & Law*, p. 6, answer to questions 8–13.

the guardian are contestable, and legal transactions made by a ward for whom the guardian is the sole representative are null and void.[48] Are these sanctions referring to a limitation of legal capacity due to the organisation of a state-ordered measure? Many legal systems provide for comparable sanctions (e.g. null and void or voidable) for a violation of the lack of legal capacity.[49]

Following Spain's report, the limitation of legal capacity is no longer legally possible in Spain.[50] However, Article 1302.3 Civil Code stipulates that a contract can be annulled if a person with a disability concludes it without using support measures. This has triggered different interpretations among Spanish scholars. For some authors, it is irrelevant whether the person in question had the necessary mental capacity to agree to the contract; if they made it without the intervention of the support person, the contract should be void. Other authors believe that the support measures must have been required in the case at issue. If the person concerned had sufficient mental capacity to enter into a contract, it should be valid, even if they did not use the support that was available.[51] Again, it is arguable whether the first interpretation does not refer to a limitation of legal capacity in the sense of legal agency.

The Swedish rapporteurs mention the existence of a special provision on contracts in their legal system, which allows a contract to be declared void if it was concluded under the influence of a psychiatric disorder.[52] Furthermore, they indicate that this only affects the legal action in question and has no implications for the person's legal capacity in *general terms*. The country rapporteurs of several legal systems indicate that a contract concluded by or a declaration of intent of a person lacking the mental capacity to contract is void or voidable in their legal system.[53] There might be differences in approach between the legal systems

48 Ibid., p. 22, answer to question 24.

49 See for example F. Swennen and T. Wuyts, 'Country report Belgium', *Family & Law*, p. 38, answer to question 28 c); V. Todorova, 'Country report Bulgaria', *Family & Law*, p. 22, answer to question 9 a) and b); T. Uusen-Nacke and K. Raud, 'Country report Estonia', *Family & Law*, p. 16, answer to question 9 a), and p. 39, answer to question 24; C. Bidaud, E. Fongaro and G. Millerioux, 'Country report France', *Family & Law*, p. 22, answer to question 28; N. Dethloff and F. Leven, 'Country report Germany', *Family & Law*, p. 14, answer to question 9; O. Szeibert, 'Country report Hungary', *Family & Law*, p. 14, answer to question 9; C. Morgana Cascione, 'Country report Italy', *Family & Law*, p. 18, answer to question 24; P. Fiedorczyk and B. Kamil Truszkowski, 'Country report Poland', *Family & Law*, p. 22, answer to question 8: 'absolute invalid'; S. Florescu, 'Country report Romania', *Family & Law*, p. 10, answer to question 9; A. Shirvindt, 'Country report Russia', *Family & Law*, p. 21, answer to question 9 a); Y. Litins'ka and I. Senyuta, 'Country report Ukraine', *Family & Law*, p. 33, answer to question 28.

50 J. Ribot Igualada, 'Country report Spain', *Family & Law*, p. 13, answer to question 8.

51 Ibid., pp. 14–15, answer to question 14 a).

52 M. Brattström and T. Fridström Montoya, 'Country report Sweden', *Family & Law*, p. 16, answer to question 8 f).

53 V. Todorova, 'Country report Bulgaria', *Family & Law*, p. 30, answer to question 14 a); N. Dethloff and F. Leven, 'Country report Germany', *Family & Law*, p. 20, answer to question 14; K. Blankman and R. Stelma-Roorda, 'Country report the Netherlands', *Family & Law*,

under study. The fact that a contract can be declared void in that case could be interpreted as a limitation of legal capacity.[54] But it could also be interpreted as a form of ex lege invalidity.[55] For instance, according to the Swiss report, an adult person who is deemed incapable of judgement (for example, as a consequence of mental disability, mental disorder, etc.) in relation to a certain act loses their full active capacity ex lege concerning this particular act.[56] Some other rapporteurs refer to the distinction between legal capacity related to a precise and readily ascertainable fact, while the absence of mental capacity should be proved.[57]

As shown, differences in the approach to the notion of 'legal capacity' and the link with mental capacity exist between the national reports. Although the notion is well known, it has become increasingly challenging to determine whether a (state-ordered) measure constitutes a limitation or deprivation of legal capacity. Some national rapporteurs indicate that incapacitation is no longer possible in their legal system. However, if the vulnerable adult acts without the approval or assistance of their support person, the act is voidable or void. Other national rapporteurs mention that legal capacity cannot be removed prospectively. Nevertheless, mechanisms exist to limit a person's freedom to contract. Finally, in most of the legal systems studied, an act can be declared void or is void if it is concluded at a time when one of the contracting parties was mentally incapable of concluding a contract. A discussion exists as to whether this mechanism is a limitation of legal capacity.

5.2. EXAMPLE 2: EX LEGE MEASURES

A second example illustrating the challenges associated with designing questionnaires and interpreting results pertains to ex lege measures. These constitute a distinct category of adult protection measures, warranting

p. 11, answer to question 14; E. IGNOVSKA, 'Country report North Macedonia', *Family & Law*, https://www.familyandlaw.eu/pagina/country_reports, pp. 25–26, answer to question 15; P. Fiedorczyk and B. Kamil Truszkowski, 'Country report Poland', *Family & Law*, pp. 28–29, answer to question 14; S. Florescu, 'Country report Romania', *Family & Law*, pp. 14–15, answer to question 14; A. Shirvindt, 'Country report Russia', *Family & Law*, pp. 57–58, answer to question 14; G. Kovacek Stanic and S. Samardzic, 'Country report Serbia', *Family & Law*, p. 24, answer to question 14; Y. Litins'ka and I. Senyuta, 'Country report Ukraine', *Family & Law*, p. 20, answer to question 14.

54 Compare this with the North Macedonia report, pp. 25–26: 'It was concluded that lower Courts decided rightfully when they annulled the Contract due to a lack of/non-existence of mental (therefore, legal) capacity to fully comprehend the meaning, rights and responsibilities'.

55 N. Dethloff and F. Leven, 'Country report Germany', *Family & Law*, p. 21, answer to question 14.

56 M. Cottier and C. Crevoisier Abdel Aziz, 'Country report Switzerland', *Family & Law*, p. 6, answer to question 8 and 28 c).

57 K. BLANKMAN and R. STELMA-ROORDA, 'Country report the Netherlands', *Family & Law*, p. 11, answer to question 14.

the inclusion of specific questions to capture a comprehensive overview of existing legal frameworks. In terms of the comparative method used, this was based on an institutional functional method rather than a problem-solving one. The questionnaire asked about the existence of ex lege provisions in the jurisdiction.[58] Ex lege measures are not often the topic of legal research and are relatively unknown. Where the main topic of adult protection measures is in all jurisdictions easy to identify, such as guardianship, ex lege measures are not. These measures might be part of different legal fields outside the law of persons, for example in medical law or social security law. In order to avoid collecting information on quite different legal instruments, the drafters of the questionnaire attempted to guide the answers as far as possible.

In this regard, two issues are at play: the term and the definition. The term was the most straightforward. During the discussions on drafting the questionnaire, consensus emerged regarding the term. There is no universally understood term beyond 'ex lege measures', even if this term does not resonate in all jurisdictions.

Concerning the definition, there is no globally accepted definition of ex lege representation. Comparative legal research rarely addresses ex lege measures. An existing definition is one employed in international law to delineate the material scope of the recommendation of the Council of Europe on principles concerning continuing powers of attorney and advance directives for incapacity. It describes ex lege measures as follows: 'arrangements under which powers, similar to some of those which might otherwise be derived from a CPA [continuing power of attorney] or guardianship order, are conferred by operation of law, usually upon a specified relative, without any procedure beyond establishment of relevant incapacity'.[59]

We opted for a definition without a comparison in the definition of the powers of a continuing power of attorney or a guardianship order. The FL-EUR definition of ex lege measures reads as follows: an adult protection measure providing legal authority to other persons to act ex lege (by operation of law) on behalf of the adult, requiring neither a decision by a competent authority nor a voluntary measure by the adult.[60] The aim was to emphasise that these measures are distinct from state-ordered mechanisms, since no state/court intervention

---

58 FL-EUR, *Questionnaire Legal Protection and Empowerment of Vulnerable Adults: definitions*, https://fl-eur.eu/working_field_1__empowerment_and_protection/country-reports (questions 50–64).

59 A.D. Ward, *Enabling Citizens to Plan for Incapacity – A review of follow-up action taken by member states of the Council of Europe to Recommendation CM/Rec(2009)11 on principles concerning continuing powers of attorney and advance directives for incapacity*, European Committee on Legal Co-operation (CDCJ), CDCJ(2017)2 final, 2018.

60 FL-EUR, *Questionnaire Legal Protection and Empowerment of Vulnerable Adults: definitions*, https://fl-eur.eu/working_field_1__empowerment_and_protection/country-reports (introduction).

is needed to establish the measure. Instead, representation powers arise automatically when predefined legal conditions are met. In contrast, voluntary measures require prior action, such as the creation of a power of attorney or an advance directive. Ex lege measures, however, operate independently of the adult's activity or consent, but are based directly on the law. This unique feature makes them particularly relevant for addressing challenges faced by ageing societies, such as the growing demand for representatives and the associated costs. The international law definition specifies that the powers are usually conferred upon a specified relative. The FL-EUR definition does not limit – unlike the Council of Europe's definition – the recipient of legal authority to family members, because it is important to obtain as much information as possible about the categories of possible ex lege representatives, family or otherwise. Another difference between the two definitions is that the Council of Europe's definition requires the establishment of relevant incapacity as a condition for the operation of ex lege measures. The FL-EUR definition does not. Here again, the aim was to obtain a full picture of the legal reality.

We further categorised ex lege measures into three types: (1) ex lege representation of vulnerable adults (in general); (2) ex lege representation in marital law; and (3) ex lege representation in the form of *negotiorum gestio* (management of affairs without a mandate). We first asked about ex lege measures in general, followed by the two more specific contexts of ex lege measures.[61] We also added a general introduction explaining that first a number of general questions would be posed, followed by a specific scenario dealing with marital and matrimonial property representation.

Despite the efforts to streamline the answers, during the comparative analysis of the country reports a significant variation in the responses was observed. This demonstrates that the FL-EUR definition of ex lege measures was not always understood as intended and did not always fit the legal realities in the European countries. The responses from the national rapporteurs revealed varying interpretations of ex lege measures. In some jurisdictions, these measures grant extensive representation powers to family members and others, while in other jurisdictions they are more narrowly defined. For example, one report highlighted provisions that determine that consent for an abortion when a pregnant woman is 'psychologically incapable' should be given by the ascendants, descendants or any relatives in the collateral line. This was not qualified by the country

61 FL-EUR, *Questionnaire Legal Protection and Empowerment of Vulnerable Adults: definitions*, https://fl-eur.eu/working_field_1__empowerment_and_protection/country-reports (question 50: general question on existence; questions 51–53: legal grounds and procedure; question 54: representatives; questions 55–56: powers and duties of the representatives; question 57: interaction with other instruments; question 58: safeguards and supervision; question 59: end of measure; questions 60–61: reflection and data; questions 62–64: specific cases of ex lege representation.

rapporteur as an ex lege measure, but according to the FL-EUR definition it was.[62] This occurred more often.[63]

Another challenge involved the classification of specific instruments as ex lege measures. This ambiguity primarily centres on the role of the court: does it establish the representation authority, or does it merely register a power already conferred directly by law? In both Bulgaria and the Czech Republic, provisions exist for ex lege representation; however, a court decision is required for these measures to take effect. In the Czech Republic, the court must approve the ex lege representation, while in Bulgaria, a decision on the deprivation of legal capacity is necessary.[64] Due to the requirement of judicial intervention, these forms of representation fall outside the scope of the FL-EUR definition of ex lege representation, which explicitly excludes measures that require a decision by a competent authority.

To overcome these issues, we refined the legal and qualification issues by delivering presentations in FL-EUR meetings and at conferences presenting comparative overviews. We also posed questions on this qualification to the country rapporteurs, accompanied by a more detailed explanation of the intention of this part of the questionnaire. This worked quite well. We are now more certain about the results and the comparative analysis. At the same time, this example illustrates how complex it is to capture diverging legal realities. A complicating factor is that when a legal term does not ring a bell, or rings different bells, the information might be less accurate. When legal instruments are less recognisable and hidden in different parts in the law, across legal fields and specific expertise, this requires even more care to be taken. A second option is to request the country rapporteurs to provide feedback on the qualifications made in the comparative analysis. On the basis of the issues at hand, one can ask very specific questions, which might result in other qualifications than originally thought of.

---

62 P. Távora Vítor, 'Country report Portugal', *Family & Law*, p. 58, answers to question 50 (not applicable) and question 51.

63 T. Uusen-Nacke and K. Raud, 'Country report Estonia', *Family & Law*, p. 58, answers to question 50 (Estonia has no specific provisions on the ex lege representation of vulnerable adults; some provisions are found in the Law of Obligations Act regarding the rights of patients with restricted active legal capacity) and question 51 (not applicable).

64 V. Todorova, 'Country report Bulgaria', *Family & Law*, answer to question 50 (the Bulgarian Family Code allows for the ex lege representation of an adult in the case of the deprivation of their legal capacity *by the court*; this measure is different to the definition adopted under this questionnaire because it is only applicable following the incapacitation of the adult by the court); Z. Králíčková, K. Lach, D. Elischer and O. Frinta, 'Country report Czech Republic', *Family & Law*, answer to question 50 (the Czech Civil Code allows for an adult who cannot enter into legal acts autonomously due to a mental disorder to be protected through representation by a member of his or her household. Although representation commences ad hoc, i.e. when such need arises in the life the individual, and the limitation of legal capacity as a protective measure of last resort would be an inadequate measure in the given case, *prior approval by the court* is nevertheless required).

6. CONCLUSION

FL-EUR is a relative newcomer when it comes to large-scale comparative law projects. The CEFL has been a pioneer in the area of family law. Is it a matter of coincidence that at least two of Europe's largest comparative law projects concern family law? Perhaps not. Comparative law projects in the law of persons and family law have the potential to affect *all* citizens in Europe. In this day and age, with ever increasing globalisation, a growing number of partners and parents with different nationalities, and a global reproduction market, the existing differences in national law might affect citizens' free movement rights within the EU and can make life more complex than necessary. Creating more insight into the similarities and differences in family law in Europe is the basis for identifying a common core and better law or best practices.

FL-EUR's working method has been detailed in this contribution. The first topic it has addressed is a strong human rights driver for changes to be made to adult support and protection measures. It thus aims not only to contribute to ideas that inspire a better realisation of human rights at the national level, but also to provide an insight into the existing diversity among and the terminology of human rights bodies such as the ECtHR, the Council of Europe and the CRPD Committee. The comparative work of FL-EUR might well inspire the ECtHR concerning the existence of a common core, which is relevant in deciding on the extent of the margin of appreciation and the fair balance to be struck. Our results might also lead to putting human rights norms, including those of the UNCRPD, into the context of legal and social reality, meaning that the outcomes of the project might demonstrate that some human rights are not very feasible.

As to the methodology of comparative projects, the inherent nature of comparative legal work will result to some extent in problems related to the misunderstanding of concepts and terminology. We have exemplified this with legal capacity and ex lege measures in FL-EUR's current topic. Much depends on the existing level of comparative knowledge when starting with a new topic. A good comparative law practice is to work with a quick scan, accompanied by questions on the main topics. This helps to gain a clear overview of the basic differences between jurisdictions. Drafting a questionnaire is then made easier. The risk of having one's own legal system in mind when drafting is thereby reduced, which hopefully leads to results that are of higher quality. At the analysing stage, an option is to ask the country rapporteurs whether the classifications made in the comparative work are correct, after having pointed out the difficulties that are inherent in the qualification.

Last but not least, we should not forget that working in these academic, independent, large-scale comparative law projects is a great deal of fun!

THE HUMAN RIGHTS PARADOX AND THE PRACTICAL CHALLENGES OF CROSS-BORDER ADULT PROTECTION

Katja KARJALAINEN

1. INTRODUCTION

The importance of the cross-border protection of adults has begun to emerge as the population of European countries ages rapidly while being more mobile than ever.[1] In addition, the Convention on the Rights of Persons with Disabilities[2] (UNCRPD) has laid down, in a new way, the right of persons with disabilities to have equal opportunities in life. The consequences of sicknesses and conditions caused by old age, such as dementia, may constitute a disability, meaning that ageing and disability rights are connected.

If an adult's legal capacity diminishes and they have connections to more than one jurisdiction, the issue falls within the scope of private international law. Which jurisdiction is competent to provide protective measures? What law is applicable? Is the decision given in one jurisdiction recognised in another? Under what framework, if any, can authorities cooperate? Nonetheless, with these brief remarks I argue that the issue of cross-border adult protection cannot be fully grasped if one only approaches the topic from the perspective of private international law. Securing the fundamental and human rights of vulnerable adults in cross-border situations calls for a knowledge of comparative law and socio-legal information on the *de facto* conditions/situations that adults in vulnerable situations face.

---

1 This chapter is loosely based on my doctoral dissertation: K. KARJALAINEN, *Ikääntyminen, liikkuvuus ja kansainvälinen yksityisoikeus Euroopassa: Vertaileva tutkimus rajat ylittävistä ongelmista sekä edunvalvonnasta Suomessa ja Espanjassa (Ageing, Mobility and Private International Law in Europe: A Comparative Study about Cross-border Problems and Guardianship in Finland and Spain)*, Suomalainen lakimiesyhdistys, Helsinki 2016, https://edition.fi/lakimiesyhdistys/catalog/book/462. It also draws from, among other sources, the collaboration behind the article: P. FRANZINA, C. GONZÁLEZ BEILFUSS, J. VON HEIN, K. KARJALAINEN and T. KRUGER, 'Cross-border protection of adults: What Could the EU Do Better?' forthcoming in the *Journal of Private International Law*, Vol 21 issue 1 2025, 1–29.

2 Convention on the Rights of Persons with Disabilities of 12 December 2006, which came into force on 3 May 2008.

2. THE UNCRPD, THE HAGUE ADULTS CONVENTION AND EU PROPOSALS

The UNCRPD sets the standards for adult protection. All EU Member States are parties to the UNCRPD, and it is also the first human rights convention to which the EU itself has become a party. The UNCRPD strives for a society that is on an equal basis, accessible for all individuals regardless of their personal characteristics. It seeks to facilitate the equality of opportunities by removing hindrances and obstacles to participation (Article 3). In principle, the Convention did not create new rights but reframed the existing human rights, as it turned the focus from individuals themselves onto society, which may not be accessible to all individuals. In accordance with the Convention, a disability should not be understood as a deficiency in an individual but as a structural challenge. Consequently, the core element of disability lies in the dynamics between impairment and the environment – impairment or insufficiency in personal capacities constitutes a hindrance that affects interaction and may impede full participation in society.[3]

As the rationale behind the UNCRPD is that a society should be inclusive in such a way that it provides 'equality of opportunities' for people with disabilities, the legal rules on cross-border adult protection can be seen as an accessibility tool.[4] They can create a step that removes hindrances and obstacles to participation, namely legal barriers, in a cross-border context and can, in this way, contribute to creating a more inclusive society.[5]

Substantially, the issue of cross-border adult protection is particularly tied to Articles 12(3), 18, 19 and 25 of the UNCRPD. Article 12(3) requires appropriate measures to be taken to provide access by persons with disabilities to the support they may require in exercising their legal capacity. This refers, among other things, to the fact that people with disabilities also have the right to individual autonomy, and the right to have their will and preferences respected in all areas of life. Articles 18 and 19 recognise the rights of persons with disabilities to the liberty of movement and to the freedom to choose their place of residence, on an equal basis with others. Article 25 recognises that persons with disabilities have the right to the enjoyment of health without discrimination on the basis of disability. The care should be provided on the basis of free and informed

---

3 As specified in Article 1(2), the Convention applies to 'those who have long-term physical, mental, intellectual or sensory impairments which in interaction with various barriers may hinder their full and effective participation in society on an equal basis with others.'

4 See e.g. the Committee on the Rights of Persons with Disabilities, General Comment No. 6 (2018) on equality and non-discrimination (CRPD/C/GC/6), 9 March 2018.

5 Communication from the Commission to the European Parliament, the Council, the European Economic and Social Committee, and the Committee of the Regions. Union of Equality: Strategy for the Rights of Persons with Disabilities 2021–2030, COM/2021/101 final, p. 14.

consent and awareness should be raised regarding the human rights, dignity and autonomy of persons with disabilities.

The only multilateral instrument that addresses these issues in the cross-border context is the 2000 Hague Convention on the International Protection of Adults.[6] The Convention applies to the international protection of adults who, by reason of an impairment or the insufficiency of their personal faculties, are not in a position to protect their interests (Article 1(1)). The purpose of the Convention is to determine the state whose authorities have jurisdiction to take measures directed towards the protection of the person or the property of the adult; to determine which law is to be applied by such authorities in exercising their jurisdiction; to determine the law applicable to the representation of the adult; to provide for the recognition and enforcement of such measures of protection in all Contracting States; and to establish necessary cooperation between the authorities of the Contracting States (Article 1(2)).

The European Commission published two proposals for the protection of adults on 31 May 2023. The first proposal is for a decision to oblige Member States to become or remain parties to the Hague Adults Convention in the interests of the EU.[7] The second is a legislative proposal to supplement the Convention's rules. This proposal introduces, among other issues, a clause on the choice of jurisdiction (Article 6), stricter grounds for refusing to recognise a foreign protective measure than the Hague Adults Convention (Article 10) and abolishing exequatur (Article 11). It also proposes practical tools, such as a European Certificate of Representation, which will make it easier for representatives to prove their powers in another Member State, and the establishment of interconnected registers that will provide information on the existence of protection in another Member State.[8]

The EU proposals will enable adults in vulnerable situations to benefit from the EU's principle of free movement and residence as they aim to ensure that the protection of adults is maintained in cross-border cases and that their right to individual autonomy, including the freedom to make their own choices as regards their person and future arrangements, is respected when they move within the EU.[9] As EU citizens, all adults should be able to fully exercise their right of free movement regardless of any disabilities (Articles 21(1) and 45 Charter of Fundamental Rights of the European Union; Article 21 TFEU). They are entitled

6 Convention of 13 January 2000 on the International Protection of Adults. The Convention came into force on 1 January 2009.

7 Proposal for a Regulation, COM(2023) 280 of 31 May 2023.

8 Proposal for a Council Decision, COM(2023) 281 of 31 May 2023.

9 See 'Commission proposes to better guarantee the rights of adults in need of protection or support in cross-border situations', Press release, https://ec.europa.eu/commission/presscorner/detail/en/ip_23_2955; 'Vulnerable Adults in Europe: European added value of an EU legal instrument on the protection of vulnerable adults in European Parliamentary Research Service', 2016, pp. 4, 16.

to have equality of opportunities; to be able to decide where, how and with whom they live; and to move freely within the EU regardless of their support needs.[10]

In this short contribution, it is not possible to go into detail, but the existing private international law rules of the Hague Adults Convention and the proposed rules provided by the EU do reasonably well when assessed in the light of the framework provided by the UNCRPD.[11] In many ways the Hague Adults Convention's rules create and the EU rules will create, if put in place, accessibility at the cross-border level and indirectly give rights, such as the right to choose where to live and the right to move freely, to people with disabilities. Furthermore, particular provisions of the instruments can be interpreted in compliance with the UNCRPD, that is, respecting the will and preferences of an adult as well as their personal autonomy and right to self-determination. Nonetheless, the rules of private international law do not work in a vacuum.

3. MUTUAL TRUST AND THE RECOGNITION OF FOREIGN DECISIONS

The effective circulation of voluntary and involuntary measures of protection is a key issue in the field of cross-border adult protection.[12] The measures must be movable in order for private international law to remove the barriers of participation and to function as an accessibility tool. Aiming to guarantee the effective circulation of protective measures, the Hague Adults Convention and the EU legislative proposal adopt the approach of direct recognition. Article 22(1) of the Hague Adults Convention provides that 'the measures taken by the authorities of a Contracting State shall be recognised by operation of law in all other Contracting States'. Similarly, Article 9(1) of the EU legislative proposal lays down that 'a measure taken by the authorities of a Member State shall be recognised in the other Member States without any special procedure being required'.

---

10 Strategy for the Rights of Persons with Disabilities 2021–2030, COM/2021/101 final, p. 14.

11 See e.g. P. Franzina et al., above n. 1.

12 The distinction is noteworthy as private instruments' voluntary measures do not in fall within the scope of recognition. However, they are subject to cooperation provisions (Chapter 5) and may constitute a power of representation (Articles 15 and 16). See, HCCH, Practical Handbook on the Operation of the 2000 Protection of Adults Convention, HCCH 2025, 224. In the review of CM/Rec(2009)11, voluntary measures are determined as follows: powers of attorney, advance directives, representation agreements, supported decision-making arrangements, co-decision-making arrangements, advocacy arrangements where the advocate is chosen by the person represented, and all other measures established by people to be supported by such measures themselves, as contrasted with involuntary measures imposed by a court, tribunal, authority or other mechanism, including by operation of law, rather than by the people subject to such measures themselves. See A. Ward, *Enabling Citizens to Plan for Incapacity: A review of follow-up action taken by member states of the Council of Europe to Recommendation CM/Rec(2009)11 on principles concerning continuing powers of attorney and advance directives for incapacity*, European Committee on Legal Co-operation, 2017, p. 12.

The recognition of foreign protective measures may only be restrictively refused to guarantee the effective circulation of the measures of protection. Article 22(2) of the Hague Adults Convention lays out standard grounds for non-recognition related to: a lack of competence (Chapter II of the Convention); a lack of minimum procedural requirements (the adult's right to be heard in non-urgent cases); conflicting decisions; and non-compliance with the mandatory provisions or public policy of the receiving jurisdiction. Furthermore, a receiving jurisdiction may refuse to recognise a decision given in another Contracting State if the procedure required in cross-border placements has not been complied with (Article 22(2)(e)). The EU legislative proposal's Article 10 limits the grounds for the refusal of recognition when compared with the Hague Adults Convention in two ways. The proposal excludes a lack of competence and non-compliance with mandatory provisions as grounds for the refusal of recognition or enforcement. Importantly, as a measure of protection taken in one jurisdiction is to be recognised in another jurisdiction as simply as possible, its merits cannot be re-examined in the receiving jurisdiction (Article 24 Hague Adults Convention; Article 13 EU legislative proposal).

Direct recognition requires trust in the legal system of another jurisdiction, trust that is most implausible in the EU area where the concept of mutual trust entails, in addition to restrictions on the grounds for the refusal of recognition, the abolishment of exequatur (Article 11 EU proposal).[13] At first sight, the swift and simple proceedings provided by direct recognition seem to simply enhance much-needed predictability and efficiency in the field of cross-border adult protection. However, legal systems differ when it comes to addressing the question of how to strike a balance between respecting the will and preferences of adults and protecting them, as there are significant differences in substantive adult protection laws. This means that comparative notions lead to a number of very difficult questions in the field of cross-border adult protection.

For example, it may be the case that a law of the country 'Sunshine' provides that an adult's legal capacity is first restricted and only afterwards is a protective measure put in place, but the law of the country 'Snow and Ice' only limits the legal capacity of an adult in very exceptional circumstances. It may also be that the law of Sunshine lays down that if a representative has been appointed for an adult, the representative decides on behalf of that adult, but the law of Snow and Ice provides that an adult must always decide for themselves concerning personal matters (such as choosing a care facility/nursing home and making care and medical decisions) if they are able to understand the meaning of the decision at the moment of decision-making.

A decision entailing a restriction on legal capacity and a protective measure is given in Sunshine, where at that point in time the adult is habitually residing. Later the adult moves back to their country of nationality, Snow and Ice. The

13 See e.g. M. Weller, 'Mutual trust: in search of the future of European Union private international law' (2015) 11(1) *Journal of Private International Law* 64.

decision given in Sunshine is directly recognised in Snow and Ice. In this case, it may be impossible to know whether the scope of the protective measure given in Sunshine, which restricts the legal capacity of the adult, is acceptable and reasonable in Snow and Ice as its merits should not be investigated in another jurisdiction. It is also very difficult to assess who should be responsible for investigating the human rights compatibility of the measure given in Sunshine as, in principle, the purpose of direct recognition is that there is no judicial investigation whatsoever in the receiving jurisdiction. Hence, it is an open question regarding by whom, at what point and on what grounds an investigation into human rights compatibility should take place.

However, if such an investigation does not take place, it may be that when a measure of protection given in Sunshine is recognised and takes effect in Snow and Ice, the adult's legal capacity is not restricted due to their need for protection, but because the decision was made abroad in a jurisdiction that may take a different approach to achieving a balance between individual autonomy and protection. This may lead to, among other things, a situation where one adult, who has a protective measure of domestic origin, has their will and preferences better protected than another adult, who has a protective measure of foreign origin, originating from a more paternalistic jurisdiction. One may also ask who has the decision-making powers with respect to an adult's personal matters when the adult has relocated back to Snow and Ice, as the applicable law provides that the representative is responsible for making care and medical decisions on behalf of the adult, but the *lex fori* gives the adult themselves the right to decide if they have the capacity to decide at the moment of decision-making. It is difficult to imagine that an adult's will and preferences can be wholly ignored in the receiving jurisdiction, even though that is the message sent by the applicable law.

As the recognition of a measure of protection originating from Sunshine in Snow and Ice poses questions related to the proportionality and necessity of the protection and equal treatment of adults in vulnerable situations, the public policy exception and mandatory provisions cannot be disregarded. For example, it may be argued that a protective measure laid down by another jurisdiction that does not fulfil the requirements of necessity and proportionality that are applicable to protective measures made in the receiving state should not be recognised because such a limitation would be at odds with the public policy in the receiving state. Illustratively, the Finnish *travaux préparatoires* on the international protection of adults maintain that the public policy exception could be used if a decision on a protective measure given abroad manifestly conflicts with the substantive Finnish adult protection legislation. Such decisions include, for example, one under which the representative's competency is significantly disproportionate.[14]

14 'Hallituksen esitys Eduskunnalle aikuisten kansainvälisestä suojelusta tehdyn yleissopimuksen hyväksymisestä ja laeiksi sopimuksen lainsäädännön alaan kuuluvien määräysten

It might be possible to argue that the aforementioned problems should be seen as issues of the conditions of implementation that are governed by the law of the jurisdiction where the given powers are exercised, as provided in Article 14 of the Hague Adults Convention.[15] However, one may question whether rectifying such drastic differences in terms of legal approaches really fits within the scope of the 'conditions of implementation' as 'the nature of the measure' should not be changed due to adaptation.[16]

4. ON NON-LEGAL CHALLENGES

In addition to challenges stemming from differences in legal systems, the field of cross-border adult protection is affected by various practical challenges that unfortunately have not yet attracted wide academic interest but are obvious when assessing real-life adult protection situations.[17] Many of the problems encountered come to the fore in purely domestic situations, but they are likely to either be much more common or escalate more easily in a cross-border context.

There are many practical obstacles ahead when a representative appointed in one jurisdiction assists or represents a vulnerable adult in another jurisdiction. The representative likely lacks at least any extensive knowledge regarding the functions of the foreign society and legal system, for example with regard to the banking system, the tax authorities or social and healthcare authorities. They may not speak the language used in the other jurisdiction. One may easily argue that these barriers lessen the possibilities of a representative appointed in one jurisdiction effectively operating and handling affairs in another jurisdiction with the adult themselves or on behalf of the adult.

The issue of language barriers in a cross-border context extends to the issue of respecting the adult's will and preferences. Illustratively, advancing dementia causes a reversion to one's primary language, one's mother tongue.[18] Hence, it is reasonable to ask, for example, how an adult originating from Snow

voimaansaattamisesta ja sopimuksen soveltamisesta sekä eräiden siihen liittyvien lakien muuttamisesta', 61/2010, p. 33.

15 The EU legislative proposal's Article 8 lays down that the law applicable to the cross-border protection of adults shall be determined in accordance with Chapter III of the HCCH 2000 Protection of Adults Convention (Article 8).

16 P. Lagarde, *Convention of 13 of January on the International Protection of Adults. Explanatory Report: New and Revised Edition*, The Hague Conference on Private International Law, 2017, paras 93–94, pp. 76–77.

17 See, however, the edited collection: M. Echezarreta, *El lugar XVI europeo de retiro. Indicadores de excelencia para administrar la gerontoinmigración de ciudadanos de la Unión Europea en municipios españoles*, Editorial Comares, Granada, 2005.

18 U.S. Goth and B.S. Strøm, 'Language Disintegration: Communication Ability in Elderly Immigrants with Dementia' (2018) 12(3) *Lancet Public Health* 3e563.

and Ice can articulate their will and preferences to the relevant authorities or healthcare personnel in Sunshine. In particular, if a representative has already been appointed on behalf of an adult, it is reasonable to suspect that there is hardly any interest in using many resources for investigating the adult's current/prevailing will and preferences. For example, in Spain there are suspicions that notaries do not investigate the *de facto* legal capacity of an older adult of foreign origin due to, among other reasons, language barriers.[19] One may reasonably assume that if an adult has an appointed representative, there is even less space for investigating the adult's current will and preferences.

An unfortunate fact is that, for an adult in a vulnerable situation, it is crucial to have close relatives or acquaintances. As they keep track of the adult's situation, they have the willingness and knowledge to start to assist the adult and possibly initiate sufficient proceedings in this respect. Otherwise, it may be that it takes some time, or way too much time, for the authorities even to discover that there is an adult in need of protection. In a similar vein, in the case of an adult without close relatives or acquaintances who is placed, under a protective order, in an institution located in Sunshine and who wishes to relocate back to Snow and Ice, one may ask who would start to investigate and promote the issue as, again, it may be that is very likely that there are language barriers and communication issues between the adult and care staff, and between the adult and their locally appointed representative whose general workload may be excessively burdensome.[20]

Finally, financial issues cannot be overlooked. There are also costs involved in domestic adult protection situations, and these costs are obviously higher in cross-border situations as there may be an extra decision-making level and, for example, a need for translation or legal assistance. If a vulnerable adult or their close relatives or acquaintances cannot cover these costs, even the best possible regulations may be inefficient in practice. On the other hand, it may be that there is less interest – at least, private interest – to protect and handle the affairs of those who have very limited means.

It is questionable to what extent cross-border adult protection matters are tied to private (international) law and private relations. In cases where a vulnerable adult does not have sufficient funds or close relatives, adult protection is an issue of social welfare law that does not wholly fall outside the scope of private international law either. However, it may very well be that, due to a lack of personal resources, the application of the rules of private international law does not come to the fore so easily. For example, would the authorities in Sunshine

19 See K. Karjalainen, above n. 1, p. 9.

20 See on the problems in terms of cross-border placements, A.R. Keene and C. Cordone, 'Distributed Rights Protection: The 2000 Hague Convention on the International Protection of Adults and the Challenge of Securing Fundamental Rights Across Borders' (2023) 91 *International Journal of Law and Psychiatry* 101936.

start to fully evaluate whether the competence to take protective measures lies within their jurisdiction in a case where it is uncertain where the adult has a habitual residence? If they would, to what extent would they do this? In a similar vein, one may ask what the possibilities are for the authorities to even find out about the continuing power of attorney granted by an adult, let alone start to investigate the law that is applicable to the powers granted.

5. CONCLUSIONS

The field of cross-border adult protection tackles a paradox. On the one hand, private international law rules on adult protection are crucial in producing rights for adults in vulnerable situations. They create accessibility at the cross-border level and facilitate free movement among all EU citizens. On the other hand, for private international law rules to be effective, in principle blind trust in the legal system of another jurisdiction is required, which can easily turn out to be problematic from the UNCRPD perspective. However, if the compatibility of a measure of protection with prevailing human rights standards should be automatically investigated in the receiving jurisdiction, the aim and benefits of direct recognition would cease to exist.

There are also many practical challenges that weaken the effectiveness of cross-border adult protection. Representatives lack knowledge of the functions of foreign legal systems and societies. Language barriers limit communication with adults who have a foreign origin. The number of adults without close relatives or acquaintances is likely to be even higher in cross-border cases than in purely domestic situations, and financial resources may be needed to cover the different costs involved, for example, among other costs, the legal fees in the two jurisdictions. To some extent, cross-border cooperation between authorities and, for example, the proposed EU rules may contribute to eliminating practical challenges by introducing EU-wide registers and an EU certificate of protection, but the main challenges for the cross-border protection of adults, in terms of differences in legal systems and language barriers, remain.

Transparency in terms of the various challenges that are present in the field of cross-border adult protection is crucial in order to protect the interests and human rights of adults in vulnerable situations. Private international law solutions in relation to adult protection ought to follow the same principles and approaches set up in the human rights framework as any form of substantive law solution must do. Private international law rules may also only have a limited impact in legal reality, but this does not imply that they are altogether meaningless. More socio-legal research is needed in the field of cross-border adult protection to properly embrace the challenges present in the field.

PART V

ASSISTED REPRODUCTION TECHNIQUES, ETHICS AND THE RIGHT TO KNOW ONE'S ORIGINS

BALANCING THE CHILD RIGHT TO KNOW IN EUROPE

Current Views of the Committee on the Rights of the Child

Velina TODOROVA

1. INTRODUCTION

Scholarly attention devoted to the identity rights of children[1] and the recognition of these rights in some European states[2] precede the adoption of the UN Convention on the Rights of the Child (CRC). Attention has been triggered by a variety of factors impacting on different directions. One could think, for example, of the commitment to uphold children's rights and the increasing numbers and social acceptance of children of non-married parents. On the other hand, there are also influential factors such as the growing demand for children, the decreasing number of children that are available for adoption and developments in reproductive medicine. Also on the increase is pressure from adopted persons and persons born as a result of third-party reproductive techniques to know their origin.

The child's right to know has had to confront certain established traditions in legislation (family law and the law on personal status), child protection and related policies in Europe.[3] Probably because of this, the proposal for such a right did not emanate from European states but from a group of Islamic states claiming that the right to know had a certain value for the child's development.[4]

---

1 For example, the powerful book by J. TRISELIOTIS, *In search of origins, the experience of adopted people*, Routledge, London 1973. More sources in: R. BLAUWHOFF, *Foundational Facts, Relative Truths. A comparative law study on children's right to know their genetic origins*, Intersentia, Antwerp 2009.

2 For example in Sweden and Germany, see R. BLAUWHOFF, above n. 1.

3 N. LOWE, *A study into the rights and legal status of children being brought up in various forms of marital or non-marital partnerships and cohabitation. A Report for the attention of the Committee of Experts on Family Law to the Council of Europe*, 2009, pp. 24–26.

4 Upon the drafting of the Convention, the right to a nationality was the initially proposed text of Article 7 that provoked lengthy debates. The text of Article 7 CRC that was finally adopted

This right created tensions in Europe and many European states subsequently made reservations to Article 7(1) CRC.[5] Another point of concern was the renaissance of anonymous births in Europe after 2000.[6] Returning to ancient and medieval traditions could be attributed to the ideologies behind the contemporary backsliding in children's rights[7] that are based on religion, conservative movements (e.g. 'pro-life') and political populism finding easy solutions to child abandonment and feeding the demand for children.[8]

Article 7 CRC acknowledged that the child has the right to an identity, including a name, a date of birth[9] and a nationality, and, 'as far as possible, the right to know and to be cared for by his or her parents'.[10] All the elements of a child's identity should be registered in a birth certificate immediately after birth. Children should be able to preserve their identity, as recognised by law, without unlawful interference and, if they are illegally deprived of some or all of the identity elements, these should be expeditiously re-established (Article 8 CRC).

---

was proposed by the delegation of Egypt on behalf of Algeria, Egypt, Iraq, Jordan, Kuwait, the Libyan Arab Jamahiriya, Morocco, Oman, Pakistan and Tunisia. According to the delegate of Egypt, the purpose of the first amendment was to ensure the psychological stability of the child, which was of equal importance to his or her physical and mental development and helped to form his or her personality. In most cases the right to know the identity of one's parents was fairly essential for the child and equal to his or her right to a name or a nationality, which were only important when the child in question reached a certain age. With regard to this proposal, the German Democratic Republic, the Union of Soviet Socialist Republics and the United States referred to the exceptions in their legislation concerning the right of a 'secret adoption', that is when the adopted child did not have the right to know the identity of his or her natural parents, and pointed out that 'the right to know one's parents' could not be applied everywhere. *Legislative History of the Convention on the Rights of the Child: Volume 1*, 2007, pp. 377–378 in: https://digitallibrary.un.org/record/602462?ln=en&v=pdf. See also R. Blauwhoff, above n. 1, pp. 5–51.

5 For example Poland, the Czech Republic and Luxembourg.

6 See M. Obladen, 'Exposed and Abandoned. Origins of the Foundling Hospital' (2023) 120 *Neonatology* 134.

7 The backsliding in children's rights formed the core of the CRC Committee Chair Prof. Ann Skelton's statement upon the closure of the January 2025 session: https://www.ohchr.org/en/documents/news/committee-rights-child-closes-ninety-eighth-session-after-adopting-concluding.

8 B. Willenbacher, 'Legal transfer of French traditions? German and Austrian initiatives to introduce anonymous birth' (2004) 18 *International Journal of Law, Policy and the Family* 343, 343–344; J. Sjöberg and J. Sköld, 'Selling Anonymity: The Market for Secrecy around Illegitimate Births' (2022) 47(3) *Journal of Family History* 261; K. Scheiwe, 'Legal Provisions that allow Women to Give Birth Anonymously – APT to be exported from France to Germany?' in P. Lødrup and E. Modvar (eds), *Family Life and Human Rights*, Gyldendal, Copenhagen 2004, pp. 681–694.

9 See: CRC General comment No. 20 (2016) on the implementation of the rights of the child during adolescence, para. 41.

10 Article 7 CRC: '(1) The child shall be registered immediately after birth and shall have the right from birth to a name, the right to acquire a nationality and as far as possible, the right to know and be cared for by his or her parents. (2) States Parties shall ensure the implementation of these rights in accordance with their national law and their obligations under the relevant international instruments in this field, in particular where the child would otherwise be stateless.'

In many European states the child's right to an identity is understood in the context of diverse national policies concerning marriage, filiation, adoption and child protection. Another important interpretative tool is the European Convention on Human Rights (ECHR) of 1950, which recognises a human right for everyone to have their private and family life respected (Article 8). Since the holders of this right under Article 8 are not only children, but also adults having various relations to children such as birth mothers, legal parents, adoptive parents, gamete donors, siblings, surrogate mothers and commissioning parents, the child's right to know could be protected following a balancing of all of the interests involved.[11] There are claims that a balancing of public interests or even other interests of the child is also necessary.[12] Although in its balancing exercise the European Court of Human Rights (ECtHR) has adopted some powerful interpretations of Article 8, the Court's jurisprudence is inconsistent and in most of its judgments it tends to favour the interests of adults but not those of children.[13]

In 2004, the Council of Europe's Committee of Experts on Family Law (CJ-FA) did recognise that the child does not have a right to know but rather a legitimate interest that would justify withholding information on the child's biological origin in certain situations.[14]

The states parties' understanding of the rights and obligations under the CRC is facilitated by the UN Committee on the Rights of the Child (CRC Committee). The CRC Committee considers the states parties' reports and addresses their concerns and recommendations in the form of 'concluding observations'; it also holds days of general discussion and publishes its evolving interpretation of the Convention's provisions in the form of general comments on thematic issues.[15]

This chapter aims to discuss the child's right to know and the way in which this should be balanced with the rights of others, in the context of recommendations issued by the CRC Committee to some European states. The first section focuses on

---

11 One could think of the interests of infertility clinics, doctors and pharma companies as well. M. Freeman, 'The Rights of the Artificially Procreated Child' in M. Freeman, *The Moral Status of Children: Essays on the Rights of the Child*, Martinus Nijhoff, The Hague 1997, pp. 200–201.

12 S. Besson, 'Enforcing the child's right to know her origins: contrasting approaches under the Convention on the Rights of the Child and the European Convention on Human Rights' (2007) 21 *International Journal of Law, Policy and the Family* 137.

13 In *Odièvre v France*, no. 42326/98, 13 February 2003, the Court stated that France had acted within 'its margin of appreciation which it must be afforded in view of the complex and sensitive nature of the issue of access to information about one's origins, an issue that concerns the right to know one's personal history, the choices of the natural parents, the existing family ties and the adoptive parents'.

14 Report on principles concerning the establishment and legal consequences of parentage – 'The White Paper', working document, as adopted by the European Committee on Legal Co-operation at its 79th plenary meeting on 11–14 May 2004, paras. 87–89.

15 The CRC Committee is a body of 18 independent experts that monitors compliance with the CRC: https://www.ohchr.org/en/treaty-bodies/crc/introduction-committee.

the CRC Committee's interpretation of the right to know in light of the European debate on balancing the rights of children and birth mothers. The practice and legislation on secrecy concerning birth in France and other European states belonging to the Roman law legal family will be critically examined in the second section to reveal the slow pace of reforms to address the disparities between international law and the national implementation of the right to know. The third section deals with the modern practices that violate the child's right to know in selected states in Europe. The last section presents the CRC Committee's views on how this right should be implemented by the states parties to the Convention.

At the time of writing and for the last eight years, the author has been a member of the CRC Committee. This chapter focuses on that time period with view to providing an insight into the Committee's thinking when issuing concluding observations to the respective states parties.

2. THE CHILD'S RIGHT TO KNOW AND ITS 'INNER CORE' INTEREST

There are different perspectives on the interpretation of the child's right to know that lead to an understanding that the realisation of this right depends on the way it is balanced with the rights of others who are involved.

The need for the balancing of rights in the European context stems from the universality of the right to respect for everyone's private life (Article 8 ECHR). For example, both the child and the mother have rights protected under the ambit of private life that are in conflict with each other. From this perspective, the claim is that the balancing should not lead to a violation of the 'inner core' of any of those rights in order not to make the right devoid of any content. The proposal is that in the case of conflicts between the fundamental rights' inner core, pragmatic solutions need to be sought in this balancing exercise and the child's right to know should not be given absolute abstract priority.[16] The solutions suggested by the CRC Committee to fulfil the child's right will be discussed later.

The CRC Committee's perspective is the one of the rights of the child but not the rights of adults, including of mothers, donors or any other parties. In the Committee's view, the right to know is an absolute and standalone child's right that is linked to many other children's rights. It creates obligations for the states parties to ensure access to information that could reveal the truth about children's biological or genetic origins.

The Committee considers that Article 7 rights facilitate the recognition of the legal personality of the child as an independent human being with evolving

[16] S. Besson, above n. 12, p. 148.

agency to exercise their rights (Article 5) in all situations from birth onwards.[17] This understanding is akin to the ECtHR's interpretation that the 'inner core' of the right is respect for one's private life: 'the person has a vital interest, protected by the ECHR, in receiving the information necessary to know and to understand their childhood and early development'.[18]

The CRC Committee observes that the right of the child to an identity could be compromised in various contexts that tend to be extended, most often by means of discriminatory regulations on establishing filiation, in adoption (national and inter-country), and assisted reproduction, including surrogacy, but also in conflict situations where the identity of children might be forcibly changed (enforced disappearances and abductions) and in other contexts.[19]

The Committee's view is that a denial of the right to know amounts to *discrimination* (Article 2). The Committee raised concerns about discrimination on the ground of childbirth and related to 'unknown origin' in its three consecutive review cycles on France and Luxembourg between 1994 and 2009.[20] Following the review of the initial report by France, the Committee observed that: 'regarding the right of the child to know his or her origins, including in cases of a mother requesting that her identity remain secret during the birth and declaration of the birth, adoption and medically-assisted procreation, the Committee is concerned that 'the legislative measures being taken by the State party might not fully reflect the provisions of the Convention, particularly its general principles' (CRC/C/15/Add.20, 1994, para. 14). France never responded to these concerns. The same concerns, but expressed more strongly, were published in 2004 and a recommendation was made that France should 'take all appropriate measures to ensure that the provisions of article 7, especially the right of the child to know his or her parents, be fully enforced in the light of the principles of "non-discrimination" (art. 2) and the "best interests of the child" (art. 3)' (CRC/C/15/Add.240, 2004, para. 24). The same recommendation was made with regard to Luxembourg in 1998 (CRC/C/15/Add.92, 1998, para. 29).

In contrast, the ECtHR did not find 'that confidentiality, as protected in France, amounted to discrimination on the ground of birth'.[21] According to the Court

---

17 Similarly in R. Hodgkin and P. Newell, *Implementation Handbook for the Convention on the Rights of the Child*, fully revised 3rd ed., UNICEF, Geneva 2007, pp. 103–108.

18 *Gaskin v the United Kingdom*, 7 July 1989, Series A no. 160, p. 20, §49; *Odièvre v France*, Joint Dissenting Opinion of Judges Wildhaber, Sir Nicolas Bratza, Bonello, Loucaides, Cabral Barreto, Tulkens and Pellonpää, para. 7. See also the discussion on justifications for a right to know one's origins and the autonomy-based approach, R. Blauwhoff, above n. 1, pp. 10–29.

19 C. Baglietto, L. Bordier, M. Dambach and C. Jeannin, 'Preserving "family relations": an essential feature of the child's right to identity', Child Identity Protection (CHIP), Geneva 2022, https://child-identity.org/images/files/CHIP-Preserving-Family-Relations-EN.pdf.

20 Concluding observations on France, CRC/C/15/Add.20, 1998, para. 14. In its second periodic report, France elaborated on its plans for the equalisation of legitimate, adulterous and natural children.

21 *Odièvre v France*, no. 42326/98, 13 February 2003, para. 56.

in the case in question, the plaintiff, Ms Odièvre, had not been discriminated against because instead of a biological mother she had an adoptive mother and because the birth mother simply did not exist. Ms Odièvre had rightly defined her status as a legal fiction, because the mother was deemed never to have given birth when she had expressly sought confidentiality.[22]

The opponents of the recognition of the right to know usually justify their position by giving priority to the right to life and the best interests of the child. It should be noted, however, that this prioritisation does not have any legal basis in the Convention. The Convention does not recognise that some rights are more important than others.[23] Rather, the Committee's view is that a denial of information violates the harmonious development of children (Articles 6 and 24). In 2012, the Committee reiterated its concerns to Austria and it perceived that the practice of anonymous abandonment through the use of 'baby flaps' or 'baby nests' was in violation of, inter alia, Articles 6, 7, 8, 9 and 19 of the Convention (CRC/C/AUT/CO/3–4, 2012, paras. 29–30). In 2015, a similar and serious concern was expressed with regard to Poland 'about the absence of regulation and the increasing number of baby boxes that allow for the anonymous abandonment of children …, which is in violation of, inter alia, articles 6 to 9 and 19 of the Convention' (CRC/C/POL/CO/3–4, 2015, para. 20).[24] The Committee interprets the child's right to development (Article 6) in its broadest sense as a holistic concept, embracing the child's physical, mental, spiritual, moral, psychological and social development.[25]

With regard to 'best interests', it is clear that Article 7 does not make the right to know conditional upon a best interests assessment, which should mean that having access to birth-related information should always be in the best interests of the child. This is in line with the recent non-paternalistic approach taken by the Committee.[26] The Committee considers that the policy of retaining the

---

22 Ibid., para. 30.

23 A discussion on the best interests and birth under X in M. Freeman, 'The new birth right? Identity and the child of the reproductive revolution' (1996) 4(3) *International Journal of Children's Rights* 273.

24 Following this criticism, the Polish government strongly defended the practice in a special letter to the Committee (a very rare occurrence). The government referred to the Ombudsman for Children's position in retaining baby hatches: 'I would like to stress that … when a conflict between the natural right to life and another right arises, the right to life must be given a priority. This statement also applies to the conflict between the right of the child to know and be cared for by his parents (Article 7 of the Convention) and the right of the child to preserve his identity (Article 8 of the Convention). The right of the child to know his biological parents may not be given primacy over the fundamental right to life. Article 6 of Convention on the Rights of the Child says that the States Parties recognise that every child has the inherent right to life.' INT_CRC_COB_POL_23260_E.

25 General Comment No. 5 (2003) on general measures of implementation of the Convention on the Rights of the Child (Arts. 4, 42 and 44, para. 12).

26 According to Hodgkin and Newell, the wording of Article 7 implies that children are entitled to know their parentage if this is possible, even if this is deemed to be against their best

secrecy of birth does not give priority to the best interests of children and is therefore in violation of Article 3 CRC.

In interpreting the right to know, the Committee has never engaged in the debate on 'who is the parent' since it is a matter for national legislation to regulate biological, genetic and social parenthood; and neither does the Committee consider this right to be a right to a family[27] or to a family life. But in specific contexts the right is meaningful for keeping families together (Articles 9 and 18 CRC),[28] facilitating contact with families across countries (Article 10), and maintaining continuity concerning a child's ethnic, religious, cultural and linguistic background (Article 20).[29] As for the qualifier of the right to know 'as far as possible', the Committee's view is that if the state withholds information whenever it is available, it would breach its obligations under the Convention.[30]

In the European context, the 'best interests' principle is applied in the context of balancing the rights of all people who are involved. The position of the majority of the Council of Europe Member States, as stated in 2004, is that 'all children have a legitimate interest with respect to their origins. At the same time it recognised that in certain situations, the best interests of the child or of other persons involved may justify withholding from the child such information or certain parts of it'.[31] Still, there is a shared notion that retaining secrecy and denying children access to their 'own personal map' protects not only the

---

interests. But the holistic nature of the Convention suggests that a child who would definitely be harmed by the discovery of his or her parent's identity could be prevented from obtaining this information. This interpretation is supported by the fact that 'as far as possible' also covers the child's right to be cared for by his or her parents – and no one could maintain that 'as far as possible' in that context does not include a consideration of the child's best interests. But it is clear that children's right to know their parentage could only be refused on the grounds of best interests in the most extreme and unambiguous circumstances, and children should be given the opportunity for this decision to be reviewed at a later date. R. Hodgkin and P. Newell, above n. 17, pp. 107–108. This notion can be seen in states that allow access to information on the child's origin when the child in question reaches the age of majority.

27 General Comment No. 14 (2013) on the right of the child to have his or her best interests taken as a primary consideration (art. 3, para. 1), para. 59: the term 'family' must be interpreted in a broad sense to include biological, adoptive or foster parents or, where applicable, the members of the extended family or community as provided for by local custom (Article 5).

28 As Fenton-Glynn rightly points out, allowing mothers to abandon their babies at birth prevents any investigation of the ability of the wider birth family to provide kinship care. C. Fenton-Glynn, 'Anonymous Relinquishment and Baby-Boxes. Live Saving Mechanisms or a Violation of Human Rights?' in K. Boele-Woelki, N. Dethloff and W. Gephart (eds) *Family Law and Family Culture in Europe*, Intersentia, Cambridge/Antwerp 2014, p. 190.

29 General Comment No. 14 (2013), on the right of the child to have his or her best interests taken as a primary consideration (art. 3, para. 1), para. 56.

30 R. Blauwhoff, above n. 1, p. 51.

31 Committee of experts on Family law to the Council of Europe. Report on principles concerning the establishment and legal consequences of parentage – "The White Paper", CJ-FA (2006) 4 e, para. 88. in: https://rm.coe.int/16807004c6.

interests of children but also the interests of the 'ideal family' and others.[32] The same justification was presented by France and Luxembourg while being reviewed by the Committee.[33]

The denial of the child's right to know is also grounded on certain public policies, such as the natalist and anti-abortion policies in France (in 1870 and 1945) promoted by medical professionals that resulted in the establishment of secret departments in maternity homes to prevent abortion and infanticide.[34] The ECtHR seems to share that notion: 'There is also a general interest at stake, as the Italian legislature has consistently sought to protect the mother's and child's health during pregnancy and birth and to avoid illegal abortions and children being abandoned other than under the proper procedure'.[35] In such cases, the Court has sought to find a balance between the competing interests of the child and those of parents and has not so far given priority to the child's best interests.

3. '*ACCOUCHEMENT SOUS X*': BALANCING IN FAVOUR OF ANONYMITY

Birth secrecy in France has been a topical subject in research, judicial judgments and advocacy initiatives. This is an important case to start with for several reasons, probably the leading one being the highest attention devoted to France by the CRC Committee (in all of the review cycles from 1997 to 2021). From a children's rights perspective, the French case demonstrates the inherent tensions between harmful traditions and rights and the dead end which may await reforms even in a free and democratic society. As Lefaucheur points out, the mere fact that the history of *accouchement sous X* dates back to the French Revolution and the Vichy Regime has made its defence politically popular and

32 J. Haderka's defence of the secretive practices in operation in Czechoslovakia before the adoption of the CRC (1987) is a good example: allowing a child to have knowledge of their genetic origins is 'an unthinkable intrusion into the privacy of the family'. Cited by M. Freeman, above n. 11, pp. 200–201. It is essential to determine the age of the child – particularly in the context of criminal proceedings and migration.

33 In its Initial Report (CRC/C/3/Add.15, 1993), France explained that 'in order to prevent any risk of infanticide or the abandonment of a child, the law recognises the mother's right to request that the birth remains confidential' (para. 174) and that 'as regards the right to know which is a specific aspect of the right to identity … which is not an absolute right because the Convention states 'as far as possible', adopted children have the right to ascertain their origin …' (para. 197). The reservation concerning Article 7 was justified by the government of Luxembourg according to the belief that the legal process in respect of anonymous births is deemed to be in the interest of the child, as provided under Article 3 of the Convention. Initial Report, CRC/C/41/Add.2, 1997, para. 53 (3).

34 That policy was developed by the Family Code of 1939 providing for family allowances and penalties for abortion.

35 *Godelli v Italy*, no. 33783/09, 18 March 2013, para. 51.

effective.[36] In fact, this is an argument in favour of the traditional family (values) since marriage-based filiation and the condemnation of illegitimate children is nothing other than this.[37] For a comparison, anonymous births were utilised for the same reasons in other parts of Europe as well, but they were abolished a long time ago.[38] In France and other closely related states, however, although some reforms were undertaken, the system largely remained non-receptive to the voices of people affected by the ban on biological truth.[39] As the dissenting judges in the *Odièvre v France* judgment stated: 'in practice, French law accepted that the mother's decision constituted an absolute defence to any requests for information by the applicant, irrespective of the reasons for or legitimacy of that decision'.[40]

Another reason for starting with this subject is the impact that the French system had on many European states, which also developed and defended various forms of birth secrecy. In reality, it is nothing other than legalised child abandonment. The third reason is the inconsistent jurisprudence of the ECtHR, as its method of balancing the conflicting rights creates further obstacles to the realisation of the child's right to know.

3.1. MATERNITY BY RECOGNITION

Maternity by recognition for children born to non-married parents (natural or illegitimate children) is the basis for the legality of '*accouchement sous X*'.[41] Nowadays, it is termed as 'the legal path to anonymous birth',[42] which

---

36 N. Lefaucheur, 'The French "Tradition" of Anonymous Birth: The Lines of Argument' (2004) 18 *International Journal for Law, Policy and the Family* 319, 328–330.

37 See I. Pretelli, 'Identity and Civil Status of Children Conceived through Cross-border Procreation Contracts: Perspectives on filiation and the best interests of the child' (2023–2024) 25 *Yearbook of Private International Law* 241.

38 For example in Sweden, where during the 17th and 18th centuries extramarital sex was a criminal offence, which meant that an illegitimate child was the ultimate proof of a criminal act. As a response to the numerous infanticide verdicts that were handed down in Sweden, King Gustav III established the Infanticide Act in 1778, which protected unmarried mothers by giving them the right to give birth anonymously and to leave their children in someone else's care. Both parents could be registered as unknown in the parish records and the midwife had no right to inquire about the father. In 1917, the Infanticide Act was replaced by the Act on Illegitimate Children, which stated that men should take more financial responsibility for their illegitimate offspring. This meant that anonymous births were no longer possible. J. Sjöberg and J. Sköld, above n. 8.

39 Child Identity Protection (CHIP), 'Legal Memorandum: Right to know one's origins – *Gauvin-Fournis and Silliau v France*', https://www.child-identity.org/wp-content/uploads/2023/12/CHIP-LegalMemorandum-EN.pdf.

40 *Odièvre v France*, no. 42326/98, 13 February 2003, para. 7.

41 N. Lefaucheur, above n. 36, pp. 320–327.

42 K. Scheiwe, above n. 8, p. 682.

is equivalent to the 'legal abandonment of infants at birth'.[43] Motherhood by recognition and the prohibition on pursuing the father in the case of non-marital children were part of the legal developments (1792–1793) that took place during the French Revolution and were linked to the regulation of marriage and the inferior position of women.[44]

Stemming from the legal concept of filiation based on recognition, '*accouchement sous X*' still survives as a 'French tradition' to this very day and it also applies in countries from the Roman law family, such as Belgium, Luxembourg, Italy and Spain.[45] It is also influential in some states in Eastern Europe that do not belong to that legal family.[46] The pressure from child 'victims' and former children, empowered by international and regional law, only slowly encouraged reforms from 2002 onwards.

It took France 27 years to reform its filiation legislation and to eliminate the distinction between legitimate and natural (or illegitimate) children.[47] Belgium only abolished the discriminatory rule on the mother's filiation based on recognition providing for the illegitimate status of children born to non-married

---

43 K. O'Donovan, 'Interpretations of children's identity rights' in D. Fottrell (ed.), *Revisiting Children's Rights. 10 Years of the UN CRC*, Kluwer Law International, The Hague 2000, p. 79.

44 The rule stating that 'establishing paternity is forbidden' (Article 340 Civil Code) was invented by revolutionary legislators (decree of 2 November 1793), U. Gerhard, 'Civil Law, a Tool of Masculine Domination?' in *Encyclopédie d'histoire numérique de l'Europe* [online], 22 June 2020, https://ehne.fr/en/node/12265. The only aspect that eventually remained of the revolutionary laws was the equal division of inheritance among all children, which included the abolishment of the eldest son's prioritisation. The question of whether this, in fact, already set in motion the father's 'dethroning' is a matter for discussion. M. Lanzinger, 'Paternal Authority in Western Europe', *Encyclopédie d'histoire numérique de l'Europe* [online], 26 June 2020, https://ehne.fr/en/node/21309.

45 In Spain, the unconstitutionality of the provisions allowing the mother to give birth in secret was declared by the Supreme Court in 1999, decision RJ 1999, 6944. J. Ribot, 'Spain' in O. Szeibert (ed.), *Developments in Family Law, Year by Year*, I. Elte Universiyu Press, Budapest 2018, p. 190.

46 "K. O'Donovan, above n. 43, p. 79. For example, the French model was adopted in Bulgaria in the Recognition of Illegitimate Children, their Regularisation and Adoption Act of 1890. That regulation was modified in 1940 by the Extramarital Children and Adoption Act. The status of illegitimate child was abolished in 1949 by the Persons and Families Act.

47 In its third and fourth periodic reports to the CRC Committee (CRC/C/FRA/42, 2007), France explained that the reform of filiation began with the Law of 3 January 1972 and was completed by the Order of 4 July 2005. The Law abolishes the distinction between legitimate and natural filiation, introducing a new concept of the law of filiation. Pursuant to Article 20, the Order of 4 July 2005 applies to children born before, as well as after, its entry into force. Certain exceptions are however provided, thereby modifying the principle of immediate application to accommodate situations where cases are already in progress. Article 310(1) of the Civil Code is an introductory provision providing a generic list of ways in which filiation can be established, no longer distinguishing between children born within and outside marriage: filiation can be established by the authoritative effect of the law, by the voluntary recognition of maternity or paternity, by a legal judgement or by the *de facto* possession of a filiated status confirmed in an affidavit.

parents in 1987, following the landmark ECtHR *Marckx* judgment of 1979.[48] That judgment, however, has never been considered by Italy and Luxembourg as a driver for change.

The Italian anonymous birth regulation gained the attention of the CRC Committee somewhat later than the French equivalent. Only in 2003, under the title 'The right to identity', did the Committee make strong recommendations that Italy should:

1. as far as possible ensure respect for the child's right to know his or her parents' identity should it be an adopted child or a child born out of wedlock who has not been recognised by either of his or her parents;
2. urgently review and amend legislation in order to ensure that children born out of wedlock legally have from birth a mother (in accordance with the ECtHR decision in *Marckx v Belgium* and the rule *mater semper certa est*), and encourage the recognition of these children by their fathers (as a way of preventing the 'easy' abandonment of children); and
3. ratify the European Convention on the Legal Status of Children Born out of Wedlock (CRC/C/15/Add.198, 2003, paras. 27–28).

The reform of the Italian Civil Code of 2012[49] did not change 'birth in anonymity' (D.lgs. 396/2000).[50] The children of unmarried mothers were declared to be 'born from an unknown person' and were immediately placed for adoption. The ECtHR found the Italian system to be in breach of Article 8 considering that it was founded on the principle of *absolute and irreversible anonymity*, which did not strike a fair balance between the mother's right to privacy and the right of the child to have information on their origins.[51] The Italian Constitutional Court (decision no. 278/2013) also declared that the child's right to know must be balanced against the mother's right to privacy and it requested

48 *Marckx v Belgium*, no. 6833/74, 13 June 1979, paras. 44–68.

49 Article 315 of the Italian Civil Code (with the effect of the Law of 10 December 2012, no. 219 and D.lgs 28 December 2013) states that '[a]ll children have the same legal status' and the terms illegitimate and natural children have been abolished. M.-D. Panforti, 'Italy' in O. Szeibert (ed.), *Developments in Family Law, Year by Year*, I. Elte Universiyu Press, Budapest 2018, pp. 101–116.

50 The government's position is that: 'a request by the child for access to information about its identity could conflict with the freedom which all women enjoyed to decline their role as mother or to assume responsibility for the child. Under Italian law, maternity was considered an aspect of private life and received statutory protection on that account'. *Godelli v Italy*, no. 33783/09, 18 March 2013, para. 44.

51 *Godelli v Italy*, no. 33783/09, 18 March 2013, paras. 57–59. The Court also noted that, unlike the French system examined in *Odièvre*, Italian law does not attempt to strike any balance between the competing rights and interests at stake. In the absence of any machinery enabling the applicant's right to discover her origins to be balanced against the mother's interests in remaining anonymous, blind preference is inevitably given to the latter (para. 56).

Parliament to enact a law to this effect.[52] Italy has not yet implemented the CRC Committee's recommendations, even though 22 years have now passed since these recommendations were issued.

In 1998, the CRC Committee recommended that Luxembourg should 'take all appropriate measures to ensure that children born out of wedlock do not suffer discriminatory treatment or stigmatization, and that the terms "legitimate" and "illegitimate", which are currently used in the Civil Code, be eliminated' (CRC/C/15/Add.92, 1998, paras. 27, 29).[53]

3.2. 'NON-EXISTENT' MOTHERS

Birth secrecy was first gradually legalised in France in penal and social legislation and thereafter – as a right for the woman giving birth – in the Civil Code. In 1941, a governmental decree introduced the penalisation of any refusal to admit pregnant women requesting secrecy along with a duty to provide assistance to the mother.[54] Currently, the amended regulation is part of the Social Action and Families Code (Article L. 222-6). It provides that mothers who request that their identity remains confidential are entitled to psychological support, practical advice and the reimbursement of costs for hospital accommodation and confinement by the Child Welfare Service.[55] It is even the case that the parents (not only the mother) of a child up to the age of 12 months are allowed to entrust the child to the Child Welfare Service and request that their identity be kept secret (Article L. 224-5 (4) Social Action and Families Code). The filiation stated in the civil-status documents is annulled and a fictitious birth certificate, known as a provisional civil-status certificate, is issued in lieu thereof.[56] This regulation questions the whole justification for 'birth under X' as serving the mothers in distress.

Opponents of *accouchement sous X* gained momentum in 1978 with the adoption of the law on access to administrative documents and the creation of a

---

52 M.-D. Panforti, above n. 49, p. 115. The same decision made a reference to a legal procedure that would allow a judge to request a woman for authorisation to disclose her name to a child born under X even in the absence of specific statutory indications to this effect. However, the refusal of the mother would be an insuperable ban on any disclosure.

53 The government replied to this recommendation as follows: 'In Title VII the Civil Code distinguishes between lawful descent and natural descent. The term illegitimate descent does not appear in the Civil Code. Article 351-1 of the Civil Code expressly provides for the child born out of wedlock to have the same rights and the same duties as the legitimate child. Thus there is no discrimination.' CRC/C/104/Add.5, 2005, para. 20.

54 Government decree by the Vichy Government of September 1941. That provision was repealed and subsequently reintroduced by the decrees of 29 November 1953 and 7 January 1959. *Odièvre v France*, no. 42326/98, 13 February 2003, para. 15.

55 *Odièvre v France*, no. 42326/98, 13 February 2003, para. 15.

56 Abolished by Law no. 2002-93 on access by adopted persons and people in state care to information about their origins.

special Commission for this purpose. Persons born 'under X' started to approach the Commission seeking the identity of their birth parents. The Association of Children in Public Care was also established to support children in requesting information about their birth.[57]

Following the example of France, Luxembourg started on reforms after a proposal by the National Consultative Commission on Life Sciences and Health Ethics (CNE),[58] which however only reached the status of a Bill on parentage (*projet de loi portant réforme de la filiation*). Meanwhile, the CRC Committee issued several repeated recommendations. In 2004, Luxembourg was urged to take all necessary measures to prevent and eliminate the practice of so-called anonymous births (CRC/C/104/Add.5, 2005, para. 23).

3.3. INTERNAL DEBATES AND INTERNATIONAL CONVENTIONS

In 1993, just prior to presenting its initial report under the Convention, the debates in France on abolishing birth secrecy, as well as donor anonymity in assisted reproduction,[59] reached Parliament. However, they ended up instead reinforcing this women's right by codifying it in the Civil Code (Articles 341 and 341-1), which provide that choosing to give birth in secret affects the determination of filiation by establishing an estoppel defence to proceedings to establish maternity.[60] As a result, the child's legal status was cleared for adoption since the 'unknown' parent(s) does/do not therefore need to give consent for the

---

57 More in *Odièvre v France*, no. 42326/98, 13 February 2003, para. 20.

58 The Luxembourg concept for reforms was presented in the second periodic report to the Committee. The government also made known that the Central Statistical and Economic Research Service (STATEC) had only recorded one case of an anonymous birth during the period from 1995 to 1999 (CRC/C/104/Add.5, 2005, paras. 25, 26).

59 The principle of donor anonymity introduced by the Bioethics Act of 1994 was abolished by the Bioethics Act of 2021, under which donors' explicit consent to the recording of their identity and non-identifying information (age, physical characteristics, marital and professional status, country of birth, reasons for donation) is a condition for all gamete donations. Persons conceived through medically assisted reproduction can apply to the Commission on Access to Third-Party Donor Data for Persons Born through Medically Assisted Reproduction (CAPADD) in order to access information about their biological parents. Children born from gametes donated before 1 September 2022 may instead apply to the CAPADD to contact the third-party donors to obtain their consent to the disclosure of the relevant information: 'Legal Memorandum: Right to know one's origins – *Gauvin-Fournis and Silliau v France*', https://www.child-identity.org/wp-content/uploads/2023/12/CHIP-LegalMemorandum-EN.pdf and https://strasbourgobservers.com/2023/12/12/is-it-safe-to-bury-the-truth-under-the-family-tree-the-ecthrs-response-in-gauvin-fournis-and-silliau-v-france/.

60 N. Lefaucheur, above n. 36, p. 323. Ms Odièvre defined this as a legal fiction, because the mother was deemed never to have given birth when she had expressly sought confidentiality. *Odièvre v France*, no. 42326/98, 13 February 2003, para. 30.

child's adoption. The government of Luxembourg also confirmed that the status of 'unknown parents' facilitates adoption.[61]

It is probable that the Committee's observations (CRC/C/15/Add.20, 1994, para. 14) on the French legislation's non-conformity with the Convention, as well as the debates on the Hague Adoption Convention, fuelled national campaigns held in 1995.[62] The law on intercountry adoption passed in 1996 provided for the collection of non-identifying data on birth mothers who requested secrecy and stated that these mothers could reveal their identity at any time. However, birth secrecy has never been legally forbidden and mothers have never been subject to the obligation to reveal the truth.[63]

The next attempt to reform filiation and to repeal birth secrecy was initiated in 1997 by the Minister of Justice, Elisabeth Guigou, supported by a report by the prominent legal sociologist Irene Thery, but it again failed. The role of medical professionals and lawyers in this failure was prominent.[64] In 1998, Ms Pascale Odièvre lodged an application with the ECtHR.[65]

In 2002, a progressive step was made by the creation of National Council for Access to Personal Origins (CNAOP), which was mandated to collect and preserve information on the identity of birth parents and the child's history that would be disclosed upon the child's request if the parent(s) agreed to this.[66] Anonymous birth was not abolished, but the law establishing the CNAOP stipulated that mothers seeking secrecy should be informed about the importance for their children to know their origin and these mothers would be requested to leave a record of their identity in a sealed envelope to be sent to the CNAOP.[67] Following an amendment to that law in 2007, the child was allowed to

---

61 In its Initial Report under the Convention, 1997, para. 135, the government of Luxembourg stated that: 'The subsequent adoption of a *child of unknown parents is considerably facilitated* by the inclusion in the Civil Code of a new provision allowing the issuance of a birth certificate not giving the names of the father and mother. As a general rule, such children are entrusted at birth to a foster-family wishing to adopt a child. However, for a period of three months the natural parents retain the possibility of making a declaration of recognition to the registration officer and requesting the return of the child.'

62 France signed the 1993 Hague Convention on Protection of Children and Cooperation in Respect of Intercountry Adoption in 1995, and ratified it on 30 April 1998. The Convention entered into force in France on 1 October 1998.

63 N. Lefaucheur, above n. 36, p. 324.

64 Ibid.

65 The applicant alleged that the fact that her birth had been kept secret, with the result that it was impossible for her to find out her origins, amounted to a violation of her rights as guaranteed by Article 8 of the Convention and constituted discrimination contrary to Article 14.

66 National Council for Access to Personal Origins – France Enfance Protégée established under Law no. 2002-93 on access by adopted persons and people in state care to information about their origins.

67 The parents are not obliged to leave personal information, but must fill in questionnaires concerning the child, particularly their medical history. The children in question are then

take action, subject to the proviso that they had reached the age of accountability and with the agreement of their legal representatives.

That reform persuaded the ECtHR to accept that France had already struck a fair balance between the conflicting rights of children and mothers. In two judgments (on similar facts but separated by 20 years), *Odièvre v France* and *Cherrier v France*,[68] the Court applied the same reasoning and reached the same decision that there had been no violation of the applicants' right to private life. It found that a procedure for the confidentiality of a mother's identity to be waived, subject to her consent, and for accessing non-identifying information on the child's origins was a suitable mechanism for ensuring a fair and reasonable balance between the rights and interests at stake.[69] To put it another way, the Court found that birth secrecy amounted to proportionate interference in the right of the child 'to achieve the aim of reconciling those interests', which did not amount to a violation of Article 8 ECHR, although France was included in the minority of states applying this rule.

In the above judgments, the Court stepped back from its own jurisprudence by interpreting the Convention as being 'intended to guarantee not rights that are theoretical or illusory but rights that are practical and effective'.[70] The Court merely accepted the government's contention that a mechanism had been established that improved the prospect of mothers 'agreeing to waive confidentiality, something which, it will be noted in passing, they have always been able to do even before the enactment of the law of 22 January 2002.'[71] As for the dissenting judges in *Odièvre*, as a result of the domestic law and practice, no balancing of interests was possible either in practice or in law. The mother thus has a discretionary right to bring a suffering child into the world and to condemn it to lifelong ignorance. The effect of the mother's absolute 'right of veto' is that the rights of the child, which are recognised in the general scheme of the Convention, are entirely neglected and forgotten.

The CRC Committee was also not at all convinced by the French 'reform' of 2002. After reviewing the second periodic report of France in 2004 and noting the Law of 22 January 2002, it remained concerned that the rights under Article 7 of the Convention 'may not be fully respected by the State party and that the right to conceal the identity of the mother if she so wishes is not in conformity with the provisions of the Convention'. Therefore France received the

---

placed provisionally with a foster family, and are later adopted when the rights of the biological parents have expired.

68 *Cherrier v France*, no. 18843/20, judgment of 30 January 2024. The case concerned a refusal by the National Council for Access to Information about Personal Origins (CNAOP) to inform the applicant, who was born to anonymous parents, of the identity of her biological mother based on the mother's refusal to reveal her identity.

69 *Cherrier v France*, no. 18843/20, judgment of 24 June 2024, paras. 80, 82.

70 *Artico v Italy*, no. 6694/74, 13 May 1980, para. 33.

71 *Odièvre v France*, no. 42326/98, 13 February 2003, para. 49.

recommendation to 'take all appropriate measures to ensure that the provisions of article 7, especially the right of the child to know, as far as possible, his or her parents, be fully enforced in the light of the principles of non-discrimination (art. 2) and the best interests of the child (art. 3)' (CRC/C/15/Add.24, 2004, paras. 23-24). In 2009, the CRC Committee expressed concern about the delays in inquiries before the CNAOP and the mother's right of veto; in addition, it reiterated its previous recommendation and also extended it: France should take all appropriate measures to fully enforce the child's right to know his or her biological parents *and siblings*, as enshrined in Article 7 of the Convention and in the light of the principles of non-discrimination (Article 2) and the best interests of the child (Article 3). The Committee further recommended the state party to 'ensure that new inquiries are treated in a timely fashion'(CRC/C/FRA/CO/4, 2009, para. 44).

In 2023, the Committee, under the cluster title 'Birth registration, nationality and the right to identity', addressed the issue of children not being allowed to seek information and unlawful intercountry adoption. France received the recommendations to ensure that: (1) 'children born through assisted reproduction technologies have access to information about their origins before they reach the age of 18, whenever they make a request to that effect' (CRC/C/FRA/CO/6–7, 2023, para. 20 (b)).; and (2) 'all children, including those who were adopted long ago, are provided with assistance in accessing information about their origins' (CRC/C/FRA/CO/6–7, 2023, para. 34 (b)).

4. EUROPE GOING BACK TO BIRTH 'UNDER X'

The French 'anonymous birth', which is rooted in discriminatory traditions towards women and children, but also in the philosophy of social versus biological parenthood, could be considered inspiration for the recent developments in Europe. Those practices, however, have their political and religious determinants as well and could be understood as an example of backsliding in children's and women's rights.[72] This subject matter has even spurred open attacks against the CRC Committee because of its critique of baby boxes and anonymous births.[73]

---

72 In Germany, the push for legalising anonymous births came from Protestant clinics, Catholic lay organisations and private welfare organisations. In Austria, the push factors were medical doctors, the social (state) welfare institution and the Socialist Party. B. Willenbacher, above n. 8, pp. 345–347. It is very likely that the recent developments have been influenced by the expansion of the 'safe haven' laws in the USA after 1999, see https://www.hrsa.gov/sites/default/files/hrsa/advisory-committees/infant-mortality/meetings/infant-abandonment-prevention.pdf. One should not forget that the USA is the only state that has not ratified the CRC.

73 R. Ramesh, 'Spread of "baby boxes" in Europe alarms United Nations', *The Guardian* 10 June 2012, https://www.theguardian.com/world/2012/jun/10/unitednations-europe-news: 'Bernd Posselt, Christian Social Union MEP for Munich who signed the letter to the UNCRC last year, told

Unlike in France, a legal basis for anonymous births did not exist in the countries from the Germanic law families, the common law states and the Nordic states in Europe. Their systems establish filiation for the mother based on the biological fact of childbirth (the *mater semper certa est* rule); there was therefore no legal means for the birth mother to escape from establishing motherhood.[74] Anonymous births were abolished in Sweden in 1917, with the opportunity for babies to be cared for by the child welfare services if the mothers had relinquished them.[75]

Since 2000, several Central European states have allowed for anonymous births under penal law and health law regulations, but not under family law. In Austria, anonymous births were not expressly legalised but were made possible in 2001 by waiving the criminal liability for abandoning the child in a *Babyklappe*.[76] In Czechia, the Health Services Act of 2004 allowed unmarried mothers to request the healthcare provider not to reveal her identity on the birth certificate and baby boxes were created by a private foundation in 2005.[77] In 2014, Germany enacted two laws legalising confidential births but also ensured that children born secretly still had the right to know their own ancestry by giving them the opportunity to enquire about the identity of their biological mothers once they have reached the age of 16.[78] It is this German 'nuanced' approach to

the Guardian that "our experiences with baby-boxes here in Munich, for example organised by a monastery, have been positive. I know also the problems, but for me it is essential to protect and to safeguard the life of children in extreme situations. All other problems can be solved with good will as long as the child is alive. *It is not the decision of an United Nations committee what we are doing to help born or unborn children*"' and 'In an email to the Guardian, Manfred Weber, German MEP and vice-chairman of the European People's Party – the largest grouping on the centre right – who signed the anti-UNCRC letter, said the issue was one of competing "rights". "Although I am convinced that a child is best raised within an intact family, the safety of children is of higher priority than their desire to know their biological parents"'.

74 K. Scheiwe, above n. 8, p. 682. M. Lanzinger, above n. 44. As Margareth Lanzinger states, 'the French Code civil of 1804 can be read as paradigmatic of the restorative thinking which was at work, since it served as a model for numerous codifications within Europe – particularly in Southern and Eastern Europe, and beyond in addition to being applied in large parts of Europe in the wake of Napoleon's conquests'.

75 J. Sjöberg and J. Sköld, above n. 8.

76 It was not expressly legalised but made possible by waiving criminal liability for abandoning a child in a *babyklappe*. The Austrian Ministry of Justice has issued a decree on baby boxes and anonymous births, according to which a maternity clinic may refrain from collecting the mother's personal data if she is in a situation of distress. I. Schwenzer (ed.), *Tensions between Legal, Biological and Social Conceptions of Parentage*, Intersentia, Antwerp 2007, p. 34. See the second periodic report of Austria (CRC/C/83/Add.88, 2004, paras. 152–153). In its third to fourth periodic report, Austria defended its practice by referring to the ECtHR's jurisprudence on Article 8 (CRC/C/AUT/3-4, 117, 2011).

77 Z. Kralickova, 'New Family Law in the Czech Republic: Back to Traditions and Towards Modern Trends' in *The International Survey of Family Law*, Jordan Publishing, Bristol 2014, pp. 85–86. See also https://www.babybox.cz/?p=english.

78 Fifth and sixth periodic reports of Germany, CRC/C/DEU/5-6, 2020, paras. 72–75. The German Constitution recognises everyone's right to know.

anonymity that allows the mother to provide a false name when giving birth in a hospital and for the provision of the birth certificate, but still requiring her personal data to be stored at a central agency for eventual access by the child once they turn 16 years of age.[79] This is the so-called 'confidential birth' and could be seen as a compromise between the two rights, but it is still based on the falsification of a child's identity.

5. BABY BOXES

Michael Obladen provides a useful insight into the ancient history and Christianity era of foundling hospitals and baby boxes in Europe.[80] He informs us that throughout the 18th century, abandoning newborn infants was widely practised, particularly among the descendants of the Roman Empire: Italy, Spain, France and Austria. It was not only premature malformed babies and infants born out of wedlock that made their way into foundling asylums; in Paris around 10% and in Vienna up to a fifth of babies admitted to these institutions had been abandoned by married couples. Obladen, after thoroughly reviewing the perspectives of the proponents and opponents of this practice, has come to the conclusion that it took decades before people realised that the mere existence of foundling hospitals – and even more so, the anonymity of the revolving boxes – encouraged abandonment and thus exacerbated infant mortality.

Although the revolving boxes had been removed in France by 1870, and in Belgium the last was closed in Antwerp in 1860,[81] recent years, since 2000, have seen the rise of these practices in Europe, with the abandonment of babies in so-called 'baby boxes' or the 'baby flap' (*Babyklappe*), 'baby window'[82] or 'hatches'. These practices are not explicitly regulated or prohibited by law.[83] Nowadays, 'baby boxes' are in operation in 12 of the 27 EU Member States: Austria, Belgium, the Czech Republic, Germany, Hungary, Italy,[84] Latvia,

---

79 C. Fenton-Glynn, above n. 28, p. 196.

80 M. Obladen, above n. 6.

81 Ibid.

82 I. Schwenzer, above n. 76, p. 345.

83 Health professionals are however in favour of their wider advertisement, including by holding information campaigns for the general public and in schools. C. Grylli et al., 'Anonymous birth law saves babies – optimization, sustainability and public awareness' (2016) 19(2) *Archives of Women's Mental Health* 291.

84 More in: https://www.euronews.com/2023/04/14/anonymous-births-and-safe-heaven-baby-boxes-italys-new-controversy.

Lithuania, Poland, Portugal, Slovakia[85] and Switzerland[86].[87] This practice is spreading beyond Europe, which testifies to its attractiveness.[88]

According to research carried out into child abandonment and its prevention in Europe, the primary causes of child abandonment in Europe in the 21st century were found to be poverty or financial hardship, being a single parent, postnatal depression, mental illness and substance misuse, a lack of sexual health education, poor knowledge regarding family planning, restrictions regarding access to abortion, the child having some form of disability, the child being HIV positive, and pregnancy as a result of rape or abuse.[89] Reasons such as the cultural background of the mother and domestic violence should also be noted.[90] Willenbacher refers to research suggesting that the institution of anonymous birth sets up a new market for the legal abandonment of children and can hence lead to pressure on pregnant women which is similar to the pressure faced by women who decide to have an abortion or to give up their child for adoption.[91] It could be further claimed that 'baby boxes' facilitate state-care policies, thereby diminishing the need for investment in prevention and case management, and supporting stigma and gender-based discrimination. In some cases, abandoning the baby in such a place completely erases any opportunity for the child to trace

85 The Committee's position on baby boxes created a platform for politicians in the former Communist bloc even to attack the Convention: 'Miroslav Mikolášik, a Christian Democrat MEP from Slovakia, stated that the "communist idea" was "to take away violently a child from a family that they considered as an enemy of regime and place him or her in a state orphanage … If UN convention on the rights of the child's article 8 that guarantees children's right to know their own identity means the death of only one unwanted baby, it is a very wrong article and very wrong convention."' R. Ramesh, above n. 73.

86 Reviewing Switzerland in 2015, under the title 'Right to identity', the Committee expressed deep concern about the absence of regulation and the increasing number of baby boxes that allow for the anonymous abandonment of children in violation of the Convention and urged Switzerland to prohibit the use of baby boxes, to strengthen and promote the already existing alternatives and to consider introducing, as a last resort, the possibility of confidential hospital births (CRC/C/CHE/CO/2–4, 2015, paras. 34-35).

87 More in C. Baglietto, L. Bordier, M. Dambach and C. Jeannin, above n. 19.

88 Baby boxes are now widespread in South Korea, Japan and other states. In 2018, an International Association of Baby Boxes was created: http://www.iabb.info/english/#link1.

89 University of Nottingham, *Child Abandonment and its Prevention in Europe*, University of Nottingham, UK with financial support from the European Commission's Daphne Programme (DG Justice), 2012, https://bettercarenetwork.org/sites/default/files/attachments/Child%20Abandonment%20and%20Its%20Prevention%20in%20Europe.pdf.

90 'One of the chaplains of the Waldfriede Clinic in Berlin, Gerhard Menn, compares his work at the clinic with that of a priest receiving a confession: "Some women who come to us are ashamed to be pregnant. If they come from a Muslim background, the issue of honour killings should also be considered. Some experience domestic violence or rape. They do not want a government agency to have their information so that they know they are pregnant. This does not work for a confidential birth" (Isenson, 2009)'. A. Lemrová et al., 'A Conflict of Three Rights – Which Prevails?' (2022) 7(2) *Social Pathology and Prevention* 35.

91 B. Willenbacher, above n. 8, p. 346.

their life history and to know their origin since the parent(s) does/do not leave any identifying information.

The CRC Committee maintains a strong position in condemning the practice of baby boxes. For Austria, strong recommendations were issued in three review cycles, under the title 'The right to identity'. In 2005, concern was expressed about the practice of anonymous births (also known as 'baby flaps' or 'baby nests') and about the fact that some data on the parent(s) are collected in an informal manner. Austria was given a recommendation to undertake all necessary measures to prevent the use of the so-called 'baby flaps' (CRC/C/15/Add.251, 31, 2005, paras. 29–30). In 2021, the Committee again urged Austria to completely abolish the practice of the anonymous abandonment of infants (CRC/C/AUT/CO/5–6, 2021, para. 20). The same advice was given to Slovakia in 2025: to take urgent measures to 'uphold the right of children to have their identity protected by ending the practice of anonymous abandonment of children, including by prohibiting the use of baby boxes, "public incubators" or "rescue nests"' (CRC/C/SVK/CO/6, 2025, para. 18). In 2019, Hungary received a recommendation to phase out the so-called 'baby box' (incubator) programme (CRC/C/HUN/CO/6, 2014, para. 26).[92] On the other hand, the Netherlands received a positive comment in 2022 that 'no newborns have been placed in "baby rooms" without information about their mother during the reporting period' (CRC/C/NLD/CO/5–6, 2022, para. 20),

6. HOW TO BALANCE THE RIGHTS FROM A CHILDREN'S RIGHTS PERSPECTIVE

The CRC Committee's position on solutions for the realisation of the child's right to know but also the right to life for babies and the prevention of abandonment can be found in the concluding observations and in some of its general comments.

In drafting its concluding observations after reviewing the state, the Committee follows the articles of the Convention, grouped in thematic

---

92 Hungary, like Poland, made a statement after receiving its concluding observations in 2014 defending its baby boxes programme where it says, inter alia, that 'the baby box system serves to guarantee the right to life of the child by ensuring safe conditions until the decision with regards to adoption takes place. Within 6 weeks from the birth, the mother or father can decide to reveal their identity and undertake the raising of the child themselves (or within the family, with the help of another family member /e.g. parents, brother or sister/). Placing the infant into the baby box is a last resort possibility for the mother, as there is a solid child protection and family support system for pregnant women in crisis to opt for in the first place. That is why the use of the baby boxes remains low, 3 to 8 times a year. However, when used, baby boxes prevent the abandonment or the death of the infant.' Supplementary information regarding certain issues raised during the constructive dialog with Hungary, in: https://tbinternet.ohchr.org/_layouts/15/treatybodyexternal/Download.aspx?symbolno=INT%2FCRC%2FCOB%2FHUN%2F19688&Lang=en.

clusters, but starts with Article 4, which lays down the general measures for the implementation of the Convention: 'The states shall undertake all appropriate legislative, administrative, and other measures for the implementation of the rights recognized in the Convention'.[93] In 2003, the Committee issued General Comment No. 5 with the aim of supporting the states parties in their implementation and reporting obligations.[94]

6.1. LEGISLATION

The Committee's view is that legislation is crucial and therefore all domestic legislation should be fully compatible with the Convention, and that the Convention's principles and provisions can be directly applied and appropriately enforced. With regard to the right to know, first of all the Committee recommends changes in the legislation in order to abolish discrimination against illegitimate children and to prohibit anonymous births. France and Luxembourg, for example, have received repeated recommendations regarding their legislation, ranging from a more general recommendation (i.e. 'to fully enforce the right to know') to much more concrete recommendations in the most recent reviews. In 2013 and 2016 respectively, Luxembourg and France were urged 'to adopt the necessary measures for all information about parent(s) to be registered and filed ... and to consider removing the requirement of the biological mother's consent to reveal her identity' (CRC/C/FRA/CO/5, 2016, para. 33). Another concrete recommendation for both France and Luxembourg was to 'urgently adopt the necessary measures for all information about parent(s) to be registered and filed, in order to allow the child to know, to the extent possible and at the appropriate time, his or her parents' (CRC/C/LUX/CO/3-4, 2013, para. 29).

In 2021, taking note of Luxembourg's Bill No. 7674 on arranging access to information on an individual's origins following adoption or conception through egg or sperm donation, the Committee recommended that the state party should

---

93 Article 4, while reflecting states parties' overall implementation obligation, suggests a distinction between civil and political rights and economic, social and cultural rights in its second sentence: 'With regard to economic, social and cultural rights, States Parties shall undertake such measures to the maximum extent of their available resources and, where needed, within the framework of international cooperation.' There is no simple or authoritative division of human rights in general or of Convention rights into the two categories. The Committee's reporting guidelines group Articles 7, 8, 13–17 and 37(a) under the heading 'Civil rights and freedoms', but indicate, according to their context, that these are not the only civil and political rights contained in the Convention. General Comment No. 5 (2003) on general measures of implementation of the Convention on the Rights of the Child (Arts. 4, 42 and 44, para. 6), para. 6.

94 General Comment No. 5 (2003) on general measures of implementation of the Convention on the Rights of the Child (Arts. 4, 42 and 44, para. 6).

ensure that the draft legislation contains a provision for children to have access to information regarding their identity if they were adopted or were born via an anonymous birth or assisted reproduction technology, including technologies involving gamete or embryo donation, or via surrogacy arrangements concluded abroad for parents who are resident in the state party (CRC/C/LUX/CO/5–6, 2021, para. 16).

In 2021, the Committee welcomed the legislative measures undertaken in Switzerland to ensure the rights of adopted children, and that children conceived by medically assisted reproduction have access to information regarding their biological origins. It also recommended that Switzerland should remove legitimate interests as a precondition for a child's right to information regarding his or her biological origins (CRC/C/CHE/CO/5-6, 2021, para. 22).

6.2. CONFIDENTIAL HOSPITAL BIRTHS

The Committee became deeply concerned by the rapidly spreading practice of 'baby boxes' in Europe. In 2012, Austria was strongly urged 'to undertake all measures necessary to end the practice of anonymous abandonment and expeditiously strengthen and promote alternatives such as the possibility of anonymous births at hospitals as a measure of last resort to avoid abandonment and or death of the child, and to keep a confidential record of the parents to which the child could access at a later stage, taking into account the duty to fully comply with all provisions of the Convention' (CRC/C/AUT/CO/3–4, 2012, para. 30).

Around 2020, the Committee accepted that the *possibility of confidential hospital births* could be considered as a form of care of last resort for the child in order to end the anonymous abandonment of children in 'baby boxes'. As explained above, the concept of confidential births differs from anonymous births. It is a way to balance the rights of the child and those of the mother, but also the public interest in safe births, by creating an obligation for mothers to leave identifying data, which could be revealed to the child once he or she has reached a certain age (i.e. 16+). For example, this practice was developed in Germany under its 2014 legislation. In 2022, Germany received a recommendation 'to strengthen measures to promote the use of confidential births and ensure that information about the biological origins of such children are preserved, with a view to eliminating the use of baby boxes' (CRC/C/DEU/CO/5–6, 2022, para. 19). Several European states also received such a recommendation: Poland (CRC/C/POL/CO/5–6, 2021, para. 23), Czechia (CRC/C/CZE/CO/5–6, 2021, para. 22), Hungary ('to introduce confidential birth registration to prevent the abandonment of children while phasing out the so-called "baby box" (incubator) programme') (CRC/C/HUN/CO/3-5, 2014, para. 32).

6.3. STORING INFORMATION

Storing (filing) and preserving information on birth parents in order to be able to provide this data for children seeking such information is a common recommendation for the states parties. It was issued to Luxembourg[95] and the Netherlands.[96] Switzerland received a more detailed suggestion to 'develop a standardized procedure for confidential birth services to ensure that information about the biological origins of children are preserved, and promote its use with a view to eliminating the use of baby boxes' (CRC/C/CHE/CO/5-6, 2021, para. 22).

Austria received an urgent recommendation to introduce and implement legal provisions and regulations on the separate registration of all relevant medical and other data, in particular the name and date of birth of the parent(s), and to allow the child at an appropriate time to have access to these data (CRC/C/15/Add.251, 31, 2005, paras. 29–30).

6.4. POLICIES

Beyond legislation, the respective states received many recommendations in the field of social policies, the training of professionals and education.

A common recommendation was issued to states to study and address the root causes of the anonymous abandonment of children and to strengthen family support measures (Poland and Czechia in 2021). In 2012, the Committee urged Austria to increase its efforts to address the root causes which lead to the abandonment of infants, including the provision of family planning as well as adequate counselling and social support for unplanned pregnancies and the prevention of risky pregnancies (CRC/C/AUT/CO/3-4, 2012, paras. 29–30). The same recommendation was issued to Slovakia (CRC/C/SVK/CO/6, 2025, para. 18).

6.5. SEXUAL AND REPRODUCTIVE HEALTH EDUCATION AND COUNSELLING

As a means of preventing adolescent pregnancies, the Committee strongly recommends that the states parties should pay particular attention to education and the accessibility of counselling and contraception. In this regard, the

95 Children should have access to information regarding their identity in case of anonymous births ... 'The State party should ensure that the legislation provides clear procedures for managing and storing data regarding children's origins.' (CRC/C/LUX/3-4, 2022, para. 16).

96 Recommendation to continue to ensure that the right of children left at hospitals to know their origins is respected (CRC/C/NLD/CO/5-6, 2022, para 20).

Committee always recalls its General Comment No. 4 (2003) on adolescent health and development in the context of the Convention, and its General Comment No. 20 (2016) on the implementation of the rights of the child during adolescence, as well as referring to and targeting 3.5, 3.7 and 5.6 of the Sustainable Development Goals.

Lithuania received a detailed recommendation to:

> (a) Ensure mandatory sexual and reproductive health education for adolescents, with special attention to preventing early pregnancy and sexually transmitted infections;
> (b) Ensure that all children, including those who are out of school and those in rural areas, receive confidential and child-friendly sexual and reproductive health information and services, including easy access to contraceptives, notably by removing any obstacles such as the referral requirement and the need for a prescription; ...
> (d) Develop and implement a policy to protect the rights of pregnant teenagers, adolescent mothers and their children, and combat discrimination against them;
> (e) Take measures to raise awareness of and to foster responsible parenthood, with particular attention to boys (CRC/C/LTU/CO/5–6, 2024, para. 38).

As for the Netherlands, the Committee recommended that it should:

> (a) Adopt a comprehensive and effective gender-sensitive sexual and reproductive health policy for adolescents;
> (b) Integrate sexual and reproductive health education into all levels of education, and ensure that it includes age-appropriate education on gender equality, sexual diversity, sexual and reproductive health rights, responsible parenthood and sexual behaviour and violence prevention (CRC/C/NLD/CO/5–6, 2022, para. 30).

6.6. ABORTION

The recommendation given to Lithuania represents all the requirements of the Committee with regard to the issue of abortion: to decriminalise abortion in all circumstances, and ensure, in law and in practice, access to safe abortion and post-abortion care services for adolescents, making sure that their views are always heard and are given due consideration as part of the decision-making process (CRC/C/LTU/CO/5–6, 2024, para. 38). Czechia received the following recommendation to ensure that the notification of the legal guardians in the case of abortion is done with the prior and informed consent of the girl concerned and is consistent with her right to privacy (CRC/C/CZE/CO/5–6, 2021, para. 38). Latvia was given the recommendation to ensure free medical abortion services to all girls under the age of 18 and to ensure that their views are always heard and respected in abortion decisions (CRC/C/LVA/CO/3–5, 2016, para. 51).

6.7. TRAINING AND CAPACITY-BUILDING

The Committee emphasises states' obligation to develop training and capacity-building for all those involved in the implementation process – government officials, parliamentarians and members of the judiciary – and for all those working with and for children. Healthcare professionals are a particularly important group bearing in mind their influence in decisions related to pregnancy, childbirth and care for mothers and babies. Training needs to be systematic and ongoing with the purpose of emphasising the status of the child as a holder of human rights, increasing knowledge and understanding of the Convention and encouraging active respect for all its provisions. The Committee expects to see the Convention reflected in professional training curricula, codes of conduct and educational curricula at all levels. The understanding and knowledge of human rights must, of course, be promoted among children themselves, both through the school curriculum and in other ways.[97]

7. CONCLUSION

The expansion of the practice of anonymous births in several states in Europe 36 years after the adoption of the UN Convention on the Rights of the Child is a trend that deserves special attention. The potential of these practices to undermine the position of the child as a holder of rights as well as the gendered aspects thereof should be studied even more carefully at a time when we are seeing the backsliding of women's and children's rights.

The Committee's jurisprudence has not been effective in halting this development, despite being grounded on the clear rights enshrined in the Convention. As already mentioned, states that rely on 'baby boxes' to save children probably rely less on their investment in child welfare policies and on the promotion of children's rights. The need to balance the rights of all persons involved should be respected, but only when concrete measures, as opposed to abstract constructions, are already in place. The Committee as a CRC monitoring body, established by the states parties themselves, expects its interpretations and recommended solutions as presented here to be discussed nationally and to be reflected accordingly. Otherwise, the Convention will lose its value and the rights of children will turn out to be merely illusory in Europe; however, Europe still remains the best place in the world for a child to be born and raised.

97 General Comment No. 5 (2003) on general measures of implementation of the Convention on the Rights of the Child (Arts. 4, 42 and 44, para. 6), para. 53.

THE SPANISH LAW ON ARTIFICIAL REPRODUCTIVE TECHNOLOGY

A Troublemaker or a Frontrunner?

Jordi Ribot Igualada*

1. INTRODUCTION

Despite their longstanding existence among us and their notorious impact on the traditional ways of creating legal parenthood bonds,[1] artificial reproductive technologies (ART) are one research field where European Family Law remains unsettled. What can we make of the current situation across European jurisdictions? Is it fit for a reflection that could lead us to a certain 'common core'? Or is a 'better law' approach the only alternative capable of reaching a reasonable consensus that may influence the development of national legal systems? If so, which elements can provide a taste of what a 'better law' might look like?[2]

This chapter aims to critically overview the issue using Spanish legislation and practice as a viewpoint for change. Spanish law offers a unique perspective. The relevant statute is 36 years old. Despite its overhaul in 2006, its main operative principles have remained substantially unchanged. Spanish law could thus be

---

* I am indebted to Dr Esther Farnós Amorós (University Pompeu Fabra, Barcelona) for her generous support in compiling the materials needed to write this chapter and her insightful advice on prior drafts. Any errors remain my own.

1 Many people in the world are facing fertility problems – approximately 150 million, of whom 25 million are in the European Union. Despite all their legalistic uncertainties, ART are here to stay. More than 10 million children have been born through ART since 1978. See the European Society of Human Reproduction and Embryology (ESHRE)'s Factsheet on ART at https://www.eshre.eu/-/media/sitecore-files/Press-room/ESHRE_ARTFactSheet_Nov_2023.pdf (last accessed 02.12.2024).

2 Underlying the whole area is whether we can envisage a right to form a family *beyond natural reproduction* and whether this right could also be framed as a human right to have a child *by any lawful means*. See the Call-to-Action 2023 launched by Fertility Europe (FE) and the European Parliamentary Forum for Sexual & Reproductive Rights (EPF), which aims to 'Recognise the right to try to have a child as a universal right across the EU'. https://fertilityeurope.eu/cta2023/ (last accessed 02.12.2024). The contours of those *lawful means* are however not self-evident.

viewed as a frontrunner, anticipating legal developments that occurred much later in other European jurisdictions. And yet, it can also be disparaged as a troublemaker when the decisions adopted by the Spanish legislator put pressure on other European jurisdictions concerning their regulation of ART or on principles governing their law on parenthood. Moreover, it could also become an annoyance if it does not evolve with other jurisdictions in advancing towards more sensible approaches to issues such as donor anonymity or even surrogacy.

The chapter starts with a brief overview of the differences across Europe, particularly regarding the scope of ART and the contested issue of donor anonymity. Next, it assesses the standing of Spanish law, calling attention to some non-legal factors that led Spain to become a champion for cross-border reproduction services. It also points to the barriers that a highly profitable business poses to the creation of a fairer regulation on ART, one that may also count as what a better European law could look like.

2. MAPPING THE DIFFERENCE

The Atlas of Fertility Treatment Policies in Europe, published by Fertility Europe and the European Parliamentary Forum for Sexual and Reproductive Rights, outlines the common ground and differences between European ART laws.[3] It is based on data from the European Society of Human Reproduction and Embryology, the European IVF Monitoring Consortium, and several national organisations and country experts.

The only absolute consensus seems to exist in allowing opposite-sex couples – the Atlas does not mention the couples' civil status – to use their own gametes in ART procedures. From then onwards, the Atlas shows that a marked contrast between jurisdictions remains.

Conception through sperm donation by opposite-sex couples now seems to be commonly available everywhere except in Turkey and Albania. The first main difference is whether female couples can have access to ART, a possibility that is still unavailable in Italy, as well as in most Eastern European countries except for in Estonia, Romania and Bulgaria.

Access to ART for single women is generally not an issue, including not in most Eastern European countries. However, it is still prohibited in some traditionally Catholic countries like Italy, Austria, Lithuania and Poland, and some other restrictive jurisdictions, including Switzerland, Albania, Bosnia-Herzegovina and Turkey.

3 https://fertilityeurope.eu/european-atlas-of-fertility-treatment-policies/ (last accessed 02.12.2024). An interactive map is also available at https://cm.eshre.eu/cmCountryMap/home/index/2021 (last accessed 02.12.2024).

Like conception through sperm donation, egg donation is today also commonly available for opposite-sex couples. Switzerland and Germany stand as exceptions in Western Europe, however, thereby aligning themselves with Turkey and Bosnia-Herzegovina. Many more countries, including most Eastern European states, Norway and Sweden, restrict procedures involving egg donation when requested by female couples. On the other hand, according to the data compiled in the Atlas, access to ART involving egg donation would be granted to single women in Russia, Belarus and Hungary despite these countries forbidding the technique for female couples.

Some of the data contained in the Atlas may now be outdated or even simply incorrect, but it does provide a tool to map the differences. In particular, it reveals a persistent marked bias against single-mother families and LGTBQ+ families. On the other hand, the Atlas does not show a clear dividing line between Eastern and Western European states. Socio-cultural factors do not seem to play the same role in culturally related jurisdictions either.

A brief overview of the issue of anonymity shows that there are also noteworthy differences there too. Most European countries still follow the rule of strictly anonymous donations. In addition, around ten states already have different systems where anonymous and non-anonymous donations coexist. In contrast, the number of jurisdictions that stipulate that the identity of the donors must be revealed to children is increasing – ten states in 2021. Since then, some have changed their regulations,[4] and the ECtHR has recognised that Article 8 ECHR protects the right of children born from anonymous ART to know their origins. The Court has also stated that although there is no clear European consensus on access to the origins of individuals conceived through gamete donation, there is a trend towards lifting donor anonymity,[5] a statement that could well be the prelude to a more demanding position of the Court on national regulations still based on the anonymity rule.

3. WHERE DOES SPAIN STAND?

Spain produced one of the first sets of ART rules worldwide in 1988.[6] The law was based on anonymous gamete donation (sperm and eggs) and was deemed to

4 That is the case for France where Act no. 2021–2017 of 2 August 2021 concerning bioethics (JORF no. 0178, 03.08.2021) introduced, in Article 16-8-1 of the *Code civile*, the right of persons born from medically assisted procreation with third-party donors to access the identity of their donor.

5 *Gauvin-Fournis and Silliau v France*, nos. 21424/16 and 45728/17, 7 September 2023, ECLI: CE:ECHR:2023:0907JUD002142416.

6 ART are currently primarily governed by Act 14/2006, of 26 May 2006 (BOE no. 126, 27.05.2006), which updated the original Act 35/1988, of 22 November 1988 (BOE no. 282, 24.11.1988).

be one of the most progressive and permissive in Europe. A great deal of water has flowed under the bridge since then. However, according to the overview provided by the Atlas, most, if not all, of its once adventurous provisions eventually became standard rules in many later regulations.

3.1. LEGAL FRAMEWORK

Since 1988, the law's focus has been the woman who wishes to become pregnant through ART.[7] From the beginning, women could become single mothers using gametes from anonymous donors. The new technologies were also available to married and *de facto* couples. In these cases, the informed consent of the husband[8] or the male partner,[9] furnished before starting the procedure, was required to establish their legal paternity over the children born therefrom. No distinction was made depending on the basis of where the gametes came from. Only posthumous fertilisation, which was also allowed, must be performed using gametes obtained from the husband or male partner before he died.[10]

After the introduction of same-sex marriage in 2005,[11] ART was opened up to same-sex female couples, but only if they were married.[12] The parental projects of *unmarried* lesbian couples did not benefit from the ART law's special rules to establish legal (co-)motherhood. The different legal treatment of married and unmarried female couples led to somewhat contradictory and controversial case law concerning the establishment of the (co-)motherhood of the children born from ART procedures undergone during the relationship.[13] The Spanish legislature addressed the issue only very recently, in 2023.[14]

---

7 Article 6.1 Act 35/1988. A second paragraph was introduced verbatim by Act 14/2006, which states that the woman 'may use or receive the techniques regulated in this act regardless of her marital status and sexual orientation.' That changed nothing because it had been allowed since 1988. In this sense, see E. Farnós Amorós, 'Legal Parenthood in Spain' in C. Fenton-Glynn (ed.), *The Law of Parenthood: A Comparative Guide*, Edward Elgar, Cheltenham 2025 (forthcoming).

8 Article 6.3 Act 35/1988.

9 Articles 6.4 and 8.2 Act 35/1988.

10 Article 9.2 Act 35/1988.

11 Act 13/2005, of 1 July 2005 (BOE no. 157, 02.07.2005).

12 Article 7.3 Act 14/2006 (as amended by Act 3/2007, of 15 March 2007 (BOE no. 65, 16.03.2007)).

13 See among the most recent judgments, nos. 15/2022, of 27 January 2022, ECLI.ES.TS.2022.243; 558/2022, of 11 July 2022, ECLI:ES:TS:2022:3002; and 351/2024, of 11 March 2024, ECLI:ES:TS:2024:1436.

14 The prevailing view is that Act 4/2023, of 28 February 2023 tacitly repealed the marriage requirement laid down in Article 7.3 Act 14/2006. Currently any 'non-pregnant mother' is allowed to establish her (co-)maternity of a child by issuing a statement for that purpose before the Civil Registry. The current situation remains extremely complex, however, due to the reform's severe technical shortcomings. See M.S. Quicios Molina, 'Las relaciones de filiación de personas LGTBI (Tribuna)' (2023) 5 *Cuadernos de Derecho Privado* 2, 5 and

Despite the overall 'liberal' approach, Spanish law also took a resolute stance against surrogacy agreements. The law of 1988 declared them null and void.[15] The case law of the Plenary of the Civil Chamber of the Supreme Court even considers cross-border commercial surrogacy to be a serious violation of the fundamental rights recognised in the Spanish Constitution and in international human rights conventions.[16] Although the Court allows the child to be adopted by the commissioning parents, thereby relieving them of substantive hurdles such as the maximum legal age for adoption,[17] some authors claim that the Court is calling on the legislature and the government 'to do everything possible to prevent the crystallisation of family situations in our country that later have to be reconstituted through adoption.' Otherwise, 'the declaration of absolute nullity of surrogacy contracts [is rendered] ineffective and causes frustration among those who do not understand the difference between purely internal situations and international ones, for which the attenuated effect of international public policy is admissible.'[18]

3.2. THE RISE OF AN INDUSTRY

Focusing on research and innovation, a network of more than 400 reproduction centres – mostly private enterprises – meant that Spain ranked highly in the table of reported treatment cycles per year.[19] In 2023, the private industry provided

---

I. Zurita Martín, 'Voluntad procreacional y socioafectividad en la determinación de la filiación: de la doble maternidad a la pluriparentalidad' in *La modernización del derecho de familia a través de la práctica jurisprudencial*, Tirant lo Blanch, València 2024, p521.

15 Article 10.1 Act 35/1988 (= Article 10.1 Act 14/2006): 'A contract in which a woman agrees to gestate, with or without payment, and gives up her maternal affiliation in favour of the contracting party or a third party shall be null and void.'

16 See judgment no. 835/2013, of 6 February 2014, ECLI:ES:TS:2014:247, and most recently judgment no. 1626/2024, of 4 December 2024. On the issue of surrogacy in Spain, see the thorough account provided by E. Farnós Amorós, 'Surrogacy in Spain' in J. Scherpe, C. Fenton-Glynn and T. Kaan (eds), *Eastern and Western Perspectives on Surrogacy*, Intersentia, Cambridge 2019, pp. 59–82.

17 Judgment no. 1153/2022, of 31 March 2022, ECLI:ES:TS:2022:1153.

18 A. Lara Aguado, 'La encrucijada entre el derecho a la identidad personal de menores nacidos por contratos de gestación por sustitución y el respeto a los derechos fundamentales' (2022) 120 *Cuadernos Civitas de jurisprudencia civil* 243. See also the dissenting opinion of Judge María Luisa Balaguer in the judgment of the Spanish Constitutional Court no. 28/2024, of 27 February 2024. In her view 'it is contrary to the legal certainty of Art. 9.3 CE that the same legislator that prohibits a practice in Spain does not provide sufficient restrictions for equivalent practices carried out outside our country, because this legalises *de facto*, by inaction and through the necessary protection of minors, what is considered illegal in our legal system.'

19 European IVF Monitoring Consortium for the European Society of Human Reproduction and Embryology, 'ART in Europe, 2019: results generated from European registries by ESHRE' (2023) 38(12) *Human Reproduction* 2321. According to the latest data available, in 2022, 167,195 IVF cycles and 31,635 AI cycles were carried out by Spanish

services worth more than €630 million, an average yearly increase of 5%.[20] The five main private providers capture more than 60% of the market.

Private treatments are, however, unaffordable for most Spanish couples who may need ART to have a child. The average cost is €800–1,000 per artificial insemination (AI) cycle and €3,000–5,500 per in vitro fertilisation (IVF) cycle.[21] More complex techniques are much more expensive. Of all reproduction centres, only 10–20% are public hospitals where fertility treatments are included in their portfolio of services. In addition, access to free treatment on the public health service has been curtailed due to funding limitations and managerial decisions. Although the requirements vary across regions, they are subject to age limitations. Usually, public hospitals do not provide ART if the woman is older than 38–40 years old. Moreover, they offer only a limited number of techniques (e.g. the transfer of donated oocytes is regularly excluded due to a lack of donors) and unsuccessful cycles (four AI cycles and three IVF cycles).[22] Discriminatory biases against non-traditional family forms have also been reported,[23] and waiting lists are common for IVF treatments, ranging from six months to more than one year, depending on the hospital in question. Under such conditions, the fairness of the Spanish model for ART is seriously compromised.

3.3. OPENING PATHS FOR NATIONALS AND FOREIGNERS ALIKE

The variety of available techniques, the lower requirements vis-à-vis users' age, sex and status, and the relative affordability of ART treatments compared to other European countries have made Spain a popular destination for fertility

reproduction centres (see *Registro Nacional de Actividad 2022 – Registro SEF*, available at https://www.registrosef.com/public/docs/sef2022_IAFIV.pdf (last accessed 02.12.2024)).

20 https://www.dbk.es/es/detalle-nota/centros-reproduccion-asistida-2024 (last accessed 02.12.2024).

21 https://www.reproduccionasistida.org/precios-de-tratamientos-de-reproduccion-asistida/ (last accessed 02.12.2024).

22 https://www.reproduccionasistida.org/reproduccion-asistida-en-la-seguridad-social-espanola/ (last accessed 02.12.2024).

23 Single women, lesbians or trans people with the capacity to gestate were systematically denied access to ART in public hospitals because they did not meet the requirements of an 'absence of pregnancy after a minimum of 12 months of sexual relations with vaginal intercourse' or 'a documented disorder of reproductive capacity.' See FAMS – Familias monoparentales, 'Prácticas discriminatorias en Reproducción Asistida', *Análisis sobre familias monoparentales* 10/2022 (available at https://familiasmonomarentales.es/wp-content/uploads/2022/08/10.-Reproduccio%CC%81n-Asistida.pdf (last accessed 02.12.2024)). These requirements were repealed by Ministerial Order SND/1215/2021, of 5 November 2021 (BOE no. 268, 09.11.2021).

treatments, offering options that are restricted in many other countries.[24] In 2020, for example, around 15% of all treatments provided by private Spanish fertility clinics were carried out for foreign couples or individuals, mostly from Italy, France, Germany and the United Kingdom.[25]

As regards this often disparagingly termed 'fertility tourism', one may wonder whether Spain moved too quickly in allowing some individuals or couples to have access to certain kinds of procedures that were legally unavailable in neighbouring countries. Personally, I do not think so. Spanish scholars who spoke out against Act 34/1988[26] have been proven wrong by the developments in the many jurisdictions that followed suit.[27] Did it put too much pressure on these countries to adapt their regulations to changing social demands? The open approach taken by the Spanish legislature in 1988, in reality, spared them from having to move on more quickly than was needed to come to terms with their doubts and hesitations. The availability of some controversial techniques in Spain (and other European countries) even allowed reluctant countries to avoid being held in violation of Article 8 ECHR.[28]

Additional concerns flow from applying Spanish family law on parenthood to foreign citizens living in Spain, where they can establish parental relationships not recognised in their country of origin or where they would like to move to at a later point in time. The problem is not exclusive to parenthood derived from ART, and it could also arise when it is established within adoption proceedings.[29]

---

24 Instituto Bernabeu, one of the leading reproduction centres, even provides a comparative chart of the treatments and legal requirements in Spain and some other Western European countries on its website (available at https://www.institutobernabeu.com/en/spanish-law-on-assisted-reproduction/ (last accessed 27.11.2024)).

25 13,588 treatment cycles. See *Registro Nacional de Actividad 2020 – Registro SEF. Informe estadístico de Técnicas de Reproducción Asistida 2020*, p. 53, available at https://www.registrosef.com/public/docs/sef2020_IAFIV.pdf (last accessed 02.12.2024).

26 Among them, conspicuously, F. Pantaleón, 'Contra la Ley sobre Técnicas de Reproducción Asistida' (1988) 5 *Jueces para la democracia* 19.

27 See the final report of the German Commission on Reproductive Self-Determination and Reproductive Medicine, which examined in detail and in an interdisciplinary manner the possibilities of legalising egg donation and altruistic surrogacy. C. Wendland, 'Legalisierung von Eizellspende und Leihmutterschaft? Bericht der Kommission zur reproduktiven Selbstbestimmung und Fortpflanzungsmedizin', *FamRZ* 2024, 829.

28 In connection with the 'careful and cautious approach adopted by the Austrian legislature in seeking to reconcile social realities with its approach of principle in this field … the Court … observes that there is no prohibition under Austrian law on going abroad to seek treatment of infertility that uses artificial procreation techniques not allowed in Austria and that in the event of a successful treatment the Civil Code contains clear rules on paternity and maternity that respect the wishes of the parents' (*S.H. and Others v Austria* (GC), no. 57813/00, 3 November 2011, para. 114, ECLI:CE:ECHR:2011:1103JUD005781300). More recently, see *Pejřilová v the Czech Republic*, no. 14889/19, 8 December 2022, para. 60, ECLI:CE:ECHR:2022:1208JUD001488919 (posthumous fertilisation).

29 See further A. Tryfonidou, 'The cross-border legal recognition of parenthood under European law: current law and future prospects' (2024) 46(2) *Journal of Social Welfare and Family Law* 267.

As mentioned earlier, the legal framework for (co-)motherhood is not as clear as it should be.[30] However, one related set of problems is linked to the legal terminology used to record the legal motherhood of two women in the Civil Registry. It states that the child has two legal mothers and identifies them as Mother A and Mother B. But it does not mention which one has given birth. The same approach is replicated in birth certificates delivered to the interested parties. In the case of *V.M.A. v Stolichna obshtina, rayon 'Pancharevo'*,[31] the ECJ dealt with the application filed in the Sofia municipality by the Bulgarian co-mother of a child born and resident in Spain. She applied for a birth certificate that was necessary for the issuing of a Bulgarian identity document for the child. The applicant submitted a legalised and certified translation into Bulgarian of the extract from the Civil Registry of Barcelona relating to the child's birth certificate, naming her the child's 'Mother A'. The Grand Chamber of the ECJ concluded that EU law required the Bulgarian authorities 'to recognise that parent-child relationship for the purposes of permitting [the child] … to exercise without impediment, with each of her two parents, her right to move and reside freely within the territory of the Member States'.[32] It must be recalled, nonetheless, that the Supreme Administrative Court of the Republic of Bulgaria eventually dismissed the application once the available evidence led it to conclude that the Bulgarian (co-)mother was not the woman who had given birth. Since the child could not acquire Bulgarian nationality by birth, Bulgaria was not under an obligation to issue herwith an identity card or passport according to Article 4(3) of Directive 2004/38/EC.[33]

Despite Spanish law's awkward approach to birth certificates issued for children raised by same-sex parents, the problem lies elsewhere. In her 2020 State of the Union speech, European Commission President Ursula von der Leyen warned against 'LGBTQI-free zones'. She called them 'humanity-free zones' that 'have no place in our Union'. Accordingly, as part of a 'strategy to strengthen LGBTQI rights', she said that the European Commission would push for the 'mutual recognition of family relations in the EU'. She claimed, '[i]f you are a parent in one country, you are a parent in every country'.[34] As

30 See above n. 14 and the corresponding text.

31 Case C-490/20, ECLI:EU:C:2021:1008. See further Case C-2/21, *Rzecznik Praw Obywatelskich*, ECLI:EU:C:2022:502.

32 Ibid., para. 49. Conversely, EU law would not require 'the Member State of which the child concerned is a national to provide, in its national law, for the parenthood of persons of the same sex, or to recognise, for purposes other than the exercise of the rights which that child derives from EU law, the parent-child relationship between that child and the persons mentioned on the birth certificate drawn up by the authorities of the host Member State as being the child's parents' (para. 57).

33 The Court stated that he probably was Spanish and that the Spanish authorities had to issue her with an identity card or passport.

34 State of the Union Address by President von der Leyen at the European Parliament Plenary, 16 September 2020, https://ec.europa.eu/commission/presscorner/detail/en/SPEECH_20_1655 (last accessed 03.12.2024).

is well known, a new proposal for a Regulation on parenthood[35] followed, which obligates the recognition of parenthood irrespective of how the child was conceived or born and the child's type of family. The new Regulation would therefore cover a Member State's recognition of the parenthood of a child with same-sex parents when that parenthood has been established in another Member State.[36]

3.4. BECOMING A NUISANCE

A particular legal system may also become a nuisance for other jurisdictions when its inadequate or inconsistent approach undermines the operative value of rules shared by all or many legal systems. That is happening in Spain regarding the need to keep track of the number of gamete donations and the children born from the same donor's gametes or through cross-border commercial surrogacy. Besides, a system turns out to be an annoyance if it if it does not stay in step with the global or regional evolution in the recognition of international human rights, as has happened with the right of the child born through ART to know about their origins, including the identity of the donor.

3.4.1. Critical Issues in the Operations of the Reproductive Industry

All industries must be 'constantly fuelled with the stuff that keeps them going'. In the case of the ART business model, it heavily relies on a stable and affordable stream of reproductive material to cope with a growing demand. Any business would also be pleased to keep red tape and administrative supervision at a minimum to reduce costs and develop new techniques in an internationally competitive market. In Spain, such an optimal *laissez-faire* environment exists because of intelligent lobbying, industry self-regulation and the government's procrastination.

Spain ranks first in Europe in terms of oocyte supplies.[37] Spanish clinics have one of the world's largest banks of donated oocytes in absolute terms.[38] This success probably has something to do with how the gamete suppliers are rewarded and the condition of anonymity upon which donations are made.

35 Proposal for a Council Regulation on jurisdiction, applicable law, recognition of decisions and acceptance of authentic instruments in matters of parenthood and on the creation of a European Certificate of Parenthood, COM/2022/695 final, 7 December 2022.

36 See Recital (21).

37 European IVF Monitoring Consortium for the European Society of Human Reproduction and Embryology, 'ART in Europe, 2018: results generated from European registries by ESHRE' (2022) 5(3) *Human Reproduction Open*.

38 62.2% of foreign patients come to Spain to undergo oocyte donation treatments.

Concerning compensation for gamete donors, although Act 14/2006 starts from the requirement that gametes can only be provided for free as a charitable act for the sake of third parties undergoing fertility problems, it does allow for the payment of compensation for time lost, risks taken and inconveniences endured. The Act does not lay down any upper amount for this compensation. In 2015, the supervisory body unofficially set it at €950 per cycle of oocyte donation and €45 per semen donation.[39] However, the need to recruit donors has stretched the amounts, and the sums currently paid to female donors are usually up to €1,200 per oocyte donation cycle. In practice, these amounts increase if further donations are agreed upon. In the case of sperm, the donors receive around €700 for a complete cycle of one or two weekly donations during three or four months.[40]

The European Union has taken steps to address this matter and ensure minimum coherence. The recent Regulation on Quality and Safety Standards for Substances of Human Origin intended for Human Application[41] stipulates that Member States may allow for the compensation of donors through fixed allowances or non-financial forms of compensation.[42] The conditions for such compensation shall be established in national legislation. Still, they must be based on transparent criteria, considering the practices followed by the Member States as documented by the Coordination Board established by the Regulation. An upper limit for compensation must also be set to guarantee financial neutrality.[43] To that end, the European Society of Human Reproduction and Embryology has recommended that: (1) compensation should reflect actual expenses, the time invested and the inconvenience incurred by donors; (2) upper limits should be specific to the type of donation; and (3) compensation for time and effort should be determined based on a transparent indicator, such as the gross domestic product per capita of the country.[44]

Red tape and administrative supervision were limited from the beginning and favoured the growth of the ART business in Spain.

---

39 Information available through https://www.documentcloud.org/documents/21271816-informe-sanidad-compensacion-economica-donaciones-ovulos-semen, contributed by Civio.es, https://civio.es/medicamentalia/2022/03/07/donar-ovulos-esperma-compensacion-economica/ (last accessed 03.12.2024).

40 See https://www.reproduccionasistida.org/compensacion-de-la-donacion-de-ovulos/ (last accessed 21.07.2024).

41 Regulation (EU) 2024/1938 of the European Parliament and of the Council of 13 June 2024, on standards of quality and safety for substances of human origin [SoHO] intended for human application, OJ L 2024/1938, 17 July 2024, http://data.europa.eu/eli/reg/2024/1938/oj (last accessed 21.05.2025).

42 Donors may also choose not to be compensated.

43 Article 54.2. This provision must be complied with by 7 August 2027.

44 The ESHRE position paper on gamete donor compensation is available at https://www.eshre.eu/Europe/Position-statements (last accessed 03.12.2024).

For instance, since 2006, the law stipulates that the maximum number of children born in Spain through gametes from the same donor must not exceed six.[45] However, a centralised register that would compile and deliver confidential information about donors and successful cycles to all centres has been lacking for a long time. Hence, the legal limitation was impossible to enforce. In practice, a mere statement from the donor has been enough to make the donation,[46] even if the reproductive centres are required to entertain enquiries to ensure compliance with the legal limits on gamete donations.[47] Consultation with other centres seems to be the most frequent safeguard.

The register was already required by Act 35/1988.[48] It was not regulated until 1996,[49] and only in 2017 did the central government implement a platform, administered by the National Health Service, aiming to record nationwide activity of private and public fertility centres.[50] The platform must contain the long-awaited national register of gamete and embryo donors, which should record confidential information on the children born from each donor, the identity of the recipient couples or women, and the original location of both at the time of donation and its use.[51] To become fully operational, the regional authorities in charge of fertility centres needed to provide the data to the national register of donors, a task that seems to have taken longer than expected. Meanwhile, it is still impossible to control the number of donations from the same donor and the children resulting from them.

All this adds to the mounting controversy about the legal rule of donor anonymity,[52] a debate that the ART industry treats as an existential threat.[53]

---

45 Article 5.7 I Act 14/2006.

46 According to Article 5.7 II Act 14/2006, 'donors must declare for each donation whether they have made previous donations, as well as the conditions of these, and indicate the time and centre where these donations were made.'

47 According to Article 5.7 II Act 14/2006, 'it will be the responsibility of each centre or service that uses donor gametes to reliably verify the identity of the donors, as well as, where appropriate, the consequences of previous donations made in terms of the generation of children born previously.'

48 1st Final Provision Act 35/1988.

49 Royal-Decree 412/1996, of 1 March 1996 (BOE no. 72, 22.03.1996).

50 Assisted Human Reproduction Information System (SIRHA). See the basic information (in Spanish) at https://cnrha.sanidad.gob.es/registros/home.htm (last accessed 03.12.2024).

51 Article 21.2 Act 14/2006.

52 Among others, see, with different standpoints, N. Igareda González, 'La donación anónima de gametos para reproducción humana asistida en España: problemas y retos' (2016) 38 *Revista de Bioética y Derecho* 71, and M.C. Cazorla González-Serrano, *Reproducción humana asistida y anonimato ¿violación o excepción al principio de verdad biológica?*, Aranzadi, Cizur Menor 2021.

53 See M. Muñoz, F. Abellán-García, I. Cuevas, A. de la Fuente, D. Iborra, D. Mataró, R. Nuñez and M. Roca, *Documento Sobre Posicionamiento de la Sociedad Española de Fertilidad Respecto de la Regla del Anonimato en las Donaciones de Gametos*, October 2019. Restricted access via https://sef.es/publicaciones-SEF (last accessed 04.12.2024).

3.4.2. *The Anonymity of Gamete Donation at Stake*

The anonymity of gamete donors is a key aspect of the Spanish legal framework for ART. It means that the donor's identity is confidential and cannot be revealed to the recipients or the children born from the donation.[54] They can only ask for general information about the donor, which includes non-identifying details on physical characteristics and medical records.[55] Only in situations where there is a highly probable risk to the life or health of the child that requires disclosure of the donor's identity can the holders of the information be released from their duty of confidentiality.[56]

The anonymity of gamete donations has been challenged before the Constitutional Court. It ruled that anonymity did not violate the fundamental rights of any of the parties and concluded that the law had struck a reasonable balance between them. The Court also pointed out that there was a societal interest in enabling the development of fertility services, which would be compromised if the identity of the donor had to be revealed.[57] In recent years, however, an increasing number of voices have called for ending the anonymity rule,[58] because it is deemed to be in conflict with the right of children born from anonymous ART to know their biological origin.[59]

For the industry, legislative changes removing the donors' anonymity would compromise the sustainability of their activity because the fear is that the number of donors will drastically fall and that those willing to become non-anonymous donors would likely ask for more money than they currently receive for an

54 Art. 5.5 I Act 14/2006. The breach of confidentiality of donor data is punished as a serious infringement of the law with fines of up to €10,000.

55 Art. 5.5 II Act 14/2006.

56 Art. 5.5 III Act 14/2006, which also stipulates that within a criminal procedure the court can order the donor's identity to be revealed if that is essential to achieve the proposed legal aim.

57 See judgment no. 116/1999, of 17 June 1999, ECLI:ES:TC:1999:116.

58 See the statement made in 2016 by the Catalan Bioethics Committee, available at https://canalsalut.gencat.cat/web/.content/_Sistema_de_salut/CBC/recursos/documents_tematica/dret_origens_biologics.pdf (last accessed 27.12.2024).

59 The Spanish Bioethics Committee, at its plenary meeting on 15 January 2020, unanimously agreed that, under the principle of the best interests of the child, the right of a child born through assisted human reproduction techniques to know his or her biological origin should take precedence over the anonymity of the donor. See https://comitedebioetica.isciii.es/informe-del-comite-de-bioetica-de-espana-sobre-el-derecho-de-los-hijos-nacidos-de-las-tecnicas-de-reproduccion-humana-asistida-a-conocer-sus-origenes-biologicos-2/ (last accessed 04.12.2024). See also I. Riaño-Galán, C. Martínez González and S. Gallego Riestra, 'Cuestiones éticas y legales del anonimato y la confidencialidad en la donación de gametos' (2021) 94(5) *Anales de Pediatría* 337.e1 (claiming that 'the attitude of parents and professionals must gradually change towards more transparent and responsible communication, based on the experiences of adults conceived by these techniques, and those adopted. Building values such as trust and truth in the family relationships from responsibility requires placing the children, largely forgotten and the most vulnerable part, at the centre of the debate').

anonymous donation without compromises. The industry anticipates that the usual type of donor currently available – young, healthy, white students – will no longer be available, as they will be risk-averse towards unknown effects related to revealing their identities in the future. To avoid a shortage of gametes, an increase in the costs would be inevitable, reducing both the margins and the attraction of Spanish centres compared to others located abroad.

Despite being a frontrunner in many ART fields, in light of the current developments regarding donor anonymity, one can safely claim that Spanish law might soon become a nuisance because the interests of the local business will very likely prevent it from aligning with future European standards.[60]

4. CONCLUDING REMARKS

To cope with the increasing demand for reproductive services, is it possible to have both a fair regulation and a sustainable private market? The example of Spanish 'liberal' legislation shows that blocking access to certain users or to some techniques entails a competitive advantage for countries that are less reluctant to adopt new reproductive technologies. Citizens from other countries bear the costs of limited access and availability, thereby triggering issues of justice in the face of increasing fertility problems.

Spain and other countries are better equipped to respond to the growing needs of people willing to raise children. However, they must adjust their laws to prevent the industry from relying on questionable practices or circumventing regulations. Accordingly, good reasons exist to deal with the issue with a more European-focused approach. The current challenges to uniformisation, or at least regional harmonisation, in this area of family law call for a sensible approach to ART legislation that strikes a fair balance between the parties' rights and expectations and society's interests. The following remarks, partly flowing from the Spanish experience, might help set the scenario for a better, if not common, law.

Firstly, the legal exclusions based on the civil status or the gender of the users, which are still widespread across European jurisdictions,[61] should be subject to critical scrutiny based on non-discrimination grounds, thereby countering biases against single or LGTBQ+ families. Access to ART cannot be based on

60 See above n. 5 and the corresponding text. See also Recommendation 2156 (2019) of the Parliamentary Assembly of the Council of Europe on Anonymous donation of sperm and oocytes: balancing the rights of parents, donors and children, available at https://assembly.coe.int/nw/xml/XRef/Xref-XML2HTML-EN.asp?fileid=27680 (last accessed 04.12.2024). The Recommendation holds that 'anonymity should be waived for all future gamete donations in Council of Europe member States, and the use of anonymously donated sperm and oocytes should be prohibited'.

61 See above section 2.

discriminatory grounds. Regulations should not have a bias towards heterosexual couples at the expense of single women and LGBTQ+ people. Treatment with donor gametes should be provided to both female couples and single women.

Private and public provision of ART should be balanced to avoid unfairness. No unjustified discrimination should be introduced based on the use of public funding. However, striking a fair balance requires setting an optimal number of cycles, establishing certain reasonable age limits, and other requirements to gain access to services provided totally or partially at the expense of the public purse. The economic costs of private ART treatment should also be reasonably contained to make them affordable to larger sections of society. This requirement entails that costs flowing directly from the legal framework of the activity should be strictly scrutinised and eventually removed.

Moreover, attention should be devoted to the legal regulation and practical operation of registries of donors, donations and successful cycles. The market for reproductive services should be properly supervised, and the ART industry needs to be more closely monitored, for example to prevent pathological serial donations and their ramifications of growing genetic fraternity.

The rule of anonymity for gamete and embryo donations is coming under pressure, and it will likely end up being gradually removed. The main difficulty lies in setting up sensible solutions to deal with when and how, and by whom, to reveal the identity of donors to children. Simply rejecting the move forward on this issue is not an option. Dismissing the legitimate claims of children born out of anonymous sperm or egg donation as irresponsible is grossly unfair.

Finally, the Spanish experience also highlights the need to openly address the ethical stakes of both commercial and altruistic surrogacy.

Spain belongs to the majority group of countries forbidding all kinds of this practice. Surrogacy agreements are null and void. The Supreme Court also rejects the recognition of parenthood based on surrogacy agreements coming from any jurisdiction in the world, holding that they are against the human dignity of both the child and the surrogate mother.[62] And yet, a booming market for intermediation services has emerged in Spain in recent years, in which companies advertise international commercial surrogacy and offer to deal with all the administrative procedures. Children born abroad from surrogacy agreements duly executed according to the law of the country where the birth took place are, in fact, ordinarily registered as children of the Spanish commissioning parents,[63] and these are granted parental leave and other social

---

62 See above n. 17 and the corresponding text.

63 Governmental regulations allow for foreign judgments executing commercial surrogacy agreements to be easily recorded at the Civil Registry. Very critical, among many others, is P. Zouak Lara, 'La filiación de menores nacidos por gestación por sustitución: situación actual en España y perspectivas de futuro' (2024) XI(3) *Revista de Derecho Civil* 243, 257, and the further references therein. The First Chamber of the Supreme Court has even

security benefits related to the birth and care of a newborn.[64] The practical effect of restrictive case law is thus limited to the few instances brought to the courts, and to introducing a delay in the registration of parenthood until the commissioning individual or couple adopts the child. Public debate is thereby silenced amid emphatic statements against exploitative commercial surrogacy. In contrast, a black market for surrogacy is tolerated, and public bodies encourage commissioning parents to ask for ad hoc solutions.[65] In sum, it is a hypocritical policy that undermines trust in the legal system and favours social injustice in the distribution of reproductive rights.[66]

allowed these children to be registered at the Civil Registry as having been born in Spain (see judgment no. 4370/2024, of 17 September 2024, ECLI:ES:TS:2024:4370).

64 See the judgment of the Social Chamber of the Spanish Supreme Court (Plenary) no. 881/2016, of 25 October 2016, ECLI:ES:TS:2016:5375 (workers who have children born through surrogacy recorded at the Civil Registry must be recognised as having the right to enjoy maternity or paternity benefits).

65 But note that a new regulation changed the policy regarding the registration in Spain of children born abroad from surrogacy agreements. From now on, judgments made by competent courts in foreign countries, which state that the commissioning persons are the child's legal parents will no longer be recognised. See Regulation of 28 April 2025 (BOE no. 105, 01.05.2025).

66 Organic Act 1/2023, of 28 February 2023, which amends Organic Act 2/2010, of 3 March 2010, on sexual and reproductive health and the voluntary termination of pregnancy (BOE no. 51, 01.03.2023) declared surrogacy to be 'violence against women' and a 'serious form of reproductive violence'. The Preamble deplores, however, that it continues to occur, 'taking advantage of diverse international regulations', and claims that 'measures must be taken in the areas of prevention and prosecution'. However, the Act merely states that public authorities shall promote campaigns 'to demystify … surrogacy' (Article 10 quinquies §II), which means, according to Article 32, to increase awareness of the unlawfulness of surrogacy agreements. In addition, advertising surrogacy is deemed an unlawful commercial practice which allows an injunction to be issued in order to put a stop to it (Article 33).

SYNTHETIC HUMAN EMBRYOS, ARTIFICIAL WOMBS, IN VITRO GAMETOGENESIS, AND OTHER (REPRODUCTION) TECHNOLOGIES

Do We have the Laws and Regulations We Need for these Brand New Ways to Make Babies?

Nils-Eric SAHLIN*

1. PRELIMINARY REMARKS

The issues to which I would like to draw your attention in this chapter are not normally considered to involve family law. Health issues have their own legal regulation, and the same applies to the research-ethics issues raised by the examples below. Having said that, I am convinced that the problems and opportunities that I will present and discuss are in dire need of a comprehensive family law analysis. Questions to do with children's rights, mothers' rights, fathers' rights and parents' rights are at the heart of the matter. So are surrogacy, adoption and paternity.

I will present a handful of examples, too many perhaps, but there are so many more. These examples highlight technological developments that will affect our view of parenting but also, and not least, how we make and have babies. The examples are charged with ethical issues. Those issues have been discussed by a number of national and international councils on ethics. Naturally, they feature in the scientific literature, too.

2. ORGAN TRADE

The Swedish Act on Genetic Integrity (2006:351) prohibits the trade in biological material from a living or deceased human being, for example human eggs.[1] Involuntary

---

* I would like to thank Professor Maarit Jänterä-Jareborg for her many constructive comments.

1 Lagen om genetisk integritet m.m. (SFS 2006:351), Ch. 2, Section 3.

childlessness is a problem in many countries, Sweden included. The longing that childlessness creates is reflected in a relatively high demand for unfertilised eggs.

The territory of Sweden is divided into so-called regions or regional units, and they are, among other things, in charge of healthcare within their respective area. Some of these regional units were quick to find a way of circumventing the legislation.[2] Instead of paying for egg donation, which is prohibited, they increased the reimbursement for travelling to and from hospital and other costs of a similar nature. The increased compensation turned out to be a success, if we take that to mean increased access to donations in the form of reduced waiting times for treatment with donated eggs. This strategy has its ethical problems, noted at the time but not given the attention they warrant. If the reimbursement of expenses is so substantial that it becomes a payment for services rendered, a step has been taken towards trading in human tissue. This practice does not comply with the Swedish Act on Genetic Integrity, nor with the 1999 Convention for the Protection of Human Rights and Dignity of the Human Being with regard to the Application of Biology and Medicine, known as the Oviedo Convention (see Article 21, Prohibition of financial gain: 'The human body and its parts shall not, as such, give rise to financial gain').[3]

However, the issue concerns so much more than genetic integrity. Not least, it is about the desire to have children of one's own and about the boundaries that impede the satisfaction of that desire. In other words, health law and similar regulations are important, but so are some of the issues that are central to family law.

3. ARTIFICIAL GAMETES AND IVG

When I was born in the 1950s, people did not *make* babies, they *had* babies.[4] The method of reproduction used at that time was the same method that has been used successfully for the last 200,000 years. My parents got what they got, and they had to make do with it.

Today we can make babies. We can take a skin cell and turn it into the precursor of a gamete. Lesbian and gay male couples can have children where the genetic link is 'unbroken'. And there is nothing to prevent a single man or woman from contributing cells to both gametes (in principle, all that is required is, for example, two skin cells), i.e. having a baby with themselves.

2 M. Johansson and N.-E. Sahlin, '11 000 kronor för en äggdonation – oetiskt hög nivå?' (2013) 110(45) *Läkartidningen* 1968 ('11 000 Swedish crowns for an egg donation – an unethically high level?').

3 Council of Europe, Treaty No. 164 (1999), Convention for the Protection of Human Rights and Dignity of the Human Being with regard to the Application of Biology and Medicine: Convention on Human Rights and Biomedicine (ETS No. 164).

4 N.-E. Sahlin, 'Krönika: Artificiella könsceller', 2013, https://smer.se/2013/11/15/kronikan-artificiella-konsceller/.

However, a homosexual male couple lacks one important thing, a womb. But this lack can be remedied, for instance with the help of a surrogate mother or a uterus transplant.[5] Uterus transplantation is a technique that has been developed over the last few decades, and it is now being discussed as a healthcare option. In theory, it is not only women who can receive a uterus in this way; a uterus can be transplanted into a man's body. This has not been done, but in theory it is possible. I only mention this because the true potential of new technologies often goes far beyond what we believe to be possible at first. And that is not all. The development of artificial external wombs is ongoing (see section 6 below). Technological developments titillate and terrify.

Today scientists talk about in vitro gametogenesis (IVG), emphasising that the technologies come with ethical problems and that there is a need for a wide-ranging informed public dialogue about these matters. The National Academies of Sciences, Engineering, and Medicine, reporting from a workshop held in 2023, list a number of issues that have to be addressed. For example, they declare that '[i]t will be important to balance scientific progress, patient safety and autonomy, safety of the future child, human dignity, equality and nondiscrimination, and many other ethical and social considerations when determining whether and how to pursue IVG.'[6]

Reproductive technologies go beyond the provision of healthcare, and they go far beyond factors that are central in modern healthcare legislation, for instance autonomy and safety.[7] Do we have the family law we need to face the future challenges connected with the making of babies? My impression is that the family law we still apply worked well in the previous millennium, but the future that is already here calls for a rethink.

A not too bold conjecture is that the general public remains unaware of the existence and possibilities of these technologies. This means that the numerous and difficult moral issues associated with these and other new reproductive technologies are not receiving the attention they deserve.

In the broad field of reproductive medicine, a number of other techniques and methods have been developed as well. These can be used to cure and prevent serious diseases, but sometimes also to improve various human characteristics (so-called 'enhancement'). These developments may change our view of what a family is, influencing the relationships we have with one another – genetic and legal ones alike.

---

5 See, for example, M. Johansson and N.-E. Sahlin, 'När tekniken går vilse' (2011) 108(26–28) *Läkartidningen* 1348, and N.J. Williams, R. Scott and S.D. Wilkinson, 'The Ethics of Uterus Transplantation' (2018) 32(8) *Bioethics* 478.

6 National Academies of Sciences, Engineering, and Medicine, *In Vitro-Derived Human Gametes as a Reproductive Technology: Scientific, Ethical, and Regulatory Implications: Proceedings of a Workshop*, The National Academies Press, Washington, DC 2023.

7 S. Wilkinson, *Choosing Tomorrow's Children: The Ethics of Selective Reproduction*, Oxford University Press, Oxford 2010.

4. GENE EDITING

My next example has been discussed in countless scientific articles and by various ethics councils and committees around the world. What I am about to present is largely based on two statements that I was involved in: the European Group on Ethics in Science and New Technologies' *Ethics of Genome Editing* of 2021, and the Swedish National Council on Medical Ethics (SMER)'s *Redigering av det mänskliga genomet* ('Editing of the human genome') of 2022.[8] In particular, the work of SMER is clearly visible in what follows.

One of the best-known gene-editing technologies is CRISPR/Cas9. This technology allows us to modify and rebuild our genes. It can be used to modify our body cells (somatic-gene therapy) but also to modify fertilised eggs (heritable gene editing). Heritable gene editing means that the changes that are made are passed on to future generations.

The enormous potential of this technology is often emphasised, but there are good reasons to be cautious about experiments or applications on fertilised eggs. There are serious risks, some of which are unforeseeable and unpredictable, not least in terms of how these kinds of modifications can affect future generations, our grandchildren and great-grandchildren. We also need to consider how these technologies affect our human dignity: is it acceptable not to be 'bespoke', 'tailor-made'? To not be perfect (whatever that means)? It is important that we consider not only the safety and efficacy of these technologies, but also their far-reaching moral implications – for individuals, for families and for our societies.

SMER, for example, recommends that the existing ban on changes in the germline should remain. Permitting heritable genome editing in humans, it argues, requires reliable preclinical data providing evidence that it is possible to make precise modifications to genes in the human germline, safely and without unintended changes. This requirement is not met today.[9]

This is a typical recommendation. We focus on the individual. But what about the family as a whole? Heritable genome editing affects not only an individual but an entire family, not just here and now, but across generations.

Many lawyers would presumably argue that it is our health laws that should deal with these issues. In Sweden, for example, according to the Patient Safety Act, healthcare professionals must perform their work in accordance with science and proven experience.[10] This much-quoted formulation is interpreted to mean that medical interventions must be safe and effective.

---

8 European Commission, European Group on Ethics in Science and New Technologies, *Ethics of Genome Editing*, Brussels, March 2021, and Statens medicinsk-etiska råd (2022:1), *Redigering av det mänskliga genomet – somatisk och ärftlig*.

9 Statens medicinsk-etiska råd (2022:1), *Redigering av det mänskliga genomet – somatisk och ärftlig*, p. 188.

10 Patientsäkerhetslag (2010:659), Ch. 6, Section 1.

I would argue that the ethical problems we are facing are not merely health law issues. In my experience, ethics councils tend to place too much focus on how new treatments should be regulated in the health sector. The questions we face, the ethical problems on which we have to take a stance, are much broader and go far beyond science and proven experience, safety and efficacy. Other values are crucial, too. The fundamental question, as always, is 'what kind of society do we want to live in?' To answer it, we must take the family (no matter how diverse and multi faceted this constellation is) and the child (regardless of how it was 'conceived' and 'customised') as our joint starting point. To my mind, the health law perspectives involved need to be balanced against family law perspectives.

5. MITOCHONDRIAL REPLACEMENT THERAPY

In 2016, *The Guardian* reported that 'the first UK baby created with DNA from three people has been born after doctors performed a groundbreaking IVF procedure that aims to prevent children from inheriting incurable diseases'. The aim of mitochondrial replacement therapy (MRT) is to prevent the transmission of mitochondrial diseases from mother to child. In vitro fertilisation involves two persons – eggs from a woman and sperm from a man – i.e. the intended parents. MRT involves an additional egg, with healthy mitochondria, from another woman, a third person. This explains the expression 'three-parent babies'. Mitochondrial DNA contains 37 genes, the genome approximately 21,000 genes. Consequently, only approximately 0.2% of the child's DNA comes from the donor; the rest, 99.8%, comes from the intended parents.[11]

Scientists and ethicists have strongly questioned the expression 'three-parent babies', and for good reasons. However, there is no denying that MRT will result in the child being the carrier of three persons' genes, and passing these on to their children and later generations.

This brings us back to the Swedish Genetic Integrity Act. MRT is in conflict with an explicit provision in that Act, which stipulates that '[e]xperiments for research or therapeutic purposes which result in heritable genetic changes in humans must not be carried out' (my translation).[12] Incidentally, if only boys are allowed to be born using this technique, the problem is avoided; mitochondrial DNA is inherited from the mother.

Is it correct to say, from a family law perspective, that how the child was conceived is 'not our problem'? The rights of the child are not determined by

---

11 See, for example, Statens medicinsk-etiska råd (2013:2), *Mitokondriebyte vid allvarlig ärftlig sjukdom – etiska aspekter*, and Nuffield Council on Bioethics, *Novel techniques for the prevention of mitochondrial DNA disorders*, June 2012.

12 Swedish Genetic Integrity Act (SFS 2006:351), Ch. 2, Section 3.

whose or which genes the child carries. A reasonable position, one might think. But in recent decades we have seen that our genetic ancestry plays a role.

6. ARTIFICIAL WOMBS

My final example is, I suspect, one that raises many emotions and concerns. The ethical issues are numerous and challenging.[13]

An artificial womb is a medical device designed to give premature infants more time to develop. The foetus will be moved from its 'natural environment', its mother's womb, into a biobag in which it floats surrounded by fluid. This move increases the chance of survival.[14]

In a recent paper, Professor of Medical Ethics Göran Hermerén, referring to recent studies, writes:

> a great number of children born before gestation week 24 suffer from impaired functions of vital organs such as brain, lungs, eyes, bowels and kidneys. Many suffer from neuropsychological problems. One out of four children develop autism spectrum condition. 88% suffer from asthma, kidney and bowel or gut related problems. Only 15 out of 383 children born after on average 23.3 weeks gestation and with a birth weight of 565 grams did not have other documented diagnoses than 'normal'; thus they can be considered to be developed normally.[15]

A few weeks in an artificial womb can mean a great deal for the future health and well-being of children born before gestation week 24. The technology has been tested on lamb foetuses with good results. These studies have shown that the lamb can survive and develop inside the artificial womb for up to four weeks.

7. ETHICAL AND LEGAL CHALLENGES

The development and introduction of these types of medical devices and methods naturally raise a number of ethical issues.[16] Some are related to safety

---

13 F.R. De Bie, S.D. Kim, S.K. Bose, P. Nathanson, E.A. Partridge, A.W. Flake and C. Feudtner, 'Ethics Considerations Regarding Artificial Womb Technology for the Fetonate' (2022) 23(5) *The American Journal of Bioethics* 67.

14 See, for example, C. Willyard, 'Everything you need to know about artificial wombs', *MIT Technology Review* 29 September 2023, https://www.technologyreview.com/2023/09/29/1080538/everything-you-need-to-know-about-artificial-wombs/.

15 G. Hermerén, 'Care of extremely preterm born children: ethics, risks and difficult decisions' in G. Hermerén, J. Persson, R. Stenwall and E. Sjöstrand (eds), *Ethics, risks and decision-making*, forthcoming 2025.

16 Professor Maarit Jänterä-Jareborg reminded me of the new family law issues that are raised by combining IVF, donation (egg or embryo) and surrogacy – a combination of 'methods' that

and risks, to science and proven experience, to security and efficacy. Another set of questions is related to healthcare prioritisation, for example whether there are other needs that should be prioritised first. I shall leave these questions aside. I believe that there is another type of ethical issue that is of greater interest here, and that is the rights of the foetus and the child.

Professor Elisabeth Rynning, a leading expert in medical law in Sweden, posed the question: When does a foetus become a human being under Swedish law? She writes:

> In Swedish law, it appears somewhat unclear whether an unborn human being can be regarded as an independent legal entity, i.e., a person to whom certain legal rights and obligations may be ascribed. … [I]n several areas, the legislator appears to indirectly answer the question in the negative. … [T]his does not [however] prevent the legal system from offering the foetus some protection even before birth.[17]

What rights does a newborn child have? The UN Convention on the Rights of the Child (1989), Article 6, states that every child has the inherent right to life: 'States Parties shall ensure to the maximum extent possible the survival and development of the child.' This must include each child's right to develop to its full potential. Rynning argues that although there may be some uncertainty about the status of the unborn, there is no such uncertainty after the moment of birth; at that point, the right to life extends to all children.[18] That is, it applies regardless of the week in which the baby is born.

As I see it, we face a potential problem (at least in Sweden) that is in urgent need of clarification. As long as the child has not yet been born, but is still in its mother's womb, the foetus has limited rights (partly depending on the number of weeks of gestation). Once born, it has exactly the same rights (to good care, provided that this care is medically meaningful) as you and I have. But what about the 'individual' in the artificial womb? Is this individual a foetus or a child? The answer to that question will determine what we can do for and with that individual.

The Swedish Abortion Act (1974:595) states that up until the end of the eighteenth week of pregnancy, the choice of an abortion is entirely up to the woman, on condition that it cannot be assumed to cause serious danger to her

---

forces us to reconsider the principle of *mater semper certa est*. I am not sure, but there is a possibility that the development and upcoming introduction of artificial wombs will further undermine this principle (who is the mother? We may have to accept that *mater semper incerta est*). What I am sure of, however, is that we cannot take the issues one by one and regulate the 'methods' in this way; a holistic approach is needed.

17 E. Rynning, 'Åldersgräns för mänskliga rättigheter? Om rätten till hälso- och sjukvård vid livets början' in A. Hollander, R. Nygren and L. Olsen (eds), *Barn och rätt*, Iustus Förlag, Uppsala 2022, pp. 149–180.The translation above is mine, referring to p. 156 in Rynning's chapter.

18 Ibid., p. 176.

life or health owing to illness on her part.[19] When this rare condition is not at hand, her reasons are immaterial. After the eighteenth week, abortion requires permission by the Swedish National Board of Health and Welfare.[20] With a few exceptions, abortion is not allowed after the twenty-second week, when the foetus is considered viable.[21]

If the individual in the artificial womb is considered to be a child in a legal sense, we cannot terminate its life as if it were a foetus. Abortion, regardless of during which week we are talking about, is therefore not an option. If, on the other hand, the individual is regarded as a foetus, it seems reasonable to assume that abortion is allowed. But is this the case after week twenty-two as well? I do not have an answer to this question; I do not think anyone has.

However, this example, like my other examples above, shows how new medical devices compel us to reconsider our legal definitions and regulations and force us to take up positions on what kinds of law reforms should be instituted.[22] Above all, the examples are geared towards demonstrating that we should not look at the issues from too narrow a legal perspective.

---

19 Swedish Act on Abortion (SFS 1974:595), Section 1, as revised by Act 1995:660.

20 The Swedish National Board of Health and Welfare is a government authority in charge of social services, health and medical care and disease prevention in Sweden.

21 Swedish Act on Abortion (SFS 1974:595), Section 3.

22 Definitions are important: we are lost without them. So-called human pluripotent stem cells can grow and self-organise into structures that resemble a human embryo. In theory, embryo models could be created that are viable and have the potential to develop into human beings. (See, for example, 'In brief Embryo models', The Swedish National Council on Medical Ethics, May 2023, also for further references.) We are not there yet, but the future is sometimes closer than we realise. Scientists have discussed how to define these models. A special problem is that we lack a criterion by which to determine how similar an embryo model is to a human embryo. Leaving that aside, my question is whether we have the legal definitions we need to regulate this scientific development. In Sweden there is no legal definition of an embryo. The Swedish Genetic Integrity Act talks about the 'fertilised egg'. It is gametes that underpin the legislation. This is obviously a problem, since it means that the legislation is not in line with current research. Within this area, legal definitions – and therefore legislation – differ across European countries. The lack of a clear, generally accepted legal definition will lead to difficulties in the not-too-distant future. These are issues that have family law implications, and legal definitions that also encompass a family law perspective are urgently required.

PART VI

LEGAL GENDERS AND IDENTITIES IN A EUROPEAN PERSPECTIVE

LEGAL GENDERS AND IDENTITIES FROM A NORDIC AND GERMAN PERSPECTIVE

Jens M. Scherpe

1. INTRODUCTION

Unlike in other parts of Europe, where LGBTQI+ issues in general, and gender recognition and identity in particular, are being weaponised for political gain at the expense of vulnerable minority groups,[1] there is a much better acceptance and understanding of issues concerning the LGBTQI+ communities in the Nordic Countries and, albeit arguably to a lesser extent, in Germany.

That the Nordic Countries are ahead of the curve in this area of law is not a surprise. The Nordic Countries have long been at the forefront of societal and family law developments,[2] including being the first countries in the world to recognise same-sex relationships (in the form of registered partnerships).[3] In

---

1 See, for example, N. Palazzo, 'The EU Family: Surviving Ideological Familism in Times of Illiberalism' in M.-L. Öberg and A. Tryfonidou (eds), *The Family in EU Law*, Cambridge University Press, Cambridge 2024, pp. 227–248; J.M. Scherpe, 'Epilogue to the Family in EU Law: Is There a European Family Law?', in the same volume, pp. 249–261; V. Todorova, 'Gender wars in Bulgaria' in J.M. Scherpe and S. Gilmore (eds), *Family Matters – Essays in Honour of John Eekelaar*, Intersentia, Cambridge 2022, pp. 245–262; L. Vaige, *Cross-Border Recognition of Formalized Same-Sex Relationships*, Intersentia, Cambridge 2022; and the contributions by Vaige and Mair in this volume.

2 See e.g. J.M. Scherpe, 'The Nordic Countries in the Vanguard of European Family Law' (2007) 50 *Scandinavian Studies in Law* 265.

3 On this, see, for example, K. Boele-Woelki and A. Fuchs (eds), *Same-Sex Relationships and Beyond*, Intersentia, Cambridge 2017; S. Cretney, *Same Sex Relationships from 'Odious Crime' to 'Gay Marriage'*, Oxford University Press, Oxford 2006; R. Wintemute and M. Andenæs (eds), *Legal Recognition of Same-Sex Partnerships*, Hart Publishing, Oxford 2001. For brief comparative overviews, see, for example, J.M. Scherpe, 'Same-sex relationships' in J. Basedow, K.-J. Hopt and R. Zimmermann (eds), *Max Planck Encyclopedia of European Private Law*, Oxford University Press, Oxford 2012, pp. 1522–1525; J.M. Scherpe, 'From "odious crime" to family life – same-sex couples and the ECHR' in A. Verbeke et al. (eds), *Confronting the Frontiers of Family and Succession Law – Liber amicorum Walter Pintens*, Intersentia, Antwerp/Cambridge 2012, pp. 1225–1240; J.M. Scherpe, 'Gleichgeschlechtliche Lebensgemeinschaften im Recht der nordischen Länder' in J. Basedow et al. (eds), *Die Rechtsstellung gleichgeschlechtlicher Lebensgemeinschaften*, Mohr Siebeck, Tübingen 2000, pp. 7–49. See also the contributions in J.M. Scherpe and A. Hayward (eds), *The Future of Registered Partnerships – Family Recognition beyond Marriage?*, Intersentia, Cambridge 2017.

the area of gender recognition, it was Sweden that took the lead with legislation in this area in 1972.[4]

While Germany only recognised same-sex relationships relatively late by comparison, namely in 2001,[5] in 1981 it became the second country in Europe to have a statutory basis for legal gender recognition,[6] which was introduced after a decision by the German Constitutional Court.[7] This may come as a surprise, given that Germany tends to be somewhat more socially conservative than its Western and Northern neighbours, but post-war Germany has the benefit of a strong constitutional tradition and human rights protection. The atrocities committed by the German people under the Nazi regime, the horrors of the dehumanisation of people who did not conform to the officially proclaimed norms and exterminating them in concentration camps has created a special and unique awareness of the dangers of 'othering' people and minorities, at least in Western Germany. This can be seen in particular in the jurisprudence of the *Bundesverfassungsgericht* (German Constitutional Court), but also in the political debates on socially sensitive issues – at least until fairly recently, when the rise of populism and the decline of social decency in politics also reached Germany. The German Constitutional Court's human rights jurisprudence over many decades was instrumental in bringing about the new law on self-determination of legal gender[8] and also triggered the recognition of a third gender category.[9]

This made Germany the first European country where there is a full third legal gender option; third gender options will be discussed under section 3 below, after gender recognition and self-determination have been looked at more broadly in section 2. In section 4 the consequences for parent–child relationships of a change of legal gender and non-binary parenthood will be discussed before section 5 concludes.

2. LEGAL GENDER RECOGNITION: SELF-DETERMINATION

As mentioned above, Sweden was the first country to introduce legislation which allowed for a change of legal gender in 1972, followed by Germany in 1980.

---

4 Lag (1972:119) om fastställande av könstillhörighet i vissa fall; on this see L. Carlson, 'The Paradox of Trans Law in Sweden' in I.C. Jaramillo and L. Carlson (eds), *Trans Rights and Wrongs – A Comparative Study of Legal Reform Concerning Trans Persons*, Springer, 2021, Vienna pp. 541–558.

5 Gesetz über die Eingetragene Lebenspartnerschaft (Lebenspartnerschaftsgesetz – LPartG), BGBl. I 2001, p. 266 (16.02.2001).

6 Gesetz über die Änderung der Vornamen und die Feststellung der Geschlechtszugehörigkeit in besonderen Fällen (Transsexuellengesetz), BGBl. I 1980, p. 1654 (10.11.1980), in force from 01.01.1981.

7 BVerfG 11.10.1978, *BVerfGE* 49, 286 = *NJW* 179, 595.

8 On this jurisprudence see e.g. A. Dutta, 'The Legal Status of Transsexual and Transgender Persons in Germany' in J. Scherpe (ed.), *The Legal Status of Transsexual and Transgender Persons*, Intersentia, Cambridge 2015, pp. 207–221; T.A. Richarz and A. Sanders, 'Trans Rights in Germany and in Denmark' in I.C. Jaramillo and L. Carlson (eds), above n. 4, pp. 279–303.

9 BVerfG 10.10.2017, *BVerfGE* 127, 1 = *NJW* 2017, 3643.

While they were groundbreaking at the time, by today's standards these two statutes not only seem outdated, but their provisions would be unacceptable today. Of course, it needs to be acknowledged that not only societal acceptance, but also medical and psychological knowledge have advanced significantly since they were enacted. The ignorance at the time is perhaps best captured by the criticism raised in the *Bundesrat* (the Upper House of the German Parliament) against the proposed German legislation in that it was premature because

> so far it has not been possible to distinguish transsexualism from other phenomena (such as homosexuality and transvestitism).[10]

Such was the unease that the German Act in its section 8 introduced a number of 'safeguards' which even exceeded those of the earlier Swedish statute, namely a minimum age for changing one's legal gender,[11] German nationality (or statelessness), that the person in question be unmarried, permanently unable to reproduce (which essentially amounted to a sterilisation requirement), had undergone gender reassignment surgery and that the person concerned has for at least three years 'felt to be under the compulsion to live in the gender different from that under which they were registered'. Similar criteria could (and in some cases still can) be found in many comparable statutes.[12] As for Germany, almost all of these criteria were successfully challenged in the German Constitutional Court, and were rightly found to be in violation of the human rights protections embodied in the German Constitution, the Basic Law.[13] Underlying these decisions is a common thread: that attaching legal requirements to be allowed to live and to be recognised by the state as who you are is an unacceptable infringement of the concerned individual's human rights.

This is also the very clear position of Article 3 of the 2006 Yogyakarta Principles:

---

10 BT-Drucks. 8/2947, pp. 18 et seqq.

11 18 in Sweden, 25 in Germany.

12 For a comparative discussion of these criteria see e.g. J.M. Scherpe, *The Past, Presence and Future of European Family Law*, Edward Elgar Publishing, Cheltenham 2016, pp. 119et seqq. and J.M. Scherpe and P. Dunne, 'The Legal Status of Transsexual and Transgender Persons – Comparative Analysis and Recommendations' in J. Scherpe (ed.), above n. 8, pp. 615–663.

13 Age requirement of 25 years: BVerfG 16.03.1982, *BVerfGE* 60, 123 = *NJW* 1982, 2061 and BVerfG 26.01.1993, *BVerfGE* 88, 87 = *NJW* 1993, 1517. Nationality: BVerfG 18.07.2006, *BVerfGE* 116, 243 = *NJW* 2007, 900; on this see also J. Basedow and J.M. Scherpe (eds), *Transsexualität, Staatsangehörigkeit und internationales Privatrecht – Entwicklungen in Europa, Amerika und Australien*, Mohr Siebeck, Tübingen 2004. Marital status: BVerfG 27.05.2008, *BVerfGE* 121, 175 = *NJW* 2008, 3117. Surgery/sterility: BVerfG 11.01.2011, *BVerfGE* 128, 109 = *NJW* 2011, 909; on this see also P. Dunne, 'Transgender sterilisation requirements in Europe' (2017) 25(4) *Medical Law Review* 554. On these decisions in context see e.g. A. Dutta, above n. 8, and T.A. Richarz and A. Sanders, above n. 8.

> Everyone has the right to recognition everywhere as a person before the law. Persons of diverse sexual orientations and gender identities shall enjoy legal capacity in all aspects of life. Each person's self-defined sexual orientation and gender identity is integral to their personality and is one of the most basic aspects of self-determination, dignity and freedom. No one shall be forced to undergo medical procedures, including sex reassignment surgery, sterilisation or hormonal therapy, as a requirement for legal recognition of their gender identity. No status, such as marriage or parenthood, may be invoked as such to prevent the legal recognition of a person's gender identity. No one shall be subjected to pressure to conceal, suppress or deny their sexual orientation or gender identity.[14]

In line with this, and the general international developments,[15] Denmark,[16] Norway,[17] Iceland,[18] Finland[19] and most recently Germany[20] have reformed

---

14 It is worth noting that Principle 31 of the 2017 Yogyakarta Principles plus 10 (YP +10) goes further and expressly calls on states 'to end the registration of the sex and gender of the person in identity documents such as birth certificates, identification cards, passports and driver licences, and as part of their legal personality'.

15 On this see e.g. Steering Committee on Anti-discrimination, Diversity and Inclusion (CDADI), Council of Europe, *Thematic Report on Legal Gender recognition in Europe*, 2022, available at https://rm.coe.int/thematic-report-on-legal-gender-recognition-in-europe-2022/1680a729b3 (last accessed 22.01.2025) and M. van den Brink and P. Dunne, European Commission Directorate-General for Justice and Consumers, *Trans and intersex equality rights in Europe – a comparative analysis*, November 2018, available at https://commission.europa.eu/system/files/2018-11/trans_and_intersex_equality_rights.pdf (last accessed 22.01.2025) and K. Boele-Woelki, 'Humanization of private international law: The search for conflict of law rules for two new areas: *de facto* partnerships and gender identity' in J.-M. Thouvenin (ed.), *Challenges of International Law at the Time of the Centenary of The Hague Academy of International Law/Les défis du droit international au tournant du centenaire de l'Académie de droit international de La Haye*, De Gruyter Brill, Berlin 2024, pp. 392–421, 412et seqq. with further references.

16 See D. Tamm and I. Lund-Andersen, 'The Civil Status of Trans Persons in Denmark' in I.C. Jaramillo and L. Carlson (eds), above n. 4, pp. 451–462 and N. Videbæk Munkholm, 'The Legal Status of Transsexual and Transgender Persons in Denmark' in J. Scherpe, above n. 8, pp. 147–181.

17 Lov om endring av Juridisk kjønn, LOV-2016-06-17-46, on this see A.V. Grønningsæter and L. Arnesen, 'The Civil Status of Trans Persons in Norway' in I.C. Jaramillo and L. Carlson (eds), above n. 4, pp. 513–540.

18 Lög um kynrænt sjálfræð (Act on Gender Autonomy) No. 80/2019 as amended by Act No. 159/2019, No. 152/2020 and No. 154/2020, English translation available at https://www.government.is/publications/legislation/lex/2020/05/08/Act-on-Gender-Autonomy/ (last accessed 22.01.2025). On this see D. Alaattinoğlu, 'Intersex Rights in the Icelandic Gender Autonomy Act' (February 2022), available at http://dx.doi.org/10.2139/ssrn.4252270 (last accessed 22.01.2025).

19 Lag om könsfastställelse/Laki sukupuolen vahvistamisesta 295/2023. See also the editorial 'Translaki poistui – oikeudellinen sukupuoli irtautui lääketieteestä' (The Trans Act was repealed – Legal gender detached from medicine) (2023) 139(15) *Lääketieteellinen Aikakauskirja Duodecim* 1147. On this generally see M. Rantala, 'Sukupuoleen sopeutetut: Intersukupuolisten ja transsukupuolisten henkilöiden oikeusasema Suomessa' (Adjusted to sex: Legal status of intersex and transgender persons in Finland) (2016) 45(1) *Oikeus* 8.

20 Gesetz über die Selbstbestimmung in Bezug auf den Geschlechtseintrag und zur Änderung weiterer Vorschriften (SBGG), BGBl. 2024 I, No. 106 (19.06.2024). For an overview see e.g. W. Keuter, 'Das neue Selbstbestimmungsgesetz – Anmerkungen zu den status-, abstammungs-

the previously more restrictive laws to permit a change of legal gender solely on the basis of a declaration by the person concerned, i.e. self-determination.[21] Central to this development is the clear separation of the medical and the legal procedures, which is perfectly consistent with not only the demands of the communities concerned but also medical and psychological research.

However, it appears that the recent reforms in Sweden, which are scheduled to enter into force on 1 July 2025,[22] unlike the vast majority of law reforms in this area, do not quite follow this trend. According to section 2 No. 4 of the new Lag om fastställande av kön i vissa fall, it is necessary that 'it can be assumed that the person will live in this gender identity for the foreseeable future'.[23] To prove this, apparently a statement by a medical professional about the 'permanence for the foreseeable future' of the gender identity sought is required, although this only needs to be a simple assessment and not a full evaluation as was the case previously. Whether this requirement will be of greater practical relevance remains to be seen, but it not only creates additional burdens to the detriment of those concerned but also to a certain degree maintains the 'medicalisation' of the process. It certainly sets Sweden apart from its neighbours, which did not consider such a requirement to be necessary.

Maintaining a medical element in the process is contrary to the notion of self-determination and arguably is the result of an often over-heated debate, in which the same arguments are being continually raised, irrespective of in which jurisdiction this debate takes place and despite there being no evidence that any of the concerns have actually materialised in a major way in those jurisdictions which have had a right to self-determination of gender for quite some time.[24]

While legal gender based on self-determination can cause issues in specific circumstances like imprisonment, or single-sex facilities more generally, this

---

und namensrechtlichen Neuerungen', *Zeitschrift für das gesamte Familienrecht (FamRZ)* 2024, 1073, B. Rentsch and D. Valentiner, 'Selbstbestimmung über das Geschlecht in den Grenzen des bürgerlichen Rechts', *Rechtswissenschaft (RW)* 2023, 467; J. Plobner and C. Markurt, 'Hintergrunde zum Gesetz über die Selbstbestimmung in Bezug auf den Geschlechtseintrag', *Das Standesamt (StAZ)* 2024, 193. On the draft Bill see A.K. Mangold and S. Rossbach, 'Das Grundrecht auf geschlechtliche Selbstbestimmung', *JuristenZeitung (JZ)* 2023, 756. A. Dutta, 'Geschlechtsidentität statt Körper', *FamRZ* 2023, 993; D. Coester-Waltjen, 'Entwicklungen im Familienstatusrecht: Abstammung – Geschlecht – Name', *StAZ* 2014, 65.

21 Albeit in Denmark with a 'reflection' period of six months, after which the decision to change legal gender must be confirmed in writing. This period can be shortened in some cases. On this see D. Tamm and I. Lund-Andersen, above n. 16, p. 457 and N. Videbæk Munkholm, above n. 16, pp. 103 et seqq., by contrast in Norway such a period was proposed and debated but ultimately rejected, cf. A.V. Grønningsæter and L. Arnesen, above n. 17, p. 521 with further references.

22 Lag (2024:238) om fastställande av kön i vissa fall.

23 In Swedish: '*det kan antas att personen kommer att leva i denna könsidentitet under överskadlig tid*'.

24 See L. Carlson, above n. 4, and also M. Jänterä-Jareborg, 'Sweden: Family law developments 2022–2024', *FamRZ* 2024, 1456.

must and can be dealt with, both respectfully and sensitively.[25] But such issues cannot be a sufficient reason to fully deny all the persons concerned the very basic right to be recognised as who they are.

Similarly, a right to self-determination, just like any other right, obviously can potentially be abused, and some abuses may (and probably will) occur. However, just because a right *can* be abused by some, it does not mean that this right should be denied to all. To give an example: people have the right to marry, yet marriage is probably the family law institution that is most often abused, for example for immigration purposes. Nonetheless, nobody would therefore call for marriage or the right to marry to be abolished. Instead, any potential abuse of a right needs to be policed and dealt with, as is done with sham marriages and other situations of the abuse of rights. That there can be an abuse of a right in a small number of cases is not a sufficient reason to deny the vast majority of those concerned a fundamental right.

In any event, the Nordic Countries (with Sweden perhaps being a bit of an outlier) and Germany for the most part have brought their laws on the recognition of legal gender into line with the Yogyakarta Principles and national and international human rights obligations.

3. NON-BINARY GENDERS

As regards non-binary genders, of the jurisdictions canvassed in this contribution only Iceland and Germany are amongst the few jurisdictions worldwide that have more than two full legal gender options. In Germany the third gender category is called 'diverse'; in Iceland it is 'neutral'.[26] The two jurisdictions reached this position in rather different ways – but ways that were, perhaps, typical for these jurisdictions.

The *Deutsche Ethikrat* (German Ethics Council) published a position paper on the legal status of intersex persons in 2012,[27] prompted by a 2009 report of the UN Committee on the Elimination of Discrimination against Women, which had strongly criticised the German government because it had not entered into a dialogue 'with some non-governmental organizations of intersexual and transsexual people'.[28] As a reaction to this, the German *Personenstandsgesetz*

25 For some case law on this see M. van den Brink and P. Dunne, above n. 15, pp. 86 et seq.

26 The author has been assured by native speakers that in Icelandic the term 'neutral' does not carry the same negative connotations as it does in English or German.

27 *Stellungnahme des Deutschen Ethikrates zum Thema Intersexualität*, BT-Drucks 17/9088 of 14.02.2012, also available at https://www.ethikrat.org/fileadmin/Publikationen/Stellungnahmen/deutsch/DER_StnIntersex_Deu_Online.pdf (last accessed 22.01.2025).

28 *Concluding observations of the Committee on the Elimination of Discrimination against Women: Germany*, CEDAW/C/DEU/CO/6, 12 February 2009, available at https://www.refworld.org/policy/polrec/cedaw/2009/en/67133 (last accessed 22.01.2025), p. 12.

(PStG, Civil Status Act) was amended and a new subsection 3 was included in §22:[29]

> Where the child cannot be assigned to either the female or the male sex, its civil status is to be recorded in the register of births without such declaration.

Thus, the gender entry of the person in question could be left blank if assigning a male or female gender was not 'unequivocally' possible,[30] i.e. only for children with a difference in sex development (also referred to as intersex or inter*). This meant that for all intents and purposes the person concerned was without a legal gender; while it was possible for the said person to choose to be registered as male or female later in life,[31] there was no legal obligation to do so.

While it was (probably) well intended, namely to prevent misgendering intersex children,[32] the absence of a legal gender had many consequences in the gendered legal system of Germany that had not been considered[33] and was criticised,[34] because, amongst other things, it was 'othering' those concerned.[35] Most controversially, a 'blank' entry effectively told the person that, as far as gender was concerned, they were a 'nothing'. This was challenged when an individual known as Vanja sought to change their gender entry from female to 'inter/diverse' to reflect their true gender. While the *Bundesgerichtshof* (Federal Court of Justice) and previous instances had denied this registration,[36] the German Constitutional Court held in 2017 that it had to be possible to obtain a 'positive' gender entry other than male or female.[37] In other words, as long as the legal gender of every person has to be recognised/documented, being gender-labelled as a 'nothing' was held to be a violation of the German Constitution. Everybody is somebody, every person has a body, and even if that body did not conform with the existing norms of gender, this did not make them

---

29 On this provision and the issues arising therefrom see e.g. T. Helms, 'The 2013 German Law: Analysis and Criticism' in J.M. Scherpe, A. Dutta and T. Helms (eds), *The Legal Status of Intersex Persons*, Intersentia, Cambridge 2018, pp. 369–381 and also the criticism by Die Dritte Option, http://dritte-option.de/stellungnahme-zur-pstg-aenderung/ (last accessed 22.01.2025).

30 Beschlussempfehlung und Bericht des Innenausschusses vom 30.01.2013, BT-Drucks. 17/12192, p. 11.

31 Cf. §27(3) PStG.

32 Changing an entry to blank was also possible for intersex persons who had been registered with a gender before the 2013 law was enacted, cf. BGH 22.06.2016, *NJW* 2016, 2885 = *FamRZ* 2016, 1580 and T. Helms, above n. 29, p. 373.

33 See T. Helms, above n. 29, pp. 375et seqq.

34 Cf. e.g. W. Sieberichs, 'Das unbestimmte Geschlecht', *FamRZ* 2013, 1180.

35 On this see e.g. M. Carpenter, 'The "Normalisation" of Intersex Bodies and "Othering" of Intersex Identities' in J. Scherpe, A. Dutta and T. Helms, above n. 29, pp. 445–514.

36 See n. 32 above.

37 BVerfG 10.10.2017, *BVerfGE* 147, 1 = *NJW* 2017, 363 (with comment by S. Gössl) = *FamRZ* 2017, 2046 (with comment by T. Helms).

genderless or a 'blank'. They had a body, and they had a gender – albeit one that was not recognised by German law. Therefore, the Court held that the German legislature had to enact appropriate legislation by the end of 2018.[38] Parliament duly did so, passing the *Gesetz zur Änderung der in das Geburtenregister einzutragenden Angaben*,[39] which amended the PStG to allow for a gender entry of '*divers*' (diverse); crucially, this did not create a 'third gender' but rather a third gender category or option.[40]

While it was certainly a positive development, this reform was of a minimalist character and the German laws on gender and gender recognition were hopelessly outdated, not least because large parts of the legislation had been set aside as they were deemed unconstitutional.[41] Moreover, the legal position of those who did not have a difference in sex development but identified as non-binary was not entirely clear and neither was the procedure which they had to follow.[42] Given that there was now a gender option beyond the binary *and* there already was a constitutionally guaranteed right to be recognised in one's desired gender identity, it was highly questionable whether choosing a 'diverse' gender entry could be denied to all those who desired to be identified as such. All in all, there was arguably a need for a comprehensive reform, and this finally happened in 2024 with the abovementioned SBGG, which allowed for the self-determination of legal gender (including the third gender option of 'diverse').[43]

What in Germany required much controversy and numerous court cases, in Iceland was achieved comparatively calmly and rationally through an Act of Parliament, namely the Act on Gender Autonomy.[44] The express objective of the Act according to its Article 1 is to provide persons with the right to define their gender and guaranteeing the recognition of their gender identity, as well as to safeguard their physical integrity. Article 3 of the Act states that there is an unrestricted right, in accordance with age and maturity,

---

38 The Austrian Constitutional Court (Österreichische Verfassungsgerichtshof) followed suit in its decision of 15.06.2018 (available at https://www.vfgh.gv.at/downloads/VfGH_Entscheidung_G_77-2018_unbestimmtes_Geschlecht_anonym.pdf, last accessed 22.01.2025), holding that every person has the right to have a gender entry that conforms to their gender identity.

39 BGBl. 2018 I, No. 48 (18.12.2018).

40 Cf. e.g. https://www.antidiskriminierungsstelle.de/DE/ueber-diskriminierung/diskriminierungsmerkmale/geschlecht-und-geschlechtsidentitaet/dritte-option/dritte-option-node.html (last accessed 22.01.2025).

41 See above n. 13. Mangold and Wiggerich rightly called the legislation a 'legal ruin', A.K. Mangold, 'Menschrechtlich gebotene Selbstbestimmung', *Zeitschrift für Rechtspolitik (ZRP)* 2022, 180–; S. Wiggerich, 'Rechtsvergleichedne Impulse zur Reform des Transsexuellengesetzes', *StAZ* 2017, 8.

42 So much so that the Bundesministerium des Innern und für Heimat issued a circular for clarification on 10.04.2019, V II 1 – 20103/27#17, available at https://www.personenstandsrecht.de/SharedDocs/kurzmeldungen/Webs/PERS/DE/rundschreiben/2019/0122-aenderung-geburtenregister.html (last accessed 22.01.2025).

43 See above n. 20. For details on the new regulation see the references in the same note.

44 See above n. 18.

a. to define one's gender,
b. to have one's gender, gender identity and gender expression recognised,
c. to develop one's personality in keeping with one's gender identity,
d. to physical integrity and autonomy concerning changes in sex characteristics.

In addition, it is expressly stated in Article 4(2) that

> [i]t is prohibited to make a surgical operation, medication, hormonal treatment or other medical treatment, such as psychiatric or psychological therapy, a requirement for changing the registration of gender.

Crucially for present purposes, according to Article 6 this includes registration as 'neutral', i.e. a gender beyond the binary. Unlike Germany, Iceland also legislated to include parent–child relations/filiation in the new, non-binary gender system (on which see section 4 below).

While in the other Nordic Countries there has been, and will continue to be, some debate on the introduction of a non-binary legal gender, no legislation has been enacted at the time of writing.[45] However, based on past experience concerning socially progressive legislation in the Nordic Countries, it can be presumed that such legislation will be considered in the foreseeable future.

4. PARENTHOOD AND GENDER

As outlined above, the Nordic Countries and Germany have moved to a system of self-declaration when it comes to legal gender, and in Iceland and Germany that even includes the option of a non-binary gender. However, when it comes to parent–child relations/filiation, the legal developments seem to be somewhat lagging behind in some of these jurisdictions.

Sweden can take credit for being the first Nordic jurisdiction to have introduced express provisions for trans persons as parents in 2018,[46] with several subsequent changes. Now the gendered parental status is allocated on the basis of the legal gender of the parent at the time of the birth of the child. Thus, a legally male person giving birth would be designated as the father of the child

---

45 For the discussions in Norway see A.V. Grønningsæter and L. Arnesen, above n. 17, pp. 538 et seq.; for Denmark see D. Tamm and I. Lund-Andersen, above n. 16, p. 460; for Sweden H.M. Ahlström, *A third legal gender in Sweden?*, thesis, Lund Universitet, Humanistiska och Teologiska Fakulteterna 2023, available at https://lup.lub.lu.se/luur/download?func=downloadFile&recordOId=9135055&fileOId=9135059 (last accessed 22.01.2025), esp. pp. 22et seqq.

46 Lag om ändring i föräldrabalken, SFS 2018:1279. Provisions now contained in 1:10–14 §§. On this see D. Alaatinoğlu and A. Margaria, 'Trans parents and the gendered law: Critical reflections on the Swedish regulation' (2023) 21(2) *International Journal of Constitutional Law (ICON)* 603.

and their spouse would also be designated as the father or mother depending on their legal gender. But the parental designation remains gendered and Swedish law has stopped short of removing gender from the equation and merely using the term 'parent', except for, perhaps ironically, in the case of a second female parent through assisted reproduction who is indeed called 'parent' and not 'co-mother' or 'mother'. At the same time, in Sweden the trans parent concerned retains the same rights and duties according to other Acts and regulations as if they had not undergone a change of legal gender, thus a trans man who has given birth is entitled to maternity leave, etc.[47]

The legal rules on parenthood in Denmark have recently undergone some changes, including on surrogacy[48] and, importantly for present purposes, concerning trans parents, with the latter following the Swedish approach.[49] Thus, according to the new rules the gender at the time of birth will determine the legal position as mother or father, and like in Sweden, otherwise the person concerned retains the same rights and duties arising from other Acts and regulations concerning parenthood as if they had not undergone a change of legal gender. A trans woman will be regarded as the female partner of the person giving birth and, unlike in Sweden, as a co-mother (*medmor*) and not 'parent'.[50] Parenthood in cases of surrogacy is now also determined based on the legal gender at the time of the birth of the child.[51]

By contrast, in Norway it in principle remains the case that the gender allocated to the parent at their birth determines parenthood under the Children Act.[52] This was deemed 'necessary to establish the parenthood of the child' – without any meaningful discussion.[53] As a result, for parenting purposes, trans persons will be (mis)gendered as mother or father according to their gender assigned at birth – with the exception of a co-motherhood in the case of a female couple, where apparently the birth gender of the co-mother is irrelevant.[54]

Finland takes a somewhat odd 'middle position' between the Swedish/Danish (legally centred) and the Norwegian (more biologically centred) approach, and even breaks new ground. Initially, in Finland the person giving birth is always

---

47 On this particular point see D. Alaatinoğlu and A. Margaria, above n. 46, p. 614.

48 Lov nr 1687 of 30.12.2024 om ændring af børneloven, adoptionsloven, forældreansvarsloven og forskellige andre love (Familiedannelse ved surrogataftaler, medfar som retlig forælder, forenkling af familiedannelse ved voksenadoption m.v.).

49 Lov nr 227 of 15.02.2022 om ændring af børneloven, navneloven og forskellige andre love (Smidiggørelse af registrering af medmoderskab, fastsættelse af transpersoners forældreskab og navneændring for transpersoner m.v.).

50 See §§31a and 31b børneloven, inserted by Lov nr 227 of 15.02.2022, above n. 49.

51 See Kapitel 5a, 5b and 5c børneloven, inserted Lov nr 1687 of 30.12.2024, above n. 48.

52 This is regulated expressly in section 6 of the Change of Legal Gender Act, above n. 17.

53 Det Kongelige Helse- og Omsorgsdepartement, Prop. 74 L (2015–16) p. 31 and p. 37; see also A.V. Grønningsæter and L. Arnesen, above n. 17, pp. 525 et seq.

54 Section 4a Children Act, on this see A.V. Grønningsæter and L. Arnesen, above n. 17, p. 526.

considered to be the mother of the child. As for the second parent, while the gendered parental designation in principle primarily depends on the legal gender of the person concerned (so father or 'other mother' because Finnish law does not allow for a person to be a 'parent'), if that person's sperm was used for the conception, they will always at first be regarded as the father of the child, irrespective of their legal gender.[55] However, once the original registration has been made, it can be changed upon an application by the person concerned from mother to father and vice versa. The reason for this approach is presumably that there is documentation of the birth-designated parental position and the subsequent change which the child concerned can later access. In any event, while somewhat more restrictive in the first mandatory registration, Finland unlike the other Nordic jurisdictions actually then gives greater freedom to self-determine which parental designation the individuals concerned ultimately want to apply to them.

In Germany, the long-planned reform of the law of filiation/parenthood came to a halt after the government collapsed at the end of 2024 and elections were called. It can only be hoped that the new government will give this important area of law the attention it deserves and will pursue these much-needed reforms. For the time being, this area remains a complicated one in Germany. As a starting point, the German view can be summarised with the (admittedly somewhat misleading) slogan 'the biological truth must prevail'; accordingly, German law generally only operates with the terms 'mother' and 'father' despite having a third legal gender option (but see below). The person giving birth is always designated as the legal mother, irrespective of their gender, even though the relevant provision §1591 BGB (Civil Code) expressly speaks of 'the woman who gives birth' and thus, technically, does not apply to legal men giving birth.[56] Concerning fatherhood, as a starting point, only a male person at the time of birth who is married to the mother or recognises paternity is recognised as the legal father, even when they are biologically female. However, a trans woman initially is not the father, even when they are the genetic father, because they are not legally male. However, since 'the biological truth must prevail', a female trans person can also choose to be treated according to their legal gender before transitioning, so they can be the father after all if they make a declaration accordingly when the birth of the child is recorded.[57] To complicate things even further, according to a provision hidden in a statutory instrument, §42(3) *Personenstandsverordnung*,[58] in the case of adoption, a person who does not

55 See the information provided at https://dvv.fi/sv/faststallande-av-annan-konstillhorighet (last accessed 22.01.2025).

56 See §11(1)1 SBGG; see also previously BGH 06.09.2017, BGHZ 215, 318 = *NJW* 2017 = *FamRZ* 2017, 1855 ('eine klare, den biologischen Umständen entsprechenden Zuordnung von Kindern zu einem Vater und einer Mutter').

57 §11(1)1 SBBG, §45b(1) Personenstandsgesetz.

58 Verordnung zur Ausführung des Personenstandsgesetzes (Personenstandsverordnung, PStV).

have the legal gender of male or female has to be registered as *Elternteil* (parent); a registration as mother or father is not possible. Moreover, according to §48(1a) of the same statutory instrument, a person initially registered as mother or father can request for that designation to be changed to *Elternteil* on the birth certificate. Like in Finland, this presupposes a registration according to the 'general rules' first.

Iceland, as the other jurisdiction that allows for more than two legal genders, has regulated parenthood, including that of trans parents and also non-binary individuals, in a very simple and straightforward way (after some necessary amendments to the original Act on Gender Autonomy in 2021).[59] Essentially, the gendered parental designation must follow the legal gender, meaning that a 'mother' is the person who at birth is female, a 'father' is the person who at birth is male and a parent is a person whose gender at birth is 'neutral'. These designations are mandatory and the persons concerned do not have any choice in the matter.

It is worth noting that the registration of parenthood and parental designation according to the birth-assigned gender was found not to be in violation of the European Convention on Human Rights (ECHR) by the European Court of Human Rights (ECtHR) in cases concerning Germany.[60] The Court stated that the matter fell within the wide margin of appreciation afforded to the Contracting States and that a fair balance had been struck between the rights of the applicant parent and child, considerations of the child's welfare and public interests. However, given that it is well documented that the misgendering of parents causes a great deal of harm to the families concerned,[61] it is the 'public interest' aspect that seems to have been given the greatest weight, certainly by the state concerned.

5. CONCLUSION

The laws on legal genders and identities in the Nordic Countries have changed considerably in the last decades and have become more respectful of the human rights of those concerned and more accepting of persons who do not conform with the previously dominant cis-gender, hetero-normative and binary gender societal and legal structures. While the situation for the LGBTQI+ communities and individuals has improved, the above shows that there are still unresolved issues even in these progressive jurisdictions.

59 By Act no. 49/2021.

60 *O.H. and G.H. v Germany*, nos. 53568/18, 54741/18, 4 April 2023, and *A.H. and Others v Germany*, no. 7246/20, 4 April 2023.

61 Cf. D. Alaatinoğlu and A. Margaria, above n. 46, pp. 606 et seqq. with further references.

All the major Nordic jurisdictions and Germany now rightly allow for a self-determination of gender and, for the most part, the separation of the medical and legal procedures. Some aspects of these procedures, which could not be presented and discussed in detail here, can be regarded as problematic and in some cases are unnecessarily burdensome for those concerned, and there certainly is room for improvement.

While accepting of gender self-determination, so far only two of the jurisdictions looked at in this contribution allow for legal genders beyond the binary, i.e. Iceland and Germany. However, if the right to self-determine one's legal gender is taken seriously, it is difficult to justify why this self-determination is limited only to the legal genders of male and female when persons identify as neither. The legal and administrative challenges that the existence of a third gender category brings with it for a legal system based on binary genders cannot, in and of itself, be a sufficient reason to maintain this system. Administrative inconvenience should not prevent the recognition and exercise of fundamental human rights.

Interestingly, similar arguments about the system of the existing gendered law and how it could not be altered were raised against and ultimately overcome in another challenge to existing structures which until relatively recently were deemed immutable: same-sex marriages. Just like on marriage, where the ECtHR found that there is no obligation under the ECHR to allow same-sex marriages,[62] concerning the introduction of a third legal gender category the Court likewise found that this fell within the individual states' margin of appreciation.[63] However, these decisions arise from the nature of the ECHR as an international, multilateral treaty and the necessary deference to national legislatures; by contrast, national constitutional courts *have* found that there is indeed an obligation arising from the human rights obligations based on the *national* constitutions.[64] Moreover, the mere fact that the ECtHR found that there is no *obligation* to introduce a third legal gender option does not prevent national legislatures from taking action – and that a matter was 'within the margin of appreciation' has not deterred parliaments in the past, as the introduction of same-sex marriage in nearly all Western European jurisdictions shows. After all, the ECHR, as a 'living instrument',[65] provides a floor of rights but not a ceiling,[66] and the margin of appreciation can narrow over time.[67]

62 See e.g. *Schalk and Kopf v Austria*, no. 30141/04, 24 June 2010.

63 *Y. v France*, no. 76888/17, 31 January 2023.

64 E.g. in Germany, above n. 37, and Austria, above n. 38.

65 This doctrine was first expressly referred to in the 1978 ECtHR decision *Tyrer v the United Kingdom*, no. 5856/72, 25 April 1978.

66 N. Wikely, 'Same sex couples, family life and child support' (2006) 122 *Law Quarterly Review* 542, 544.

67 As it did, e.g., for legal gender recognition.

The above has also shown that changes to provisions concerning legal genders and identities should not and must not be seen in isolation as they have wider repercussions. This contribution looked briefly at the laws of parenthood/filiation as an example, highlighting the issues and presenting the approaches the jurisdictions canvassed have taken. The spectrum observed ranges from fully legally centred to fully biologically centred.

While the laws focusing solely on the legal, such as in Iceland, Sweden and Denmark, have the benefit of clarity, they are static and do not allow the individuals concerned to choose their parental designation. This is based on the assumption that the identification regarding the parental position always follows the (self-identified) gender, which is not necessarily true.[68] It seems at odds with the notion of self-determination to only allow this for one's gender but not for one's parental designation.[69]

Jurisdictions focusing solely on the biological, such as Norway, of course also do not respect the legal self-determination of a parent, with this approach causing much distress to the families concerned.[70]

By contrast, jurisdictions like Germany and Finland take their starting point in biology but then permit a subsequent self-determination of the legal parental designation, at least to a certain extent, thereby avoiding the problems that comparable families in Norway are facing.

Ultimately, it may be worth thinking about what many have suggested[71] and what jurisdictions like Malta[72] and Ontario[73] have done and purge the terms 'mother' and 'father' from the legislation (i.e. 'degender' the law of parenthood/filiation) and merely use the term 'parent' instead. In an age of same-sex, trans, non-binary and indeed multiple parenthood, this would appear to be the obvious way forward.

---

68 See also D. Alaatinoğlu and A. Margaria, above n. 46, p. 622; L. Karaian, 'Pregnant Men: Repronormativity, Critical Trans Theory and the Re(conceive)ing of Sex and Pregnancy in Law' (2013) 22 *Social & Legal Studies* 211.

69 See also A.K. Mangold and S. Rossbach, above n. 20.

70 See above n. 56.

71 See e.g. A. Brown, 'Trans (legal) parenthood and the gender of legal parenthood' (2024) 44 *Legal Studies* 168; D. Alaatinoğlu and A. Margaria, above n. 46; J.M. Scherpe, above n. 12, p. 131; J.M. Scherpe, 'Mehr Freiheit wagen im Familienrecht – Entgeschlechtlichung des Rechts' in A. Dutta and C. Heinze (eds), *„Mehr Freiheit wagen" – Beiträge zur Emeritierung von Jürgen Basedow*, Mohr Siebeck, Tübingen 2018, pp. 73–87, J.M. Scherpe, 'Breaking the Existing Paradigms of Parent–Child Relationships' in G. Douglas, M. Murch and V. Stephens (eds), *International and National Perspectives on Child and Family Law: Essays in Honour of Nigel Lowe*, Intersentia, Cambridge 2018, pp. 347–359.
On degendering the law more broadly see e.g. the 'Future of Legal Gender' Project at https://futureoflegalgender.kcl.ac.uk/ (last accessed 22.01.2025).

72 Marriage Act and other Laws (Amendment) Act 2017.

73 All Families Are Equal Act (Parentage and Related Registrations Statute Law Amendment), 2016.

LEGAL GENDERS AND IDENTITIES IN FORMER SOVIETISED EUROPEAN JURISDICTIONS

Laima VAIGĖ

1. INTRODUCTION

This chapter discusses legal gender recognition (LGR), which means the possibility to change one's sex/gender marker and name on official identity documents. 'Transgender' is understood as an umbrella term for anyone whose gender identity differs from the one typically associated with the legal sex/gender assigned to them at birth. There are no sufficient population studies, but it is estimated that only about 1% of the world's population is transgender, and increasingly more people are identifying as transgender among younger generations.[1]

Trans-affirmative healthcare is not the focus of this chapter, but a significant issue is whether any medical procedures are required prior to LGR. The ethical stance in this chapter is that LGR and trans-affirmative healthcare must be separate issues, because trans people are not identical and they might need some, none or many medical services to reaffirm their gender. It is reported that about 25% undergo some form of gender-affirming surgeries.[2]

Nine Member States of the European Union (EU) were in the past either actual members of the Soviet Union – Estonia, Latvia and Lithuania – or satellite states of the Soviet Union – Bulgaria, Czechia, Hungary, Poland, Romania, and Slovakia. Croatia and Slovenia were part on an independent communist regime, Yugoslavia and are included here for comparative purposes within the broader geopolitical context. Due to the limited scope of this chapter, the text only goes into detail concerning four of the EU Member States – Estonia, Hungary, Lithuania and Poland – with comparative tables on all 11 Member States. Each country was assigned a title that corresponds to its first letter, using a form of acrostic wordplay for mnemonic purposes. For example, Estonia is represented as 'Expert Committee', Hungary as 'Horror Zone', Lithuania as 'Late', and Poland

1 I.T. NOLAN, C.J. KUHNER and G.W. DY, 'Demographic and Temporal Trends in Transgender Identities and Gender Confirming Surgery' (2019) 8(3) *Translational Andrology and Urology* 184.
2 Ibid.

as 'Parents' Fault'. These mnemonic cues are intended for easy memorisation and to capture certain aspects of the transgender rights situation in each country and could reflect some of the challenges and conditions faced.

The key questions in this chapter are:

1. Are there procedures for LGR in the analysed states? Are these procedures provided in a legal regulation which is sufficiently stable and clear, and does not include excessive requirements? Does the law provide a possibility for LGR for trans youth and those with non-binary identities, and is LGR possible in cross-border situations?
2. If the legal regulation in the analysed jurisdictions has recently changed, what are the trends and reasons for these changes?

This chapter employs a comparative legal analysis, as well as the perspective of human rights law and private international law, where some relevant data can be found.[3] From a comparative perspective, Estonia and Hungary are analysed as being most different. Lithuania and Poland are analysed as similar, but they are only similar at first glance, and reveal interesting nuances and problems, some of which are specific to the analysed state in question, and some of which are common to the whole area.

The Baltic states were incorporated into the USSR against their will and they persistently object to being called 'Eastern' and 'post-Soviet'.[4] In Russia, the West is construed as being decadent, while the East is the stronghold of traditional values.[5] In Western contexts, the East can be seen as culturally backward, and the West as an example of civilisation. Both approaches are simplifications that contribute to the construction of a binary divide between 'us' and 'them'. This text strives to avoid contributing to this binary divide between the West and the East, and to challenge the colonial mindset that is associated with the use of the term 'post-Soviet'. Therefore, following a suggestion by legal historians in this area, the formulation 'former sovietised' was added in the title, to signify

---

3 The countries in the geopolitical area analysed in this chapter do not appear to have specific choice-of-law rules on LGR. For an analysis of emerging choice-of-law rules elsewhere in Europe, see K. Boele-Woelki, 'Humanization of Private International Law: The Search for Conflict of Law Rules for Two New Areas: *De Facto* Partnerships and Gender Identity' in J.-M. Thouvenin (ed.), *Challenges of International Law at the Time of the Centenary of The Hague Academy of International Law / Les défis du droit international au tournant du centenaire de l'Académie de droit international de La Haye*, De Gruyter Brill, Cambridge 2024, pp. 392–421.

4 D. Sagatienė, 'Challenging the Post-Soviet Label and Colonial Mindsets', *Verfassungsblog* 11 July 2023, https://verfassungsblog.de/challenging-the-post-soviet-label-and-colonial-mindsets/ (last accessed 27.02.2025).

5 'Putin Attacks West as "Satanic," Hails Russian Traditional Values', *Reuters* 30 September 2022, https://www.reuters.com/article/world/us/putin-attacks-west-as-satanic-hails-russian-traditional-values-idUSS8N2Z80G1/ (last accessed 27.02.2025).

that this region was under the direct control (or significant influence) of Soviet imperialism. It might be claimed that legal developments in these countries are still affected by Russia, and by the global anti-gender and anti-trans movement.[6]

This contribution also assesses the quality of regulation on transgender rights in the former sovietised area by comparing national rules with the human rights standards developed by the European Court of Human Rights (ECtHR). While a detailed examination of these standards is beyond the scope of this chapter, the key principles are outlined as follows. In *Christine Goodwin v the United Kingdom* (2002),[7] the Court established that some form of LGR is necessary under the Convention. Later, in *A.P., Garçon and Nicot v France* (2017),[8] the Court found that requiring medical surgery as a prerequisite for LGR was incompatible with the European Convention on Human Rights (ECHR), while the requirement of a medical diagnosis and medical examinations was considered to still be acceptable. In *X v the Former Yugoslav Republic of Macedonia* (2019),[9] the Court further clarified that states must ensure a procedure for LGR that is 'quick, transparent and accessible', a standard that was later reaffirmed, inter alia, in *R.K. v Hungary* (2023).[10] The law is considered to be of better quality where it follows these established standards.

2. PARTICULARLY DIFFERENT: ESTONIA AND HUNGARY

2.1. ESTONIA: 'EXPERT COMMITTEE'

The Estonian Vital Statistics Registration Act provides that a person may apply for a change of gender-related data in the Estonian population register.[11] The data that can be changed in the population register is the person's gender, and if relevant,[12] their name, surname and personal identification number. A person needs to submit a written application in a special form,[13] together with the

---

6 A. Graff and E. Korolczuk, *Anti-Gender Politics in the Populist Moment*, Routledge, London 2022.

7 *Christine Goodwin v the United Kingdom*, no. 28957/95, 11 July 2002.

8 *A.P., Garçon and Nicot v France*, nos. 79885/12, 52471/13 and 52596/13, 6 April 2017.

9 *X v the Former Yugoslav Republic of Macedonia*, no. 29683/16, 17 January 2019.

10 *R.K. v Hungary*, no. 54006/20, 22 June 2023.

11 Estonian Vital Statistics Registration Act, entered into force 01.01.2014, Chapter 3^1, section 49^1.

12 Provided that (sur)names reflect one's gender and the person desires to change them, in accordance with the Estonian Names Act, section 15 on 'assigning a new personal name due to a change of gender of the person in the case of adults and minors'. Names Act, entered into force 31.03.2005.

13 Estonian Minister of Regional Affairs, *Application Form to Amend the Gender Data in the Estonian Population Registry*, Regulation No. 8, 03.05.2010, amended by Regulation No. 22 of the Minister of Population, 20.06.2019.

decision of the medical assessment committee, to the local city and municipality government. The change of data in the population registry is free of charge. The person may also receive a 'sex reassignment certificate' in the form of an extract from the population register.[14]

The medical assessment committee is convened by the Ministry of Social Affairs. The expert committee's decision forms the basis for two important services: LGR and trans-specific healthcare. The latter, in the form of hormone therapy and gender-reaffirming surgery, needs to be permitted by the Ministry itself, on the basis of the committee's decision.[15] The committee considers whether certain conditions are met, such as the 'occurrence of a transsexual identity' for at least two years prior to the decision, and a psychiatrist's decision evaluating the mental health of the person concerned.[16] Hormone therapy can be started immediately after a diagnosis, and at least a year is required prior to gender-reaffirming surgery.[17]

Transgender persons who are married retain this civil status. Same-sex marriage has recently been legalised in Estonia, as of 1 January 2024. LGR is available to minors in Estonia. Regarding a change of names, section 15 of the Names Act allows a parent or a guardian to apply for a change to the names of minors.[18] Regarding a change of the gender data in the birth register, the Ministry of Social Affairs specifies that a court decision is required if the situation concerns a child.[19] Furthermore, if the gender/sex marker has been changed abroad, it is recognised in Estonia. The person in question needs to submit a document from the foreign authority to an Estonian city and municipality government.[20] The document needs to be translated or legalised, or certified by an apostille.

It is significant that trans-specific legal rules can be found at the level of parliamentary acts (since 2014),[21] rather than only in policy documents that can be changed by a newly appointed government. The ministerial regulations on Common Requirements for Medical Operations for Gender Reassignment (1999) is not a sufficiently stable legal basis. Nevertheless, it is impressive that such regulations have existed in Estonia since 1999, and that the text refers directly to the Constitution of Estonia.[22] This strengthens the argument that

---

14 Vital Statistics Registration Act, Chapter 3^1, section 49^2.

15 Minister of Social Affairs, *Common Requirements for Medical Operations for Gender Reassignment*, Ministerial Regulations, in force from 01.06.2002, passed 07.05.1999, No. 32, section 3.

16 Ibid., section 1(2).

17 Government of Estonia, 'Gender Reassignment', *eesti.ee*, https://www.eesti.ee/eraisik/en/artikkel/family/gender-reassignment (last accessed 27.02.2025).

18 Estonian Names Act, Section 15.

19 Government of Estonia, 'Gender Reassignment', *eesti.ee*, https://www.eesti.ee/eraisik/en/artikkel/family/gender-reassignment (last accessed 27.02.2025).

20 A judgment is not needed as a civil status document appears to be sufficient. Ibid.

21 The Vital Statistics Registration Act, Chapter 3^1, consisting of two sections, serves as the legal basis for a change to the sex/gender marker, and the Names Act, section 15, is the basis for a change of names.

22 Sections 26 (protection of private life) and 28 (protection of health) of the Estonian Constitution.

trans-specific healthcare is considered a justiciable constitutional right in Estonia. The requirement of a diagnosis, however, is unclear and imprecise, the language and terms being outdated. The regulations could mean that a diagnosis is only required if the person wants to have access to trans-specific healthcare, which is not the aim of all transgender individuals. In practice, however, the requirement of a diagnosis is applied even in the process of LGR.

The ministerial regulations did not establish requirements as to job title or ethical standards for the expert committee members, and the committee's mandate was broad and indeterminate in terms of time. In practice, the committee was chaired by one person, a sexologist, for over 20 years. There was some alleged inappropriate behaviour, and in 2021, the committee disbanded itself.[23] For some months, before a new committee was established, transgender people had nowhere to turn.

A simplification of the present rules was offered in 2015 and in 2020.[24] In 2015, Jevgeeni Osinovski, the former leader of the Social Democratic Party, and Margus Tsakhna, the former leader of the conservative Isamaa party, suggested rules grounded on the notion of self-determination. Self-determination or self-identification would have meant that LGR would be up to the individual to decide, rather than a decision by third parties. An individual decision on legal gender/sex markers is the most liberal idea when it comes to legal regulation, and a gold standard under international soft law.[25] In 2020, the proposed changes were less liberal and included reducing the number of required expert committee evaluations. Concerns were raised about the potential misuse of LGR and de-transitioning.

Some relevant legal amendments were adopted in 2025.[26] The most relevant is the provision of a legal ground for the adoption of a new regulation on gender incongruency to be included in the Estonian Health Services Organisation Act.[27] It applies to trans-affirmative healthcare, but the amendment is also significant for LGR, because it means that the ministerial regulations on Common Requirements for Medical Operations for Gender Reassignment will cease to apply as of 1 September 2025. By that time, new rules must be adopted.

---

23 A. Kuusik, 'Läbipaismatu süsteem ja hinnanguid andvad spetsialistid – ehk kuidas kohtleb riik trans inimesi?', *Feministeerium* 5 July 2021, https://feministeerium.ee/labipaistmatu-susteem-ja-hinnanguid-andvad-spetsialistid-ehk-kuidas-kohtleb-riik-trans-inimesi/ (last accessed 12.01.2025).

24 H. Wright (ed.), 'New draft regulation would make it easier to change gender', *ERR News* 16 September 2020, https://news.err.ee/1136150/new-draft-regulation-would-make-it-easier-to-change-gender (last accessed 12.02.2025).

25 CoE Resolution 2048 (2015), Report of the Independent Expert on protection against violence and discrimination based on sexual orientation and gender identity, Victor Madrigal-Borloz, A/HRC/47/27, UN General Assembly, 03.06.2021.

26 Public Health Act, RT I, 02.01.2025, to enter into force 01.09.2025.

27 Ibid., section 61, part 3, specifying the inclusion of a new paragraph in the Health Services Organisation Act, in subsection 56 (1), point 12.

Estonia's example is not a perfect solution. However, it stands out in contrast to other states in this region, because transgender people's rights have a legal basis in parliamentary acts, which shows both the legitimacy and a certain quality of the law. There is a long history of providing services (at least since 1999), despite some hiccups. These rights are framed as being grounded in the Estonian Constitution, and politicians on both sides of the political spectrum discuss self-determination, which is the most liberal regulation on LGR. The other two EU Member States that are at a similar level of development are Slovenia and Croatia. They are not analysed in more detail here, but Table 1 below provides some details on the legal frameworks in these two states. The legal regulations in Croatia and Slovenia differ, but the interpretation within their respective legal and cultural contexts has resulted in an outcome that is similar to the legal framework in Estonia. From the perspective of European human rights standards, this cluster of countries is considered to be an example of 'better' laws in this area.

Table 1. Legal Gender Recognition in Former Socialist EU Member States: Cluster 1 (Better-Quality Law)

Country	Legal basis (parliamentary act, policy and/or case law)	Contents of the law
Croatia	Law on Civil Registers[28] Ordinance on the collection of medical documents and establishing conditions for a change of gender and life into another gender identity[29] Decision of the Constitutional Court, 18 March 2014	LGR possible, no medical procedures required. In practice, a diagnosis appears to be required.[30] The Constitutional Court of Croatia ruled in 2014 that changing the sex marker on a birth certificate should be possible without surgery.[31]
Estonia	Vital Statistics Registration Act Names Act Ministerial Regulations on Common Requirements for Medical Operations for Gender Reassignment (in force until 9 September 2025)	LGR possible, no medical interventions required. Diagnosis currently required. May apply separately for a change of names and a change of gender data. New rules must soon be adopted

(continued)

28 Law on Civil Registers (Zakon o državnim maticama), Narodne novine br. 96/93., 76/13., 98/19., 133/22.

29 Ordinance on the collection of medical documents and establishing conditions for a change of gender and life into another gender identity (Pravilnik o načinu prikupljanja medicinske dokumentacije te utvrđivanju uvjeta i pretpostavki za promjenu spola ili o životu u drugom rodnom identitetu), Narodne novine br. 132/2014.

30 Data on Croatia was inconsistent. The Croatian legal regulation requires an *opinion* by a psychiatrist, endocrinologist, clinical psychologist and the Institute for Social Work. After consulting Helena Majer and Sandra Winkler (University of Rijeka, Croatia), it appears that the requirement of a diagnosis is nevertheless implicit.

31 Constitutional Court of the Republic of Croatia UIIIB-3173/2012 (Odluka Ustavnog suda Republike Hrvatske U-IIIB-3173/2012), Narodne novine br. 46/14.

Table 1 *(Continued)*

Country	Legal basis (parliamentary act, policy and/or case law)	Contents of the law
Slovenia	Civil Registry Act[32] Regulations for the Enforcement of the Civil Registry Act[33] Personal Name Act[34]	LGR possible, no surgery required, but the opinion of a medical institution or a doctor is required, stating that the gender has been changed.[35]

2.2. HUNGARY: 'HORROR ZONE'

Until a few years ago, transgender people could access LGR in Hungary. In practice, this possibility had existed in Hungary since 1982, and no requirement of surgery was systematically applied.[36] The right to change one's name relied on the constitutional case law.[37] In 2016, the unregulated practice of LGR was suspended and then regulated in a government decree.[38] However, the regulation lacked clarity and accessibility, and since 2018 LGR has again been suspended, this time on the pretext of the EU rules on data protection (GDPR). In 2020, on the International Day for Trans Visibility, a new package of amendments was introduced.[39] At that time, due to the COVID-19 pandemic, the Prime Minister was granted the authority to rule by decree, and this broad discretion remains until today (in early 2025); however, the anti-trans legislative package was passed by Parliament, granting it a higher degree of legitimacy.

In the 2020 legislative amendments, the binary classification of birth sex (*születési nem*) was formally codified, resulting in the elimination of all legal avenues for gender recognition. The legislative package inter alia amended the

32 Civil Registry Act (Zakon o matičnem registru), ZAKO3354, Article 4(11) provides for the registration of a change of gender.

33 Regulations for the Enforcement of the Civil Registry Act, adopted by the Ministry of Internal Affairs (Pravilnika o izvrševanju zakona o matičnem registru), PRAV5572, Article 37. The procedure for LGR requires a certificate from a medical institution or a physician, which has to provide that the person in question has changed their gender.

34 Personal Name Act of 2006 (Zakon o osebnem imenu), ZOI-1, Article 18. This is not a trans-specific article.

35 In practice, it appears to be a quick administrative procedure, and it is also available to minors. 'Slovenia: Legal Gender Recognition', *Equaldex*, https://www.equaldex.com/log/5794 (last accessed 12.02.2025).

36 'LGBT Rights in Hungary', *Equaldex*, https://www.equaldex.com/region/hungary (last accessed 24.02.2025).

37 Constitutional Court decision 58/2001 (XII. 7.) AB, which held that changing one's name is a right guaranteed under the Fundamental Law of Hungary.

38 Government Decree on the detailed rules for carrying out the duties of registration, 429/2017 (XII. 20.).

39 Hungarian Law of 31.03.2020, in particular amending Article 33 of the Act on the Registration Procedure.

Hungarian Act on the Civil Registration Procedure. After the amendments, it now provides that the register of births has to contain the 'birth sex' of the person concerned, and section 69/B(3) specifies that the sex assigned at birth cannot be changed.[40] Considering that daily life in Hungary often requires identification documents to be shown, the exposure of transgender persons is inevitable. Transgender people risk facing difficulties in proving their identities in banks or on public transport, difficulties in finding work, obstacles in everyday life, and the risk of harassment and hate crimes. That is why the words 'state transphobia' and even a 'horror zone' are suitable to describe this situation: a small minority of people are being legally harassed by the government.

In the case of *R.K. v Hungary*, the ECtHR ruled that Hungary had violated Article 8 ECHR (the right to private life) by failing to establish a 'quick, transparent, and accessible procedure' for LGR, at the material time as was relevant for the applicant (2018–2020).[41] Hungary continues to violate the rights of transgender individuals. Nevertheless, at least 70 transgender persons from Hungary have resorted to the courts[42] and, after exhausting domestic remedies, the flow of applications will inevitably reach the ECtHR.

At the EU level, Hungary has been[43] currently facing proceedings at the Court of Justice of the European Union (CJEU), including some relevant to this chapter. For instance, Case C-769/22 addresses issues related to the censoring of information on homosexual and transgender identities, under the pretext of protecting children's rights.[44] This case relates to a broader anti-LGBTQ rights legislative package introduced in Hungary in 2021 (the so-called 'Anti-LGBTQ law'). It is the first time that the Commission has directly relied on Article 2 of the Treaty on European Union, which protects democracy, the rule of law and human rights as the founding values of the EU.[45] The forthcoming decision will be adopted by all judges of the CJEU (the so-called full Court).

---

[40] Act No. I of 2010 on the civil registration procedure, section 69/B(1)b)be. The Act is available in English at https://njt.hu/jogszabaly/en/2010-1-00-00 (last accessed 26.05.2025).

[41] *R.K. v Hungary* (ECtHR, 22 June 2023) App no 54006/20.

[42] 'More Than 60 Transgender Hungarians Have Submitted Applications to the European Court of Human Rights', *Háttér Society* 15 February 2024, https://en.hatter.hu/news/more-than-60-transgender-hungarians-have-submitted-applications-to-the-european-court-of-human (last accessed 25.02.2025).

[43] Case C-4/23, *Mirin*, ECLI:EU:C:2024:845, as discussed further in part 4 of this text. Case C-247/23, *Deldits*, ECLI:EU:C:2025:172. The case concerned General Data Protection Regulation (GDPR), which was interpreted as 'requiring a national authority responsible for keeping a public register to rectify the personal data relating to the gender identity of a natural person where those data are inaccurate'.

[44] Case C-769/22, *European Commission v Hungary*. OJ C 54, 13.2.2023. Also see C-769/22, AG Ćapeta, Opinion, 5 June 2025, ECLI:EU:C:2025:408. In the Opinion, AG recommends to find Hungary has failed to fulfil its obligations under EU law.

[45] For a discussion on this pending case, see M. Bonelli and M. Claes, 'Crossing the Rubicon? The Commission's use of Article 2 TEU in the infringement action on LGBTIQ+ rights in Hungary', (2023) 30(1) *Maastricht Journal of European and Comparative Law* 3.

The example of Hungary is striking, because it demonstrates a rapid retrogression. The legislative changes have also been implemented with a certain degree of legitimacy: the act was passed by Parliament, and the Hungarian Constitutional Court subsequently confirmed its constitutionality.[46] Meanwhile, only a few years ago (in 2018), the Hungarian Constitutional Court held that: 'the State – in accordance with its obligation of protection – must develop a regulation that acknowledges gender reassignment'.[47] At that time, the Court relied on the fact that it was possible to have access to LGR in Hungary. When the legislation eliminating the possibility of LGR was passed in 2020, the initial focus of the Constitutional Court was on whether the said provision may apply retroactively. A procedural rule provided that the amended provisions were to apply to proceedings instituted before the entry into force of the amendments.[48] That procedural rule on retroactive application was subsequently found to be unconstitutional.[49] However, when the focus became the substance of the amendments adopted, the Constitutional Court confirmed, in early 2023, that the concept of birth sex is constitutional and its immutability does not infringe human dignity nor does it constitute a disproportionate restriction on the protection of private life.[50]

Another EU Member State that has recently experienced a retrogression is Bulgaria (see Table 2). In practice, Slovakia also seems to be following a similar path, which is discussed further in section 4 below.

Table 2. Legal Gender Recognition in Former Sovietised EU Member States: Cluster 2 (State Transphobia)

Country	Legal basis (parliamentary act, policy and/or case law)	Contents of the law
Bulgaria	Civil Registration Act[51] Interpretative Decision No. 2/2000 of the Supreme Court, 20 February 2023[52] Interpretative Decision of the Constitutional Court, 26 October 2021[53]	LGR impossible. The concept of sex/gender in Bulgaria is determined at birth and can only have a binary biological meaning.

(continued)

46 Constitutional Court of Hungary, No. 3058/2023 (II. 16.).
47 Constitutional Court of Hungary, No. 6/2018. (VI. 27.) §48.
48 Act No. I of 2010, on the Civil Registration Procedure, section 101/A(2). See above n. 40 for a link to an English translation.
49 Constitutional Court of Hungary, No. 11/2021 (IV. 7.).
50 Constitutional Court of Hungary, No. 3058/2023 (II. 16.).
51 Civil Registration Act, Prom. SG. 67/27 July 1999, with amendments. Article 76(5) states that a change of sex cannot be undertaken administratively.
52 Supreme Court of Cassation of Bulgaria, Interpretative Decision No. 2/2020, 20.02.2023.
53 Constitutional Court of Bulgaria, 26.10.2021, in Constitutional Case No. 6/2021, Decision No. 15 (published in State Gazette No. 93, 09.11.2021), providing a binding interpretation of the concept of sex.

Table 2 *(Continued)*

Country	Legal basis (parliamentary act, policy and/or case law)	Contents of the law
Hungary	Act on the Civil Registration Procedure	LGR illegal.
	Ruling of the Constitutional Court of Hungary of 2 February 2023	Immutability of 'birth sex' since 2020, confirmed by the Constitutional Court in 2023.

3. SIMILAR YET DIFFERENT: LITHUANIA AND POLAND

3.1. LITHUANIA: 'LATE'

The Lithuanian legal regulation initially seemed promising. The Civil Code, adopted in 2000, provided for the right to 'gender reassignment'.[54] This is admittedly an outdated term, but to entrench a right to LGR via a parliamentary act was quite progressive in 2000. The relevant provision in the Civil Code came into force in 2003, but all of the details relating to LGR and trans-affirmative care were supposed to be specified in a separate parliamentary act. That parliamentary act was not adopted, and in the case of *L. v Lithuania* (2007) the ECtHR found a violation of the Convention. The Court specifically determined that it 'would be satisfied by the enactment of the subsidiary legislation at issue in the present case within three months of the present judgment'.[55] The said law was not enacted within this three-month period, and neither has it been passed to date (as of early 2025).

In practice, judicial practice has been compensating for this legislative omission. Since 2007, transgender individuals can apply for compensation for their trans-affirmative care in the courts, and also for LGR. That has required extensive efforts by applicants. Surgery prior to LGR had been a requirement in Lithuanian judicial practice up until 2017.[56] Hormones could only be obtained on the black market (prior to 2022), and applicants had to travel abroad to undergo gender-affirmative medical procedures. Prior to addressing the court regarding LGR in Lithuania, applicants also have to ensure that they were not married and they then had to sue the civil status registry office in order to have access to LGR.[57]

---

54 Civil Code of Lithuania, 18.07.2000, No. VIII-1864, Article 2.27.

55 *L. v Lithuania*, no. 27527/03, 11 September, §74.

56 Vilnius District Court, 02.05.2017, Civil Case No. E2YT-5326-987/2017.

57 Since *L. v Lithuania*, gender affirmative care obtained abroad has to be compensated by the Government.

In 2021 and 2022, two significant ministerial orders were adopted, which clarified the procedure for a legal change of names[58] and the procedure on the provision of gender-affirmative healthcare.[59] If a person has obtained an F64.0 diagnosis (transsexualism) under the International Classification of Diseases (ICD-10), which is currently applicable in Lithuania, it is relatively easy to change one's name and surname by simply attaching the diagnosis to an online application. Furthermore, some opportunities to receive trans-affirmative care in Lithuania were provided. However, these two orders did not provide for any changes regarding LGR. That means that a person still needs to address the court in order to change their legal gender.

The procedure is as follows. The person in question first needs to apply to the civil registry office and then to receive a decision in the negative, which is then appealed before a court. According to the only trans-specific civil society organisation in Lithuania, there was only one lawyer who worked on such cases in 2024.[60] There is very little information on what actually occurs before the courts, but it appears that the procedure is individualised. The lawyer who practises in this field has reported that the Lithuanian courts no longer require surgery, precisely as a result of the case law from the ECtHR.[61] A diagnosis of transsexualism is however required. Some judges allow minors to change their legal gender, although Article 2.27 of the Civil Code provides that 'gender reassignment' shall only be available to adults. There are only two binary genders in Lithuania, male and female, so non-binary identities are not recognised. If the applicant is married, they first need to apply for a divorce because Lithuania does not allow for same-sex marriage or registered partnerships.

The court procedure is neither expeditious, transparent nor accessible. It is also an issue that has class implications, because not everyone can afford the necessary legal fees. Such fees are not compensated. Judges might also have very different approaches to transgender rights. According to the Fundamental Rights Agency of the EU, Lithuania is among those states with the highest incidents of discrimination (Bulgaria and Slovakia are also on a similar level) due to sexual orientation and gender identity.[62] It can be presumed that this also translates into

---

58 Amendment of the Order of the Minister of Justice of Lithuania No. 1R-333 of 28.12.2016 On the Approval of the Rules for Changing a Person's Name and Surname, TAR, 31.12.2021, No. 27936.

59 Order of the Minister of Health of Lithuania on the Approval of the Procedure for the Diagnosis and Treatment of Gender Identity Disorder (Transsexualism), TAR, 05.08.2022, No. 16729.

60 'Dažniausiai užduodami klausimai', *TransAutonomija*, https://transautonomija.lt/dazniausiai-uzduodami-klausimai/ (last accessed 27.02.2025).

61 'Transgender People in Lithuania: The Daily Challenge of Being Yourself', at the conference *LGBTQ+ and Mental Health: What is Important to Know for Specialists?*, organised by the Lithuanian psychologists' union, Vilnius University, Vilnius, 21.10.2022. Full discussion is also available online.

62 European Union Agency for Fundamental Rights (FRA), *LGBTIQ Equality in the EU: Challenges and Achievements*, Publications Office of the European Union, Luxembourg 2024,

diverse experiences before the courts. The judicial practice of abandoning the requirement of surgery has also not been formally established by the Supreme Court, which would provide a greater incentive for judges to adopt this stance, rather than relying on a flexible and individualised approach, which opens the door to intrusive questions and humiliating treatment.

3.2. POLAND: 'PARENTS' FAULT' (UNTIL 2025)

The Polish example is similar to Lithuania, due to the fact that court proceedings are necessary to have access to LGR,[63] which again highlights class inequalities, i.e. LGR is more accessible to those with a higher education and sufficient financial resources. At this point in time, the Polish legislation does not contain trans-specific *rights*, in contrast to the Lithuanian Civil Code. However, there is rich case law from the Supreme Court of Poland.

As early as 1978, the Supreme Court of Poland held that the gender on a birth certificate could be corrected, even though the applicant had not undergone surgical intervention.[64] The decisive role of the surgical criterion was abandoned when Poland was still a satellite state of the USSR. Later, under the new Polish legislation that was not trans-specific,[65] the Supreme Court confirmed (in 1991)[66] that there was the possibility to access LGR, and it later explained (in 1995) that the correct defendants in these contentious proceedings were the applicant's parents.[67]

In March 2025, the Polish Supreme Court issued another important decision.[68] The case was brought by Zbigniew Ziobro, the former Prosecutor General, who raised the legal question of whether proceedings for LGR should take the form of a joint application supported by the applicant's parents, spouse and children (where relevant). Although the purpose of the reference was to increase the procedural burden, the Court held that gender recognition proceedings should

https://fra.europa.eu/sites/default/files/fra_uploads/fra-2024-lgbtiq-equality_en.pdf (last accessed 31.01.2025).

63 For an excellent legal analysis of the Polish situation in 2020, see M. Wojewoda, 'Gender Modification in Poland: A Case Law Phenomenon in a Civil Law Country' in I.C. Jaramillo and L.Carlson (eds), *Trans Rights and Wrongs, A Comparative Study of Legal Reform Concerning Trans Persons*, Springer, Cham 2021, pp. 97–117.

64 Supreme Court of Poland, 25.02.1978, III CZP 100/77. The case concerned an intersex person, so it was still considered an exceptional case.

65 Civil Code of Poland, Article 23; Code of Civil Procedure, Article 189.

66 Supreme Court of Poland, 22.03.1991, Case No. III CRN 28/91.

67 Supreme Court of Poland, 22.09.1995, Case No. III CZP 118/95.Also confirmed by the Supreme Court of Poland, 10.01.2019, Case No. II CSK 371/18. The procedural legal basis for litigation was Article 189 of the Civil Procedure Code, as mentioned above, and it requires a defendant.

68 Supreme Court of Poland, 04.03.2025, Case No. III CZP 6/24.

be conducted as non-contentious proceedings.[69] As a result, only the applicant can apply for the correction of their gender in the civil register. In addition to the applicant, only the applicant's spouse may participate in the proceedings as an interested party.

The diagnosis procedure mostly takes place privately and involves four to six visits to a psychologist, up to three meetings with a sexologist, and a pause in medical testing.[70] When the person in question receives the diagnosis, an application to the courts can then be made, which until very recently involved suing the parents of the applicant for assigning an incorrect sex at birth. Strong opposition by the parents could prolong the process by several years. Judges in Poland have very different approaches and attitudes to transgender rights. There is some data on courts requesting the applicants to undergo a 'real life test' of two years.[71] Former applicants and their parents have reported that some judges could ask intrusive questions, for instance about the transgender person's sexual and bodily experiences, and use incorrect pronouns.[72] It has also been reported that hormonal treatment is usually needed, and partial surgeries can be helpful in convincing the judges.[73]

Private international law aspects were also addressed in the case law. In one case, a Polish citizen had undergone LGR in Canada and subsequently applied for this to be recognised in Polish documents.[74] However, the public prosecutor considered that the transcription of gender into Polish identity documents would violate the *ordre public* of Poland. The Supreme Administrative Court of Poland ruled in 2021 that LGR abroad must be recognised in official documents issued by the Polish state, and such transcription does not violate the *ordre public* of Poland.

In 2015, the Polish Parliament adopted the Gender Accordance Act, which would have increased the quality and accessibility of the legal regulation.[75] A key

---

69 By analogous application of Article 36 of the Polish Law on Civil Status Records of 28 November 2014, Dz. U. of 2020, which applies to *correction* of civil status documents.

70 'How to Start Medical Transition in Poland?', *Tranzycja.pl*, https://tranzycja.pl (last accessed 27.02.2025).

71 'LGBT Rights in Poland', *Equaldex*, https://www.equaldex.com/region/poland (last accessed 27.02.2025).

72 A. Gmiterek-Zabłocka, 'To change your official gender in Poland, you have to sue your parents, causing trauma for trans people', *Notes from Poland* 31 March 2023, https://notesfrompoland.com/2023/03/31/to-change-your-official-gender-in-poland-you-have-to-sue-your-parents-causing-trauma-for-trans-people/ (last accessed 27.02.2025).

73 M. WOJEWODA, 'Gender Modification in Poland: A Case Law Phenomenon in a Civil Law Country' in Isabel C Jaramillo and Laura Carlson (eds), *Trans Rights and Wrongs, A Comparative Study of Legal Reform Concerning Trans Persons*, Springer, Cham 2021, p. 109.

74 Supreme Administrative Court of Poland, 06.12.2020, Case No. II OSK 3320/20.

75 Gender Accordance Act, adopted by the Polish Parliament on 23.07.2015 (vetoed on 02.10.2015), available at: https://orka.sejm.gov.pl/proc7.nsf/ustawy/1469_u.htm (last accessed 27.02.2025). The Act is sometimes translated as Sex Reconciliation Act.

aspect was that LGR would not require medical interventions, but a diagnosis was nevertheless necessary. The Act was vetoed by President Andrzej Duda, and the newly formed Parliament, led by right-wing populists, did not override this veto. In 2024, the populists lost their grip on the Polish Parliament and it has been speculated that discussions on LGR will be reopened in Parliament after President Andrzej Duda finishes his term in June 2025.[76] Said hopes were crushed with Karol Nawrocki winning the presidential election in 2025, who during his presidential campaign, promised to fight any progress of LGBTQ rights.

Table 3. Legal Gender Recognition in the Former Sovietised EU Member States: Cluster 3 (Court-Based Procedure)

Country	Legal basis (parliamentary act, policy and/or case law)	Contents of the law
Lithuania	Order of the Healthcare Ministry of 2022 Order of the Justice Ministry of 2021 Decision of the Vilnius District Court of 2 April 2017	LGR possible, but requires a diagnosis, court proceedings, and if the person is married, a divorce. Two separate rules on trans-specific care and a change of names. It is still necessary to resort to the courts regarding a change of sex/gender.
Poland	Law on the change of name and surname, 17 October 2008 Polish Civil Code and Civil Procedure Code Case law of the Supreme Court	LGR possible, but requires a diagnosis. Available to minors. Two separate procedures for a name change and a gender marker change. It is still necessary to resort to the courts regarding a change of gender marker, but the procedure is non-contentious.

4. DEMAND FOR MEDICAL PROCEDURES: AGAINST HUMAN DIGNITY AND PHYSICAL INTEGRITY

The requirement of medical procedures prior to LGR is becoming a thing of the past throughout Europe. This demand is intrusive, unreasonable and humiliating, because there are many transgender people who do not need such procedures. Even those who need trans-affirmative care should not be subjected to the requirement of having to undergo medical procedures prior to LGR. As stated in the Yogyakarta Principles on the Application of International Human Rights Law in Relation to Sexual Orientation and Gender Identity (2017):

[76] D. Tilles, 'Top Court Rules That Sex Change Abroad Must Be Recognised in Polish Documents', *Notes from Poland* 13 January 2021, https://notesfrompoland.com/2021/01/13/top-court-rules-that-sex-change-abroad-must-be-recognised-in-polish-documents/ (last accessed 27.02.2025).

> No one shall be forced to undergo medical procedures, including sex reassignment surgery, sterilization or hormonal therapy, as a requirement for legal recognition of their gender identity.[77]

The Yogyakarta Principles are not binding but are a soft-law product of global cooperation between experts in issues of sexual orientation and gender identity. This key notion – the legal recognition of one's gender should be separate from medical procedures – is reflected in various soft-law documents at the global and European level.[78] More importantly, it is entrenched in the case law of the European supranational courts, which is legally binding.

Some of the former sovietised EU Member State have requirements for body modification prior to LGR, or have had them until very recently, and it is unclear whether they still apply. Considering that the ECtHR has consistently clarified[79] that this requirement violates the ECHR, national authorities should refrain from requiring medical procedures prior to LGR. However, various comparative reports[80] give the impression that vague or non-existent national legal rules can still be interpreted to the detriment of transgender persons.

In Czechia, LGR is governed by the Act on Registers, Names and Surnames[81] and the Civil Code.[82] The Constitutional Court has ruled against mandatory invasive surgery, including sterilisation, with this decision set to take effect in July 2025.[83] In Latvia, LGR is regulated by the Law on the Registration of Civil Status Acts, along with government regulations from 2013[84] and a Supreme Court decision from 2008.[85] LGR is possible but requires proof of a 'change of sex'. The gender/sex entry in the register can be supplemented in cases where the said 'change' has occurred.[86] Name changes are also allowed for individuals who

---

77 Yogyakarta Principles plus 10 (YP +10), extract from Principle 3. The YP were initially drafted in 2006, and then revised in 2017. The full text of the Yogyakarta Principles and the Yogyakarta Principles plus 10 are available at: www.yogyakartaprinciples.org.

78 For instance, the CoE Parliamentary Assembly Resolution No. 1728 (2010) of 29 April 2010 and No. 2048 (2015) of 2 April 2015.

79 See above n. 8, and also *S.V. v Italy*, no. 55216/08 11 October 2018, and *X and Y v Romania*, no. 2145/16, 19 January 2021. Medicalisation of transgender identities was also found to be incompatible with EU law, in case C-247/23, *Deldits*, ECLI:EU:C:2025:172.

80 Data can be found in Z. Chiam, S. Duffy, M. González Gil, L. Goodwin and N.T. Mpemba Patel, *Trans Legal Mapping Report 2019: Recognition before the law*, ILGA World, Geneva 2020. Also, for more recent and more concise information, see 'Changing Gender', *Equaldex*, https://www.equaldex.com/issue/changing-gender (last accessed 27.02.2025).

81 Act No. 301/2000 on Registries, Given Names and Surnames and amending certain acts, sections 17a and 72.

82 Civil Code of Czechia (2014), Act No. 89/2012 Coll., §29.

83 Constitutional Court of Czechia, 09.01.2024, Decision Pl. ÚS 52/23.

84 Regulations of the Cabinet of Ministers of Latvia on Civil Status Registers, No. 761 of 03.09.2013.

85 Supreme Court of Latvia, Senate Administrative Case Department, 14.01.2008, Case No. A42229505 SKA-5/2008.

86 Section 37 of the Law on the Registration of Civil Status Acts of Latvia, 2012/197.1, Latvijas Vēstnesis No. 205 (4191).

have undergone 'a complete or partial change of sex'.[87] The Supreme Court ruled in 2008 that partial surgery may be sufficient,[88] and later attempts to introduce sterilisation requirements were unsuccessful. It is unclear whether a diagnosis is sufficient to prove a 'change of sex', and Latvia was difficult to classify, because the regulation resembles the Slovenian regulation, but in practice, it appears to be interpreted in a stricter manner.[89] The legal and political culture in Slovenia appears to be more positive towards both sexual orientation and gender identity issues, which would explain the differences in practice.

In Romania, LGR is allowed,[90] but requires a court decision, and the courts tend to require invasive medical procedures. In *X and Y v Romania*, this requirement was found to be in violation of the European Convention.[91] Furthermore, in 2024 the ECJ ruled in a key case concerning the freedom of movement and private international law aspects of LGR.[92] A Romanian transgender man living in the UK, here dealt with as a EU Member State, changed his legal gender by means of a declaration there, and his gender/sex marker was denied recognition in Romania. The ECJ found this to be a restriction on free movement, ruling that Articles 20 and 21(1) TFEU prevent Romania from requiring court proceedings. These two cases, *X and Y v Romania* and *Mirin*, are very important for Romania, but also for all Council of Europe and EU Member States. It is not clear how responsive the Romanian courts will be towards this case law, however, because LGR still mostly takes place behind closed doors and the courts have broad discretion where clear rules are lacking.

In Slovakia, changing one's name and gender/sex marker has been possible,[93] and in October 2022, the Supreme Administrative Court overturned the requirement for sterilisation,[94] which had not been specified in any regulations, but was applied in practice. However, the court also ruled that Slovak law does not specify what documents are required or who can issue them. In April 2022, the Ministry of Health published standards of care for trans people, which were

87 Regulations of the Cabinet of Ministers of Latvia on Civil Status Registers, No. 761, section 137.3.

88 Supreme Court of Latvia, Senate Administrative Case Department, 14.01.2008, Case No. A42229505 SKA-5/2008.

89 'Right to Change Legal Gender in Latvia', *Equaldex*, https://www.equaldex.com/log/11354 (last accessed 18.02.2025).

90 Law No. 119/1996 on Civil Status Documents, Article 43.i, which provides that a change of sex can be recorded after a final judicial decision.

91 *X and Y v Romania*, no. 2145/16, 19 January 2021.

92 Case C-4/23, *Mirin*, ECLI:EU:C:2024:845.

93 Act No. 300/1993 on Name and Surname, as amended; Act No. 301/1995 on Personal Identification Numbers.

94 Supreme Administrative Court of Slovakia, decision of 19.10.2022, overturning the decision of the Regional Court of Banská Bystrica. Najvyšší súd Slovenskej republiky, 'Krajský súd v Banskej Bystrici musí opätovne rozhodnúť vo veci, ktorá sa týka zmeny pohlavia', 6 February 2024, https://www.nssud.sk/rozhodnutie-krajsky-sud-v-banskej-bystrici-musi-opatovne-rozhodnut-vo-veci-ktora-sa-tyka-zmeny-pohlavia/ (last accessed 27.02.2025).

revoked within a month due to political pressure; they were then readopted in March 2023, only to subsequently be revoked once again in November 2023. The said ministerial guidelines did not require medical procedures but only a medical diagnosis for access to LGR. After the guidelines were revoked in late 2023, medical interventions are reported as being necessary.[95] Moreover, it can *de facto* be very difficult to access LGR and trans-affirmative care, since it was clarified that this area is unregulated.[96] The legislature is also in the process of debating a law that would ban transgender identities. That would leave Slovakia in the same cluster as Hungary and Bulgaria (state transphobia).[97]

5. ALL JURISDICTIONS: TENDENCIES AND KEY REASONS FOR CHANGES

The entire region has a problem with regulating transgender human rights in parliamentary acts, with some notable exceptions, as discussed in this chapter.[98] That means that politically sensitive human rights[99] are often left to the executive and/or judicial branches. The regulation of human rights by the executive branch is less predictable and has less legitimacy. Rules in ministerial orders are of less quality than parliamentary acts, because there are no rigorous preparatory works. A ministerial order can be recalled very quickly, which the data discussed in this chapter exemplifies. A rule on the level of a parliamentary act is a more reliable legal ground because it is not as easy to change as a ministerial order. It must pass the test of political opposition and, hence, has greater legitimacy. Arguably, it also better corresponds to the requirements of ECtHR practice, considering that all restrictions of human rights should be prescribed *by law*, and law requires the quality of precision and stability.

Judicial practice can be similar in its effect to legislation, but if the courts operate under no clear rules, and the decisions are individualised, human rights

---

95 S. Macor Otajovicova, 'Slovakia: Surgery Once Again a Condition for Gender Change', *Deutsche Welle* 12 January 2024, https://www.dw.com/en/slovakia-surgery-once-again-a-condition-for-gender-change/a-67961893 (last accessed 27.02.2025).

96 ILGA-Europe, 'Annual Review of the Human Rights Situation of Lesbian, Gay, Bisexual, Trans, and Intersex People in Slovakia', February 2024, https://www.ilga-europe.org/files/uploads/2024/02/2024_slovakia.pdf (last accessed 27.02.2025).

97 The law has passed through its first reading but has not yet been adopted. J. Rankin, 'Slovakia Moves to Block Legal Recognition of Trans People', *The Guardian* 17 May 2023, https://www.theguardian.com/world/2023/may/17/slovakia-block-legal-recognition-trans-people-lgbtq (last accessed 27.02.2025).

98 Estonia, Lithuania and Hungary are exceptions, because they regulate LGR in parliamentary acts, although the contents of these acts are very different.

99 This chapter analyses transgender rights, but other types of politically sensitive rights, for instance the right to abortion, also appear to be regulated in executive orders in this region, rather than parliamentary acts.

are not sufficiently protected. Some judges may require real-life tests, medical interventions and passing as a woman/man for a certain period of time. Such requirements are outdated and humiliating. The real-life test, for instance, has been abandoned in most recent standards of care.[100] Court decisions that deal with LGR are informed by the culture of the particular legal system. In some geopolitical contexts, the politics of disgust and disapproval is promoted by the government, and that may potentially also affect the courts. The practice of litigating against one's parents or the state (represented by the civil registry) can also be a psychologically difficult experience. Altogether, the requirement of a court decision has a chilling effect on LGR.

There are multiple reasons for the changes in the analysed region, and they are likely to be similar in other regions. First, certain diagnoses are becoming obsolete. In 2019, the World Health Organization called for the end of the categorisation of trans-related conditions as mental and behavioural disorders. After the review of the International Classification of Diseases (ICD-11) by the World Health Assembly, trans-related categories have now been added to a new chapter on 'conditions related to sexual health'. The ICD-11 uses the term 'gender incongruence'. The said condition is 'characterised by a marked and persistent incongruence between an individual's experienced gender and the assigned sex'.[101] Some countries tend to use the Diagnostic and Statistical Manual of Mental Disorders (DSM) diagnostics system in this area. The DSM abandoned 'gender identity disorder' and has used the term 'gender dysphoria' since 2013.[102]

In the countries analysed in this chapter, the diagnosis of either 'transsexualism' or 'gender dysphoria' is still required, even in the more progressive and newer regulations. In the future, the older terminology needs to be definitively abandoned, because changes in the diagnostic systems (DSM and ICD) are significant for all countries that apply them. Gradually, states might also consider the idea of self-identification, which means that no diagnoses of 'gender incongruence' or 'gender dysphoria' would be necessary if the only aim is LGR.

Another reason for these changes is the engagement of the different states with the idea of substantive gender equality. Historically, women and men have been assigned certain roles in society and within the family. The diversification of gender roles is relatively new. Transgender identity is seen as a direct threat to the imagined tradition of gender complementarity, which has been popularised in some of the countries analysed.

---

100 Standards of Care for the Health of Transgender and Gender Diverse People, Version 8, 2022.

101 World Health Organization, 'Gender Incongruence and Transgender Health in the ICD', https://www.who.int/standards/classifications/frequently-asked-questions/gender-incongruence-and-transgender-health-in-the-icd (last accessed 16.01.2025).

102 The latest (fifth) edition was adopted by the American Psychiatry Association in 2022 (DSM-5-TR).

Furthermore, the state legislatures, executives or courts engage with the changing standards of European human rights law. As described in the introduction to this text, in the landmark decision in *Christine Goodwin v the United Kingdom*, the ECtHR held that some procedure allowing for LGR must be provided. The Court subsequently clarified that the LGR procedure should be 'quick, transparent and accessible'. It could be claimed that the developments under the ECHR have made an impact in the analysed jurisdictions. For instance, in 2017 the Court held that medical requirements, such as sterilisation, surgery or hormonal treatment, are not in compliance with the Convention.[103] Subsequently, the requirement of medical procedures was also abandoned in the case law of the Lithuanian courts.

Finally, some recent negative changes can be claimed to correspond to the trend of autocratisation.[104] On his first day in the White House (20 January 2025), US President Donald Trump signed an executive order providing that the sex/gender of an individual cannot be changed. The executive branch is entrusted 'to promote this reality' throughout the USA.[105] Exactly the same vision of 'reality' has been promoted in Russia since 2023,[106] as well as in two formerly sovietised states, Hungary and Bulgaria, as discussed in this chapter.

All of the states mentioned above (Russia, the USA, Hungary and Bulgaria) have some ongoing problems with the rule of law. There are several infringement procedures that are pending against Hungary, due to ruling by executive decrees, 'foreign interference' law that resembles that in Russia, and the legislative package on the suppression of LGBTQ rights. The instrumentalisation of minority groups to consolidate political support is a longstanding tactic employed by demagogues since the earliest forms of democratic governance.

6. CONCLUSIONS

The legal frameworks of former sovietised states exhibit a general trend towards providing for LGR, whether through statutory law, executive orders or judicial decisions. A notable early precedent dates back to 1978, when the Supreme Court of Poland partially lifted the surgical requirement for LGR. Many states in this region had gradually moved away from requiring medical intervention

103 *A.P., Garçon and Nicot v France*, nos. 79885/12, 52471/13 and 52596/13, 6 April 2017.

104 V-Dem, *Democracy Report 2024*, https://www.v-dem.net/documents/43/v-dem_dr2024_lowres.pdf (last accessed 27.02.2025).

105 Executive Order 14166, 'Defending Women from Gender Ideology Extremism and Restoring Biological Truth to the Federal Government', adopted by the US President, 20 January 2025.

106 Amnesty International, 'Russia: Adoption of Transphobic Legislation a "Horrendous Blow" to Human Rights', 25 July 2023, https://www.amnesty.org/en/latest/news/2023/07/russia-adoption-of-transphobic-legislation-a-horrendous-blow-to-human-rights/ (last accessed 27.02.2025).

earlier than 2017, when it was mandated by the ECtHR. This reflects a broader shift towards de-medicalising the legal process. While discussions on self-identification, that is, allowing individuals to change their legal gender without a medical diagnosis, are emerging, no country in the said region has yet adopted such a model. None of the states recognises non-binary identities. Some countries have adopted anti-transgender approaches, in contrast to the positive obligations under the ECtHR and EU values. Moreover, in some jurisdictions, access to LGR is dependent on court decisions, thereby reinforcing socio-economic inequalities, as the process is significantly more accessible to individuals with a higher education and the necessary financial resources.

Within the realm of private international law, specific rules on the recognition of LGR obtained abroad remain absent across these legal systems. There is little available data on how the authorities approach such cases in practice. However, the *Mirin* case[107] established that an EU Member State must recognise a legal gender registered in another EU country, as non-recognition would be an obstacle to the freedom of movement. Additionally, some case law from the analysed region suggests that the *ordre public* should not be invoked to deny a gender status gained from non-EU states. For instance, the transcription of the gender status of a Polish national in Canada into Polish documents was not considered to infringe the *ordre public* of Poland.

There are various reasons for changes in this geopolitical area and the key thereto are responses to updated medical standards, European case law and engagement with European values, such as the substantive gender equality of all people. Resistance to the case law of the ECtHR is also evident, especially in jurisdictions where transgender rights have become a focal point of broader democratic backsliding. In countries like Hungary and Bulgaria (potentially also Slovakia), legal changes reflect an anti-gender movement and a retrogression of the rights of women and minorities. Transgender individuals, as a small and politically vulnerable minority, are currently being used as scapegoats in the process of autocratisation, reinforcing exclusionary narratives and eroding fundamental freedoms. Addressing this injustice is crucial, as it is not only unethical and incompatible with international human rights law, but also poses a broader threat to democracy and the rule of law.

---

107 Case C-4/23, *Mirin*, ECLI:EU:C:2024:845.

LEGAL GENDER RECOGNITION IN SOUTHERN EUROPEAN COUNTRIES

Paula Távora Vítor

1. INTRODUCTION

The regulation of the lives of individuals by law often relies on specific categories, particularly with regard to family relations and the *status* of persons.[1] Gender is one of those key categories and, until recently, one that was legally static, given its association with sex. However, many jurisdictions have now established procedures that enable individuals to change their name and gender marker in official registers and documents. In Europe, the existence of such procedures is widespread,[2] but the conditions for implementing them differ considerably from country to country.

This chapter aims to provide an overview of the main features of legal gender recognition (LGR) procedures in four different jurisdictions: Portugal, Spain, Italy and Malta. It does not present a comprehensive survey of LGR in Southern Europe, neither does it dwell on the development of each system, nor on the debates involved,[3] but it does prove itself useful in comparative terms.

---

1 J. Eekelaar, 'Family Law and Identity' (2018) 38(4) *Oxford Journal of Legal Studies* 831.

2 In 2020 the European Commission study *Legal gender recognition in the EU. The journeys of trans people towards full equality* concluded that '[a]ll EU Member States and the UK allow for LGR of transgender individuals or have permitted individuals to be recognised in accordance with their gender identity'. European Commission, *Legal gender recognition in the EU. The journeys of trans people towards full equality*, Directorate-General for Justice and Consumers, June 2020, p. 110.

3 In the Portuguese context, for instance, the legal literature has intensely discussed the introduction of the new system of Law No. 38/2018, 7 August. See, among others, I. Espinhaço Gomes, 'A tutela multinível da identidade de género' in R. Lobo Xavier et al. (eds), *Constitucionalismos e (Con)temporaneidade. Estudos em Homenagem ao Professor Doutor Manuel Afonso Vaz*, Universidade Católica Editora, Porto 2020, pp. 249–280, and M.M. Barbosa, 'Direito à autodeterminação da identidade de género e responsabilidade civil: reflexões em torno da Lei N.º 38/2018, de 7 de Agosto' (2018) 94(2) *Boletim da Faculdade de Direito. Coimbra* 1097.

Despite their different sizes,[4] the selected jurisdictions have substantial similarities, not only from a geographical point of view – apart from Portugal,[5] they are all Mediterranean countries – but also from a social and cultural point of view, from which perspective such similarities can be traced back to several features, namely to their Latin linguistic roots[6] and to their common religious historical traditions. Additionally, these jurisdictions share a common legal background provided by the Roman law tradition[7] and, in terms of international law, by human rights protection framework laid out by common international organisations and their instruments – most notably by the Charter of Fundamental Rights of the European Union, the European Convention on Human Rights (ECHR) and the European Court of Human Rights (ECtHR), as well as the Convention on the Rights of the Child (CRC) – that shapes and enforces the legal approach to this subject.[8]

However, even though all the aforementioned jurisdictions have a legal framework that regulates gender recognition, their approaches sometimes differ. Portugal, Spain and Malta have enacted recent Acts on the subject, under the auspices of current international law, whereas the Italian legislature has long been inactive concerning this matter. Indeed, the current regime of LGR in Portugal was introduced in 2018, by Law No. 38/2018 of 7 August,[9] the most recent Spanish approach[10] was carved out in 2023, by Law 4/2023 of 28 February,[11] and the Maltese system[12] was established by the Gender Identity, Gender Expression and Sex Characteristics Act (GIGESC), which was enacted in 2015[13]

---

4 The current population of the aforementioned countries is as follows: Italy 59,223,089; Spain: 47,898,013; Portugal: 10,417,081; and Malta: 543,139. https://www.worldometers.info/population/europe/southern-europe/.

5 Even though, despite being *Atlantic by location*, Portugal may be considered *Mediterranean by nature*. J. Pequito Rebelo, *A Terra Portuguesa*, Lisbon 1929, p. 55 *apud* O. Ribeiro, *Portugal, o Mediterrâneo e o Atlântico. Esboço Geográfico*, 2nd ed., Livraria Letra Livre, 2021, p. 63.

6 The exception here is Malta, whose official languages, Maltese and English, are from different language families.

7 Even though other legal traditions may also be present, most notably in Malta.

8 See e.g. the Ruling of the Italian Constitutional Court 221/2015, which leans on the case law of the European Court of Human Rights, relating Article 8 of the European Convention on Human Rights to this issue.

9 This Act repealed Law No. 7/2011, 15 March. Later, Law No. 15/2024, 29 January, has introduced amendments. It should also be noted that the Constitutional Court has declared two provisions of this Act (Article 12(1) and (2) regarding Education and Teaching) to be unconstitutional.

10 Regarding the Spanish legal system, I have to thank Jordi Ribot Igualada, from the University of Girona, for his critical reading.

11 It was preceded by Law 3/2007, 15 March.

12 The Maltese jurisdiction has been classified by the ILGA as the one that offers better compliance with human rights standards and occupies the first place among the countries analysed and has also been given one of the best scores when it comes to the regulation of LGR. See https://rainbowmap.ilga-europe.org/countries/malta/.

13 This Act repealed the provisions introduced by Act XVIII of 2004.

and subsequently amended.[14] The Italian legal regime,[15] however, dates back to 1982 and is regulated by Law No. 164/1982. Nonetheless, as will be pointed out, there are many nuances to be considered, particularly the approach taken by case law, which has not ignored the most recent developments on this subject, particularly the ECtHR case law.[16]

This condensed overview intends to address the nature of each jurisdiction's LGR procedures, the criteria underlying them and the legal consequences of such recognition, particularly from the perspective of family law, and to focus on the particular case of LGR concerning children.

2. LEGAL GENDER RECOGNITION PROCEDURES AND THEIR NATURE

The Southern European jurisdictions addressed in this chapter foresee the possibility of the recognition and registration of a person's gender and they regulate the pathway by which to pursue this, as well as the effects of such a change. While in Italy only *a court*[17] – functioning with a collegiate composition[18] – is entitled to conduct such a process, Portugal, Spain and Malta have *administrative* procedures in place, that are, nevertheless, allowed in the context of (at least slightly) different circumstances. In the Portuguese and Spanish legal systems, the competent administrative body is the Civil Registry.[19] The Maltese procedure involves a declaratory public deed drawn up by a notary and the subsequent amendment of the acts of civil status will be authorised by the Director of the Public Registry.[20] In Portugal, the procedure is exclusively

14 The GIGESC was amended by Act XX of 2015, Act LVI of 2016, Act XIII of 2018, and Act No. XXV of 2024. It is also relevant to take into account the amendment of Article 278 of the Civil Code by Act LVX of 2020.

15 Regarding the Italian legal system, I have to thank to Giulia Binato, from the Università degli Studi di Padova, for her critical reading.

16 The role recently played by the ruling of the European Court of Human Rights in *S.V. v Italy*, no. 55216/08, 11 October 2018, should be stressed, which found a violation of Article 8 ECHR in a case in which the Italian authorities had refused to allow a transgender woman to officially change her first name before a judicial decision confirmed the successful completion of sex reassignment therapy.

17 Article 1 Law of 14 April 1982.

18 Italian law identifies this court as the court of the plaintiff's residence. Article 31(2) Decree 150/201.

19 In Portugal, the administrative procedure of gender recognition and a name change implies a decision by the registrar (Article 6 Law No. 38/2018, 7 August). The claim is filed at the Civil Registry Office (Article 8 Law No. 38/2018, 7 August) and there may be an appeal to the President of the Institute for Registry and Notaries (Article 9(3) Law No. 38/2018, 7 August). In Spain, the request may also be presented at any Civil Registry Office and it is recognised by its officer (Articles 44(1) and (2) and 45 Law 4/2023, 28 February).

20 Articles 4 and 5 GIGESC. The fact that Maltese law establishes a maximum time limit for the LGR request filed with the Director of the Public Registry to be noted in the birth certificate

administrative and the decision is issued by the registrar of the Civil Registry. In Spain[21] and Malta,[22] a court will have jurisdiction where the LGR procedure concerns children of a certain age.

All of the aforementioned jurisdictions have different regimes regarding the entitlement to request LGR and tend to make differentiations based on age.

Portuguese nationals who are 18 years of age – the age of majority in Portugal[23] – may file an LGR claim.[24] Spanish nationals are entitled to request this personally and without assistance before the general age of majority,[25] at 16 years old.[26] The same age threshold – 16 years of age – has been adopted in Malta for 'every person who is a Maltese citizen'.[27] Both the Portuguese law and the Spanish law refer to the situation of persons with diminished capacity. In Spain, the approach is more up to date with the recent reforms in the area of capacity,[28] because it expressly allows persons with disabilities to present their claim, resorting to the support measures in force and providing safeguards.[29] The Portuguese approach is a negative one, because it excludes those who are subject to a protection measure.[30] However, given the fact that not long after Law No. 38/2018 of 7 August was enacted the adult capacity regime was amended, this limitation should therefore be interpreted in accordance therewith. Since a judicial determination of a support measure does not necessarily imply incapacitation, the supported person should be allowed to personally petition for LGR when legal capacity is intact.[31]

Beyond the aforementioned thresholds, there are several different regimes. In Portugal, those who are between 16 and 18 years old may file the LGR claim through their legal representatives and subject to special requirements.[32]

---

of the applicant has been identified in the aforementioned study of the European Commission as good practice. European Commission, *Legal gender recognition in the EU. The journeys of trans people towards full equality*, Directorate-General for Justice and Consumers, June 2020, p. 115.

21 Article 43(4) Law 4/2023, 28 February.

22 Article 7(1) GIGESC refers to an application to the Civil Court.

23 Article 123 of the Portuguese Civil Code.

24 Article 7(1) Law No. 38/2018, 7 August.

25 Article 315 of the Spanish Civil Code.

26 Article 43(1) Law 4/2023, 28 February. But, in order to obtain such rectification, the person needs to ratify it after three months (Article 44(8) Law 4/2023, 28 February).

27 Article 4(1) GIGESC.

28 The reform of the Spanish Civil Code took place in Act 8/2021, 2 June. This reform aimed to address the requirements of the UN Convention on the Rights of Persons with Disabilities.

29 Article 43(3) Law 4/2023, 28 February; Article 44(11) Law 4/2023, 28 February.

30 It refers to those 'under guardianship or curatorship'. However, this Act is from 7 August 2018, while on 14 August 2018, Law No. 49/2018 was approved by the Portuguese Parliament. It revoked both guardianship and curatorship and introduced a new support measure – *acompanhamento* – in order to comply with the requirements of the UN Convention on the Rights of Persons with Disabilities.

31 Law No. 272/2001, 13 October.

32 Article 7(2) Law No. 38/2018, 7 August.

However, when it comes to intersex persons, no specific age limits have been established – the request may be filed from the moment their gender identity manifests itself.[33] In the Spanish legal system there are two groups of minors who are subject to different rules: those between 14 and 16 years of age present their claim personally, assisted by legal representatives;[34] for those between 12 and 14 years old, a court authorisation is required.[35] In Malta, persons exercising parental responsibility or the tutor of the minor may file an application at the Registry of the Civil Court on behalf of the minor in question.[36] The LGR of minors is not expressly admitted by Italian law. However, Italian case law has already dealt with this matter in several cases and allowed it.[37]

The possibility to legally reverse the recognition of the change of gender is also regulated by Portugal, Spain and Malta. However, whereas in Spain the reversal (*reversión*) of the previous LGR follows the same procedure[38] as the first,[39] in Portugal[40] and Malta[41] this subsequent procedure is judicial[42] and therefore a court order is required. In Italy, this issue is not addressed by the law.

3. CRITERIA FOR LEGAL GENDER RECOGNITION

The criteria that determine LGR are key to defining the model adopted by each jurisdiction. Portugal, Spain and Malta expressly reject the medical model for approaching this subject, by electing instead for the exercise of the 'self-determination'[43] of the claimant as the ground for obtaining LGR,[44] and

33 Article 7(3) Law No. 38/2018, 7 August.
34 Article 43(2) Law 4/2023, 28 February.
35 Article 43(4) Law 4/2023, 28 February.
36 Article 7(1) GIGESC.
37 See below section 4.
38 According to Article 47 of Law 4/2023, 28 February, after six months from registration in the Civil Registry, the LGR may be reversed by means of the same procedure; a new rectification must however be established by a court decision.
39 On this first occasion, advance information is provided regarding a reversal (*reversión*) of the gender identification. Article 44(5) Law 4/2023, 28 February.
40 Article 6(3) Law No. 38/2018, 7 August.
41 Article 8(2) GIGESC.
42 The 2024 amendments to the GIGESC clarify that the existence of previous amendments when the person was a minor does not hinder the possibility to follow the notarial procedure when the person reaches the age of 16.
43 This model is in line with the Parliamentary Assembly of the Council of Europe (PACE) *Resolution 2048 (2015): Discrimination against transgender people in Europe*, which calls on Member States to 'develop quick, transparent and accessible procedures, based on self-determination, for changing the name and registered sex of transgender people' on official documents and the Yogyakarta Principles (Principle 3: the right to recognition before the law).
44 Portugal and Spain both expressly refer to self-determination – see Article 3(1) of Portuguese Law No. 38/2018, 7 August, and Article 44 of Spanish Law 4/2023, 28 February.

refusing any requirement of a medical or psychological diagnosis or any medical intervention.[45] The requirement of a psychological report in Portugal, in the particular case of this procedure for children, has the objective of ascertaining the capacity to consent and does not refer to any medical certification of a 'gender disorder'.[46]

The Italian model is not a 'self-determination' model. However, the development of its application by the Italian courts has departed from the requirement of medical procedures. Indeed, despite the fact that the 1982 Act is still in force, it may be argued that Italian case law has enabled a transition towards a 'soft medicalisation' model.[47] The orientation of the Law of 14 April 1982 is clearly a medical one. According to Article 2 of this Law, 'the court will order that counselling will take place so that the psychosexual conditions are ascertained' – in other words, a gender dysphoria diagnosis. Additionally, Article 1 of the Law of 14 April 1982 determines that the rectification 'attributing a different sex to a person' will follow 'intervening changes in his sexual characteristics', which could be what was originally understood as requiring surgical intervention. In 2011,[48] the court procedure was amended by Decree 150/2011, such that the new formulation stated that the court authorised surgery *when necessary*. Finally, in 2015, the Corte di Cassazione[49] considered that it would be an excessive restriction of fundamental rights to require a modification of sexual characteristics before the LGR proceedings, and Ruling No. 221/2015 of the Constitutional Court dismissed any need for surgical intervention. This ruling interpreted Article 31(4) of Decree 150/2011 in the sense that it requires the court to authorise a surgical intervention, if necessary, but does not compel such an intervention. And, finally, in 2024, Ruling No. 143/2024 of the Constitutional Court deemed even the need to obtain a court authorisation before undergoing sexual characteristic adjustment surgery to be unconstitutional.

4. LEGAL CONSEQUENCES

The LGR procedures in the four jurisdictions analysed allow for the transition of genders from masculine to feminine or from feminine to masculine. The

45 Article 9(2) of Portuguese Law No. 38/2018, 7 August; Article 44(3) of Spanish Law 4/2023, 28 February; Articles 3(4), 4(3) and 5(2) of the Maltese GIGESC. The depathologisation was clearly assumed through Act No. LVI of 2016.

46 Article 7(2) of Portuguese Law No. 38/2018, 7 August.

47 G. Binato, 'A genderless family law for gender-fluid families? Parentage rules and the right to gender identity' in F. Swennen, E. Goossens and T. Van Hof (eds), *Rethinking Law's Families and Family Law*, Edward Elgar Publishing, Cheltenham 2024, pp. 198, 200.

48 Decree 150/2011 introduced Article 31(4) concerning surgical intervention, which revoked Article 3 of the Law of 14 April 1982.

49 Decision of the Corte di Cassazione No. 15138/2015.

possibility of the recognition of a non-binary gender identity is absent from any of these legal systems,[50] with the exception of Malta. Maltese law establishes the possible gender markers M or F and, since 2024, the Gender Identity, Gender Expression and Sex Characteristics (Amendment) Act (Act No. XXV of 2024) enables identification as non-binary with the gender marker X on all official documents through a declaration made via a notary.[51]

Gender transition is usually linked to a name change, and hence to the rights to demand a name change and to have identification documents and other relevant acts of civil status modified accordingly.[52] However, a name change is not a necessity and a holder may opt not to exercise this right: in the Spanish system, a name change will not take place *if the person wants to retain their original name* and according to the principles of the Civil Registry, while in Malta the right to change one's first name may be exercised '*if the person so wishes* ... in order to reflect that person's self-determined gender identity'.[53]

Portuguese, Spanish and Maltese law not only guarantee that the rights of the person are not affected by the LGR,[54] but they also expressly establish rights that support them and provide safeguards.[55]

Family rights are particularly highlighted in the legislation. As far as marriage is concerned, LGR does not affect its validity,[56] nor its effects, in Portugal,[57] Malta[58] and Spain.[59] In these legal systems, same-sex marriage is allowed, which

---

50 In 2024, the Italian Constitutional Court (Ruling No. 143/2024) considered a complaint about the failure to provide for a 'third gender' to be inadmissible.

51 Explanatory notes of the GIGESC (Amendment) Act, at https://www.gov.mt/en/Government/DOI/Government%20Gazette/Government%20Notices/Pages/2024/07/GovNotices1607.aspx.

52 Articles 6(1), 7, 8, 9 and 10 of Portuguese Law No. 38/2018, 7 August; Articles 49 and 50 of Spanish Law 4/2023, 28 February. In Italy, the court decision will order the officer of the Civil Registry of the municipality where the act of birth was recorded to rectify it (Article 3 Law of 14 April 1982).

53 Article 4(1) GIGESC.

54 Article 10 of Portuguese Law No. 38/2018, 7 August; Article 46(5) of Spanish Law 4/2023, 28 February.

55 In 2024, a new provision was added to the Portuguese Act, introducing a ban on 'forced conversion regarding sexual orientation, gender identity and expression'. Law No. 15/2024, 29 January added Article 3(3) to Law No. 38/2018, 7 August and modified the Criminal Code accordingly. Articles 11 et seqq. of the Maltese GIGESC establish measures of protection, anti-discrimination and the promotion of equality, the right to bodily integrity and physical autonomy.

56 See the Recommendations on human rights and gender identity to the Council of Europe member states by the Commissioner for Human Rights, CommDH/IssuePaper(2009)2, V. 6, Strasbourg, 29 July 2009.

57 Same-sex marriage has been allowed in Portugal since 2010 (Law No. 9/2010, 31 May).

58 A person's rights, relationships and obligations arising out of marriage shall in no way be affected (Article 3 (2) a. GIGESC). In Malta, same-sex marriage has been allowed since 2017 (Marriage Act and other Laws (Amendment) Act, 2017) and civil unions since 2014 (Civil Unions Act (CAP 540)).

59 Same-sex marriage was introduced in Spain in 2005, by Law 13/2005, 1 July.

provides a legal framework that enables this consequence. The Italian situation is more complex. Indeed, same-sex marriage is not allowed in the Italian legal system. Thus, a court decision giving effect to gender recognition would lead to the dissolution of the marriage or the nullification of the civil effects of a religious marriage.[60] Since 2016, however, upon the registration of the rectified gender, *Law Cirinnà* – the act that introduced a civil union for same-sex couples in Italy – now allows for the automatic establishment of a civil union between such partners now of the same sex if they have expressed a willingness not to dissolve or terminate the civil effects of their marriage.[61] Moreover, the safeguarding of parental rights and duties[62] is expressly mentioned in Portuguese law[63] and in the law of Malta.[64]

5. THE PARTICULAR CASE OF THE LEGAL GENDER RECOGNITION OF CHILDREN

When LGR proceedings concern children, the particular situation of those who are developing their identity and whose legal capacity is evolving may demand a different approach, and the Portuguese, Spanish and Maltese legal systems have all incorporated that perspective by creating a specific set of rules to address this issue. Therefore, although in these systems the self-determination of the person concerned is still the criterion to be taken into account, it should be understood in the context of childhood and the capacity to act independently during this period.

In Portugal, children who may apply for LGR are those between 16 and 18 years old.[65] This age limit does not apply, however, to intersex children, who are entitled to claim LGR from the moment their gender identity manifests itself.[66]

---

60 Article 4 Law No. 164/1982.

61 Article 1(27) Law of 20 May 2016, n. 76 (*Legge Cirinnà*). This is made through a joint declaration to the Civil Registry Officer in the municipality where the marriage has been registered (Article 5 Decree of the President of the Council of Ministers No. 144/2016).

62 The ruling of the European Court of Human Rights in *P.V. v Spain*, no. 35159/09, 11 April 2011, addressed the Spanish reality under the previous law. It dealt with the custody and contact arrangements of the child of a 'male-to-female transsexual', whose 'transsexualism was what had prompted the former wife to bring proceedings to amend the arrangements made at the time of their separation'. In this ruling, the ECtHR considered that 'transsexualism was indisputably covered by Article 14'.

63 Article 10 of Portuguese Law No. 38/2018, 7 August.

64 Article 3(2) a. GIGESC. LGR does not determine the loss of parental rights in Italy. However, there is evidence in the case law suggesting that the Italian courts have considered this fact to be detrimental to the child, as identified by M.G. Cubeddu Wiedemann, 'Italy' in J.M. Scherpe (ed.), *The Legal Status of Transsexual and Transgender Persons*, Intersentia, Cambridge/Antwerp/Portland 2015, p. 258.

65 Article 7(2) Law No. 38/2018, 7 August.

66 Article 7(3) Law No. 38/2018, 7 August.

In this context, the paramount consideration is the best interests of the child and the law frames this by referring to the exercise of self-determination and repealing any requirement of a gender identity diagnosis.[67] In order to guarantee the free and informed consent of the child – and given the fact that adulthood and full capacity is only attained at the age of 18[68] – some procedural guarantees have been laid down: the hearing of the child by the registrar and the presentation of a report by a physician (registered with the Medical Association) or a psychologist (registered with the Psychologists' Association) who has determined the child's capacity to decide, according to their progressive autonomy and their best interest of, as enshrined in the CRC.[69]

In Spain, special regimes apply when the applicant is a minor.[70] As far as children between 12 and 14 years of age are concerned, a request must be filed before the court.[71] Children between 14 and 16 years of age present their claim personally at the Civil Registry Office, but they have to be assisted by their legal representatives[72] and, in the event of a lack of agreement, an *ad litem* representative will be nominated.[73] Finally, the general regime applies to those who are above 16 years of age as far as legal standing and the nature of the procedure[74] are concerned. However, even when children have the ability to personally claim LGR – i.e. minors from 14 to 18 years of age – there are special safeguards that apply to them: the child has the right to be heard, to receive adequate information and to the use of appropriate language, while the best interests of the child is always the criterion to be taken into account in every case.[75]

In Malta, for the purposes of LGR, minors are those under the age of 16.[76] The law identifies those who may file an application at the Registry of the Civil Court (Voluntary Jurisdiction section) as 'persons exercising parental responsibility or the tutor of the minor'.[77] It is therefore a judicial procedure. The particular situation of minors 'whose gender has not been declared at birth' determines

67 Article 7(2) Law No. 38/2018, 7 August.

68 Despite the existence of several situations in which the legal capacity to act is granted to younger children (e.g. the capacity to consent to medical treatment or to freely choose their religion).

69 Article 7(2) Law No. 38/2018, 7 August.

70 The options under Law 4/2023, 28 February and its focus on granting autonomy to minors were influenced by the Constitutional Court's case law that referred to the previous regime, namely Ruling 99/2019, 18 July 2019, which ruled that Article 1(1) of Law 3/2007, 15 March, was unconstitutional in the sense that it restricted the rectification of the gender marker to minors with 'sufficient maturity' in a 'stable situation of transsexuality'

71 Article 43(4) Law 4/2023, 28 February and Law 15/2015, 2 July.

72 Article 43(2) Law 4/2023, 28 February.

73 Article 43(2) Law 4/2023, 28 February.

74 Article 43(1) Law 4/2023, 28 February.

75 Article 44(6) Law 4/2023, 28 February.

76 See the amendments of Act No. LVI of 2016 and GIGESC (Amendment) Act of 2024.

77 Article 7(1) GIGESC.

that persons exercising parental responsibility or the tutor of the minor may file an application at the Registry of the Civil Court in order to declare the gender and the first name of the minor if he or she wants to change his or her first name, with the express consent of the minor.[78] The evolving capacities and the best interests of the child, as enshrined in the CRC, are also expressly highlighted by Maltese law as being paramount in procedures regarding children.[79]

In Italy, the LGR of children is not specifically regulated. However, Italian case law has already decided several of these claims where parents have brought lawsuits on the behalf of their children. In the absence of a particular regime, the general rules on pleading regarding children and their representation apply,[80] meaning that the courts must take into account the child's will and maturity, in light of the legal principles on medical consent by minors (Law No. 219/2017).[81] For instance, in 2023 the Court of Parma[82] decided in favour of the gender recognition of a child in a case that contained extensive documentation from a medical point of view.

78 Article 7(4) GIGESC.

79 Article 7 GIGESC. This includes not subjecting the minors to additional processes that may negatively impact their well-being.

80 On the subject of a conflict between the child and the parents, see G. Binato, 'Mature minors and self-determination in medical consent law: a comparison between the Italian legal system and the English legal system' (2019) XXIV(1) *Interdisciplinary Journal of Family Studies* 80.

81 Court of Frosinone, C – Decision No. 1002, 25 July 2017, which also dealt with authorisation for medical procedures. See also Court of Genova, 17 January 2019; Court of Lucca, 27 August 2021.

82 Court of Parma, Decision No. 1151, 20 July 2023.

LEGAL GENDERS AND IDENTITIES

Internal Disharmony in the United Kingdom

Jane Mair

Recent decades of European family law have been characterised by terms such as 'harmonisation', 'unification', 'collaboration' and 'cooperation'. Within the context of comparative family law scholarship, ideas of commonality and the methodology of the 'common core' have become well established. As we celebrate almost a quarter century of the work of the Commission on European Family Law, the CEFL is joined by a growing number of networks, frameworks, conferences and committees designed to share knowledge, best practice and common challenges, working together across borders in the development, design and dissemination of family law and policy for contemporary family life.[1] It is against that background of cooperation and shared concerns that this chapter presents a tale of disharmony. Focusing on the recent experience of the various nations and devolved administrations within the United Kingdom, in the context of proposed reforms of the law relating to gender identity, this is a case study of how not to do it: a cautionary tale of the impact which disharmony can have on the process of legal reform.

1. MAPS AND IDENTITIES

1.1. THE UNITED KINGDOM

How we see ourselves and how others see us is all part of the complex and changing construction of identity: national, cultural, jurisdictional, political, personal. Viewed on a world map, and from the perspective of the European mainland, the

[1] Including, e.g., the European Law Institute Project on Empowering European Families, https://www.europeanlawinstitute.eu/projects-publications/publications/eli-report-empowering-european-families-towards-more-party-autonomy-in-european-family-and-succession-law/; FL-EUR, Family Law in Europe: Academic Network, https://fl-eur.eu/; Nordic Centre for Comparative and International Family Law, www.law.aau.dk/forskning/forskningsgrupper/nordic-centre-for-comparative-and-international-family-law-norfam.

British Isles sit to the northwest of the European mainland, a small, tight cluster of islands of which the two largest are Great Britain and Ireland. The island of Great Britain is made up of England, Scotland and Wales, while the island of Ireland is divided into Northern Ireland and the Republic of Ireland. Northern Ireland, together with England, Scotland and Wales form the United Kingdom.[2]

Within those national and geographical entities, there is further complexity, with England and Wales, Scotland and Northern Ireland having their own distinct legal systems. While England and Wales, and Northern Ireland are common law jurisdictions, and share much in terms of legal systems, Scotland may be described as a mixed jurisdiction with its traditions in civil law, overlaid with common law influences. Until the late 1990s, although there were separate legal systems, all law-making was centralised in the UK Parliament, situated in Westminster. Since then, however, policy and law-making in certain areas – the devolved matters – have been delegated to the Scottish Parliament, the Welsh Assembly, later renamed the Welsh Government, and the Northern Ireland Assembly – with reserved matters remaining within the power of the UK legislature.[3]

The particular entity which is the focus of this chapter is the United Kingdom. While this is not the place for detailed discussion of British and Irish constitutional law and law-making, the following description of the UK gives a sense of the complexities:

> The United Kingdom (UK) is a multinational … State with four distinct territorial units. Although formally understood as a unitary State (i.e., it has a single source of sovereign authority, located in the UK, or Westminster, Parliament), it was formed through a series of unions between England and its smaller neighbours … Scotland … Wales and Ireland (now Northern Ireland) … This historical development has left a legacy of distinct sub-state national identities, and asymmetric governance, most recently in the establishment of devolved legislatures and governments for Scotland, Wales, and Northern Ireland from 1999.[4]

The simple point being made in this chapter is that what may appear from the outside as a 'united' Kingdom, a close-knit geographical region of the British

2 The Republic of Ireland, while part of the geographical British Isles, left the United Kingdom in 1922 and became an independent state.

3 This process of devolution began with the Scotland Act 1998, the Northern Ireland Act 1998 and the Government of Wales Act 1998, all of which have been subsequently amended and extended. For an introduction to devolution, its history and current structures, see D. TORRANCE, *Introduction to devolution in the United Kingdom*, House of Commons Library Briefing Paper 8599, 2024, https://researchbriefings.files.parliament.uk/documents/CBP-8599/CBP-8599.pdf.

4 A. McHarg, 'Constitutional Law and Secession in the United Kingdom' in R.D Griffiths, A. Pavkovic and P. Radan (eds), *The Routledge Handbook of Self-Determination and Secession*, Routledge, Abingdon 2023, p. 591.

Isles, is in fact a complex interaction of national, political and legal identities and institutions.

1.2. EUROPEAN FAMILY LAW: A VIEW FROM THE EDGE

The separate jurisdictions of Great Britain and the United Kingdom have perhaps always been to some extent on the edge of the Europeanisation of family law. Whether EU or Council of Europe, and even before the impact of Brexit, the UK, and its constituent jurisdictions, can seem somewhat on 'the boundary'.[5] The discretion of the English common law system stands out against the civilian codes of much of Europe and, despite its civilian heritage, the extent to which Scotland is 'mixed' is never clearer than when it tries to find its proper place within the classifications of European comparative law. When at home, we tend to stress the differences between Scots, English and Irish family law. When we find ourselves in the company of European family lawyers, however, we often reflect on how much our domestic systems, within the constituent parts of the United Kingdom, share in contrast to the gap between us and particularly the codified systems of mainland Europe.

Following a domestic referendum in 2016 and in accordance with the European Union (Withdrawal Agreement) Act 2020, the UK left the EU with effect from 11pm on 31 January 2020 ('Brexit'). While the United Kingdom (England, Wales, Scotland and Northern Ireland) has left the EU, and arguably moved itself even further to the edge of the Europeanisation of family law, the Republic of Ireland remains as a Member State.

1.3. GENDER IDENTITY

A key feature of the emergence and narrative of European family law has been the idea of cultural identity, with earlier scepticism about the suitability of family law for harmonisation being rooted in 'strong cultural and historical constraints'.[6] For others, too much focus on cultural constraints is arguably a distraction from a longer-term view of the force of family law in 'national identity'[7] or the role of politics and political economy.[8]

---

5 N. Lowe, 'The Growing Influence of the European Union on International Family Law – A View from the Boundary' (2003) 56(1) *Current Legal Problems* 439.

6 M. Antokolskaia, 'Family law and national culture: Arguing against the cultural constraints argument' (2008) 4(2) *Utrecht Law Review* 25, 25.

7 P. Tsoukala, 'Marrying Family Law to the Nation' (2010) 58(4) *The American Journal of Comparative Law* 873.

8 D. Bradley, 'Convergence in Family Law: Mirrors, Transplants and Political Economy' (1999) 6(2) *Maastricht Journal of European and Comparative Law* 127.

A very different type of identity lies at the heart of this account – gender identity. Gender identity was at one point an unquestioned and immutable certainty at the heart of the family law institution of marriage. In recent years, gender has become much less of a concern for family law, with the widespread decoupling of marriage from heterosexual relationships, while at the same time, in the context of parenting, it continues to challenge and disrupt the structures of legal parentage and the language of mothers and fathers. Gender, and the legal recognition of gender identity, remain a core aspect of family law, albeit trans rights go far beyond the boundaries of family law.

Identities, personal and national, have been to the fore of policy, debate and reform in recent years, from the initial enactment across the United Kingdom of the Gender Recognition Act 2004 through to the various, separate attempts particularly in England and Wales, and Scotland to reform the law relating to gender identity. It is that story, and what it says about union and dis-union, harmony and disharmony, cooperation and challenge, which forms the basis for this chapter.

2. THE GENDER RECOGNITION ACT 2004

2.1. RESPONDING TO AN EXTERNAL PRESSURE

Prior to 2004, the law throughout the UK made no provision for the legal recognition of gender to be changed from that which was registered at birth, except in the very limited circumstances where there had been a mistake in the original registration. The position was as set out by Ormrod J in *Corbett v Corbett*:

> the biological sexual constitution of an individual is fixed at birth (at the latest), and cannot be changed, either by the natural development of organs of the opposite sex, or by medical or surgical means. … The only cases where the term 'change of sex' is appropriate are those in which a mistake as to sex is made at birth and subsequently revealed by further medical investigation.[9]

The direct driver for change came from the decision of the European Court of Human Rights (ECtHR) in *Goodwin v the United Kingdom*.[10] As the judgment in this case recounts, this was not the first time the issue of transsexuals had been raised in the UK context. In 1999, an Interdepartmental Working Group on Transsexual People had been established, and in July 2000 its Report[11] was

---

9 *Corbett v Corbett* [1970] 2 All ER 33.

10 *Goodwin v the United Kingdom*, no. 28957/95, 11 July 2002.

11 Home Office, *Report of the Interdepartmental Working Group on Transsexual People*, April 2000, https://www.oocities.org/transforum2000/Resources/wgtrans.pdf.

presented to the UK Parliament. Issues had also come to the ECtHR on a number of previous occasions,[12] but on each occasion the margin of appreciation had saved the UK from action. This lack of progress was highlighted in *Goodwin*, with the applicant submitting that:

> despite warnings from the Court as to the importance for keeping under review the need for legal reform the Government had still not taken any constructive steps to address the suffering and distress experienced by the applicant and other post-operative transsexuals.[13]

Set against this background, it was in *Goodwin* that the ECtHR ran out of patience, finding that 'the situation, as it has evolved, no longer falls within the United Kingdom's margin of appreciation.' The UK was found to have breached Article 8 and Article 12 of the European Convention on Human Rights (the right to respect for private life and the right to marry). As the ECtHR continued:

> It will be for the United Kingdom Government in due course to implement such measures as it considers appropriate to fulfil its obligations to secure the applicant's, and other transsexuals', right to respect for private life and right to marry in compliance with this judgment.[14]

The decision of the ECtHR in *Goodwin* was by no means an isolated incident in the path towards law reform in the UK but it was undoubtedly the most direct and powerful driver.[15] In the domestic case of *Bellinger v Bellinger*, concerning the right of a transsexual to marry, the House of Lords noted that, with *Goodwin*, 'the sands of time have run out'.[16] While reform was not immediate, the judgment of the ECtHR put in train a series of events which ultimately led to the Gender Recognition Act 2004.

2.2. A UNITED RESPONSE

On 13 December 2002, the UK government announced its intention to 'bring forward primary legislation which will allow transsexual people who can demonstrate they have taken decisive steps towards living fully and permanently

---

12 See e.g. *Rees v the United Kingdom*, no. 9532/81, 17 October 1986; *Cossey v the United Kingdom*, no. 10843/84, 27 September 1990.

13 *Goodwin v the United Kingdom*, no. 28957/95, 11 July 2002, para. 60.

14 Ibid., para. 120.

15 For an overview of key stages and developments in the campaign towards trans rights in the UK, see S. Whittle and F. Simkiss, 'A perfect storm: the UK governments failed consultation on the Gender Recognition Act 2004' in C. Ashford and A. Maine (eds), *Research Handbook on Gender, Sexuality and the Law*, Edward Elgar Publishing, Cheltenham 2020, pp. 214–218.

16 *Bellinger v Bellinger* [2003] UKHL 21, para. 21.

in the acquired gender to marry in that gender'.[17] While the decision in *Goodwin* imposed an obligation on the UK, the specific issues at stake and which required to be reformed, fell within the devolved competence of the separate nations of Northern Ireland and Scotland. It was not a devolved matter for Wales, albeit there were differences in the Welsh law on marriage which would need to be taken into account. At the point of the announcement, it remained an open question whether the Westminster Parliament 'should legislate for the whole of the UK on this matter … in view of the inter-relationship between devolved and reserved policy aspects.'[18] By July 2003, when the UK government published its draft Bill, it was clear that there was a move towards an integrated approach. While the draft Bill, as initially published, covered only England and Wales, it was confirmed that agreement had been made 'with the Northern Ireland Office for provisions covering Northern Ireland to be added before the Bill begins its passage through Parliament'.[19]

With regard to Scotland, while no final decision had been reached, it was stressed that the Scottish Executive wished:

> to comply at the earliest opportunity with the rulings of the European Court of Human Rights and to achieve an integrated solution that avoids cross-border anomalies. Accordingly, the Executive intend to invite the Scottish Parliament to approve a Sewel Motion which will enable devolved as well as reserved aspects to be dealt with in the one Westminster Bill.[20]

The intention of the Westminster government was by this point clear, namely that a single piece of legislation, which would cover the whole of the UK, was the preferred approach. It was then for the Scottish Parliament to decide if they would cooperate by approving a 'Sewel motion'. A Sewel motion, now described as a legislative consent motion, is a reference to section 28 of the Scotland Act 1998, the legislation which established devolution. It provides that 'the Parliament of the United Kingdom will not normally legislate with regard to devolved matters without the consent of the Scottish Parliament.'

The question of whether to proceed by Sewel motion or by separate legislation was considered by the Justice Committee of the Scottish Parliament on 28 January 2004. In answer to a question as to whether he was certain that UK legislation was the preferable route, the Deputy Minister for Justice responded as follows:

---

17 Ibid., para 26.

18 Written statement to House of Commons, 16 December 2002, https://hansard.parliament.uk/Commons/2002-12-16/debates/b6ad03ae-c31f-420f-81de-c1aab8bb4dd6/TranssexualPeople.

19 HL Deb, 11 July 2003, col. WA64, https://publications.parliament.uk/pa/ld200203/ldhansrd/vo030711/text/30711w01.htm#30711w01_spmin2.

20 Ibid., col. WA64–65.

> The difficulty is that we do not have a parliamentary time slot. There is a breach of the ECHR, which could have legal consequences and lead to a challenge under infraction proceedings. The matter must be addressed sooner rather than later.[21]

In his answer, and in the ensuing discussions of the Committee, it was clear that time was of the essence. In debate in the Scottish Parliament, on 5 February 2004, the Deputy Minister for Justice went further by stating that, not only was 'inclusion of Scottish provisions in the UK bill … the swiftest and most cost-effective' approach, but also a UK-wide approach would ensure 'consistency in the process of determining legal recognition and in the legal consequences that flow from recognition of a transsexual person's acquired gender, thereby avoiding difficult and complex cross-border issues.'[22]

The path was therefore set for the UK to respond to the decision in *Goodwin*, and to legislate for gender recognition, by means of a single integrated Act which would apply across the UK. While it was proposed to legislate by means of a single statute, it was clarified that 'relevant Scottish provisions have been included in the bill to ensure that the legislation takes account of Scots law.'[23] In other words, it would be a single Act but with distinct and separate sections to reflect the law of the various jurisdictions.

2.3. THE 2004 ACT: GOOD IN ITS DAY

While by no means underplaying the long and difficult struggle for trans rights, the actual period from the publication of the draft Bill in July 2003 to the enactment of the Gender Recognition Act in July 2004 was itself relatively short and the process perhaps surprisingly smooth, considering not only the contentious nature – for some – of the reforms, but also the complexity of securing cooperation among the constituent nations of the UK. The Act itself and the system of gender recognition which it introduced were welcomed as 'fit for the twenty-first century', 'state of the art legislation'.[24] The task of drafting and enacting a complex statute which accommodated multiple jurisdictional differences was no mean feat, and it was achieved relatively smoothly.

21 Scottish Parliament Justice 1 Committee, 28 January 2004, https://www.parliament.scot/chamber-and-committees/official-report/search-what-was-said-in-parliament/J1-28-01-2004?meeting=2082&iob=9802.

22 Scottish Parliament Debate, 5 February 2004, https://www.parliament.scot/chamber-and-committees/official-report/search-what-was-said-in-parliament/chamber-and-committees/official-report/what-was-said-in-parliament/meeting-of-parliament-05-02-2004?meeting=4492&iob=32909.

23 Ibid.

24 S. Whittle and F. Simkiss, above n. 15, p. 211.

The GRA 2004 introduced a framework whereby a person could apply for a Gender Recognition Certificate (GRC),[25] the effect of which was set out in section 9, as follows:

> Where a full gender recognition certificate is issued to a person, the person's gender becomes for all purposes the acquired gender (so that, if the acquired gender is the male gender, the person's sex becomes that of a man and, if it is the female gender, the person's sex becomes that of a woman).

At the time, the 2004 Act was considered 'pioneering' to the extent that it did not require gender reassignment surgery but instead it permitted application either on the basis of 'living in the other gender'[26] or 'having changed gender under the law of a country or territory outside the United Kingdom'.[27] Applications were to be made to a newly constituted body called a Gender Recognition Panel (GRP).[28] Section 2(1) provided that, where an application is made on the basis of 'living in the other gender', the GRP must grant the application if satisfied that the applicant –

> (a) has or has had gender dysphoria
> (b) has lived in the acquired gender throughout the period of two years ending with the date on which the application is made,
> (c) intends to live in the acquired gender until death.

Section 3 set out the forms of evidence to be provided in respect of each of the section 2 requirements, with a diagnosis of gender dysphoria being required by a registered medical practitioner or registered psychologist practising in the relevant field.[29]

Section 4 set out the effect of a successful application and it is here that the complexity of the 2004 Act could be seen, in order to satisfy the requirements of the different legal systems within England and Wales, Northern Ireland and Scotland. Section 4 provided that, if an application was granted under section 1, then the GRP must issue a GRC to the applicant. In its original form, the section provided that, where the applicant was unmarried, the certificate was to be a 'full gender recognition certificate',[30] whereas if the applicant was married, the certificate was to be 'an interim gender recognition certificate'.[31] This difference was required because at that time there was no provision for same-sex marriage

---

25 GRA 2004, s. 1(1).
26 GRA 2004, s. 1(1)(a).
27 GRA 2004, s. 1(1)(b).
28 GRA 2004, s. 1(3) and Sched. 1.
29 GRA 2004, s. 3(2).
30 GRA 2004, s. 4(2) (as originally enacted).
31 GRA 2004, s. 4(3) (as originally enacted).

in the UK and the issuing of a full gender recognition certificate would have had the effect of making any existing marriage void. The objective of this approach was the same across the UK, that is to save the validity of existing marriage and leave it to the parties themselves to decide whether that marriage should continue or not. The means by which the objective was to be achieved, however, were different, reflecting the different legal systems in England and Wales, Northern Ireland and Scotland. In essence, the grant of an interim GRC provided grounds for a marriage to be voidable, in England, Wales and Northern Ireland, whereas in Scotland it provided a ground for divorce. The statute has subsequently been amended on numerous occasions to incorporate the introduction of civil partnerships, same-sex marriage and the extension of civil partnership to different-sex couples from its original form as restricted to couples of the same sex.[32]

The GRA 2004 is a complex statute, with many amendments, insertions, complicated numbering schemes and separate provisions, parts and Schedules for different parts of the UK. Despite its complexity in structure and drafting, it does nonetheless demonstrate what can be achieved in terms of integrated, cross-UK legislation. It manages to take account both of devolved matters and of the distinct and underpinning legal systems and institutions, particularly around family law, that operate in England, Wales, Northern Ireland and Scotland. Both in its original development and in its considerable subsequent amendment, it reflects a shared purpose and will and, in that, it stands in stark contrast to the attempted reforms which have followed.

3. REFORM OF THE GRA

3.1. STARTING FROM THE SAME PLACE

In January 2016, the UK Parliament's House of Commons Women and Equalities Committee published a report into *Transgender Equality* in which it stated that the GRA 2004, while once 'pioneering', was 'now dated'.[33] The Committee highlighted in particular the 'medicalised approach' underpinning the GRA, which 'pathologises trans identities and runs contrary to the dignity and personal autonomy of applicants.'[34] The Committee concluded that reform of the original legislation was required 'in line with the principle of self-declaration'.[35]

---

32 Discussion in this chapter focuses on the GRA 2004, as originally enacted and does not engage in any detail with the considerable subsequent reforms.

33 House of Commons Women and Equalities Committee, *Transgender Equality, First Report of Session 2015–16*, HC 390, 2016, p. 3.

34 Ibid., p. 3.

35 Ibid., p. 3.

The Committee, part of the UK government, grounded its Report firmly in the statement that '[f]airness and equality are basic British values',[36] while noting that its 'inquiry covered a wide range of policy areas, which are affected in different ways by the current devolution arrangements'.[37] The Committee's Report provided a useful starting point for debate and policy development across the UK.

3.2. INCREASINGLY DIVIDED

From a shared UK-wide starting point in 2016, the separate nations, in particular England and Wales on the one hand and Scotland on the other, embarked on their own particular routes to reform. Development towards reform in Northern Ireland has been much more limited to date.[38] While, in the early stages, shared objectives and continuing cooperation were highlighted, over time the gaps widened and the polarisation of position became more evident in the national narratives. In this chapter, a brief chronology of events and changing focus is traced through a series of consultations, government responses, legislative activity and legal process.

3.2.1. *Scotland Leads the Way*

Scotland took the lead on reform of gender recognition, by launching its first consultation in November 2017.[39] In introducing the consultation, the influence of the Westminster Women and Equalities Select Committee's report on *Transgender Equality*[40] was acknowledged as a key source, shaping the Scottish government's decision to act. It was further stressed in the ministerial foreword to the consultation document that, while gender recognition was a devolved matter and therefore within the competence of the Scottish Parliament, the Scottish government would 'work closely with the UK Government on any potential consequential changes needed to reserved or cross-border legislation'.

Central to the consultation was a preliminary proposal to adopt a system of self-declaration for gender recognition and here the Scottish government was

36 Ibid., p. 6.

37 Ibid., p. 7.

38 See now I. Latu et al., *Gender Recognition Act (GRA) 2004 Evaluation and Policy Options*, Queens University Belfast, 2022, https://www.finance-ni.gov.uk/sites/default/files/publications/dfp/GRA_QUB_Report_19.09.2022_accessible.pdf.

39 *Review of the Gender Recognition Act 2004: A Consultation*, Scottish Government, 2017, https://consult.gov.scot/family-law/review-of-the-gender-recognition-act-2004/user_uploads/sct1017251758-1_gender_p4--3-.pdf.

40 House of Commons Women and Equalities Committee, *Transgender Equality, First Report of Session 2015–16*, HC 390, 2016.

keen to place Scotland in alignment 'with the best international practice'.[41] At this stage, there was little indication of the intra-UK divergence which would follow but it was, in retrospect, a sign of things to come. Scotland was moving ahead in its ambition, and benchmarking itself against the world-leading nations in this respect. Here too were the first references to the difference in status which would result from the proposed reform with clarification that:

> applications to the Scottish self-declaration system should be restricted to those whose birth or adoption was registered in Scotland and to people who are resident here.[42]

3.2.2. *England and Wales Follow Close Behind*

In July 2018, the UK government launched its own consultation on *Reform of the Gender Recognition Act*, in which it stated its commitment to 'making the United Kingdom a country that works for everyone'.[43] The scope of this particular consultation, however, was restricted to England and Wales. It was explained that gender recognition was 'mostly devolved to Northern Ireland and Scotland'[44] but not to Wales.[45]

While the consultation was limited to England and Wales, the tone was still one of cooperation, with reference, for example, to the UK government's commitment to 'working closely with the Scottish Government on its proposals'[46] and continuing to 'engage with the Welsh Government'.[47] It was acknowledged that the devolution of gender recognition to the Scottish government meant that 'Scotland can have its own system for gender recognition if it wants to'[48] and there was a general sense from the tone of the document that the UK government was comfortable with that possibility; that there might be 'more divergence in the future'.[49] Although the consultation clearly recognised that there might be a move away from the current UK-wide approach, at this stage there was little indication of significant divergence in policy, with the UK government explaining that it too wanted 'to make it easier for trans people to achieve legal recognition' and was consulting 'on the best way to achieve this'.[50]

41 *Review of the Gender Recognition Act 2004: A Consultation* Scottish Government, 2017, para. 3.26, https://consult.gov.scot/family-law/review-of-the-gender-recognition-act-2004/user_uploads/sct1017251758-1_gender_p4--3-.pdf.

42 Ibid., para. 3.47.

43 *Reform of the Gender Recognition Act – Government Consultation*, 2018, p. 2.

44 Ibid., p. 12.

45 Ibid., p. 59.

46 Ibid., p. 58.

47 Ibid., p. 59.

48 Ibid., p. 55.

49 Ibid., p. 12.

50 Ibid., p. 21.

3.2.3. *Scotland Responds and Reconsults*

By November 2018, the responses to the Scottish government's first consultation had been analysed and published.[51] There was generally a fairly consistent majority in favour of reform. Focusing, for example, on three key areas, there were similar rates of positive response: 60% in favour of self-declaration; 61% in agreement with the proposal to reduce the age for applicants to seek gender recognition from 18 to 16; and 62% in favour of some provision being made for the recognition of non-binary identities.

In the analysis, there were early indications of the various issues which would become flashpoints in the future: concerns about women's safety and single-sex spaces; fear of abuse of the system by 'predatory men'; and questions about the distinction – and specifically the consultation paper's failure to distinguish – between sex and gender.[52] There was also some drawing of territorial boundaries, with the specific point being highlighted that 'Scotland cannot, or should not try to, make laws that extend beyond its borders or that affect the lives of people who are not its own nationals.'[53]

With some momentum building, a statement by the relevant Scottish government minister was made to the Scottish Parliament in June 2019 to the effect that they would proceed to consult on a draft Bill. That consultation was subsequently launched in December 2019.[54] By this time, the public and political debate had become intense and increasingly hostile, a fact which was referenced in the ministerial foreword to this second consultation: 'the debate on gender recognition has become polarised, both in Scotland and elsewhere'.[55]

Unlike previous statements, policy proposals and reports, which had consistently made at least some reference to UK-wide cooperation, it was notable that there was no mention by the minister of the UK government. The previous language of 'close cooperation' was conspicuous by its absence from the consultation document. International comparisons were cited on a number

51 Craigforth, *Review of the Gender Recognition Act 2004: Analysis of responses to the public consultation exercise*, Scottish Government, November 2018, https://www.gov.scot/binaries/content/documents/govscot/publications/consultation-analysis/2018/11/review-gender-recognition-act-2004-analysis-responses-public-consultation-exercise-report/documents/00543297-pdf/00543297-pdf/govscot%3Adocument/00543297.pdf.

52 Ibid., paras 8 and 10.

53 Ibid., para. 25.

54 *Gender Recognition Reform (Scotland) Bill: A consultation by the Scottish Government*, December 2019, https://www.gov.scot/binaries/content/documents/govscot/publications/consultation-paper/2019/12/gender-recognition-reform-scotland-bill-consultation-scottish-government/documents/gender-recognition-reform-scotland-bill-consultation-scottish-government/gender-recognition-reform-scotland-bill-consultation-scottish-government/govscot%3Adocument/gender-recognition-reform-scotland-bill-consultation-scottish-government.pdf.

55 Ibid., p. 2.

of occasions as examples of good practice and, with close reading and perhaps the benefit of hindsight, Scotland was now positioning itself more firmly on the European and international stage with rather less regard for its closer neighbours within Great Britain and the UK.[56]

On the few occasions within this second consultation document where there were references to the UK government, they were strategic and somewhat defensive. There was extensive focus throughout the document on the interaction between the proposed gender recognition reforms and the Equality Act 2010 (a UK-wide statute). Concerns had been raised in responses to the first consultation, and in much debate, both formal political and on social media, about the impact of a new, simpler system for gender recognition on the sex – or gender – discrimination protections within the 2010 Act and this was becoming a central issue in the second consultation process. The Scottish government sought to provide reassurance that nothing in its proposals would affect, and specifically weaken, the equality provisions and, in doing so, it drew support from similar reassurance which had been presented in the UK government's consultation.[57] In other words, the only direct reference to the UK government in this second Scottish consultation was to present previously used words of the UK government as evidence to support the Scottish government's position.

3.2.4. *England and Wales: Analysis of Response*

An independent analysis of the responses to the UK government's consultation (2018), in the form of a report commissioned by the Government Equalities Office, was presented to the Westminster Parliament in September 2020.[58] Neither the precise questions, nor the format of the analysis were directly comparable with the Scottish consultation, making comparative conclusions difficult. Whereas, for example, the Scottish government asked for views specifically on the question of a 'self-declaration' system, the UK government broke this down into separate questions about each of the current elements of the GRA scheme: the requirement of a gender dysphoria diagnosis; the requirement of a medical report; the requirement of evidence of living in the acquired gender, etc. In response to each of these questions, there was a majority in favour of change. Of those who responded (98.6% of all respondents) to the question of whether there should be a requirement in future for a diagnosis of

---

56 See e.g. Ibid., pp. 2, 3, 11 and Annex E, which set out a summary of the gender recognition processes used in 16 other countries or territories.

57 Ibid., e.g. paras 5.20 and 5.25, where the consultation paper quoted from the UK government's consultation paper of 2018.

58 D. King, C. Paechter and M. Ridgway, *Reform of the Gender Recognition Act: analysis of consultation responses*, 2020, https://assets.publishing.service.gov.uk/government/uploads/system/uploads/attachment_data/file/919890/Analysis_of_responses_Gender_Recognition_Act.pdf.

gender dysphoria, 64.1% said 'no'[59] – a figure similar to the 60% in Scotland who responded in the first consultation in favour of self-declaration. Approximately two-thirds of those who responded (64.7%) thought that the GRA should be amended to 'accommodate individuals who identified as non-binary';[60] a similar figure of 62% had expressed support for this in the first Scottish consultation.

It was noted that, of those respondents who could be categorised by location, 73% were based in England, 6% in Scotland, 3% in Wales and 1% in Northern Ireland.[61] Some variation was noted in the responses, based on location, with there being a tendency in this group of questions for the Scottish rate of support to be slightly higher than that from England – for example, 70.5% of respondents based in Scotland were in favour of removing the requirement for a diagnosis for gender dysphoria, compared to 65.8% of those based in England.[62]

Despite these statistical nuances, the overall headlines were that there were similar levels of support for the reforms in the UK consultation as there had been in the earlier Scottish consultation. If cultural gaps were appearing between the nations, they were not evident in the consultation responses themselves.

3.2.5. Westminster Calls a Halt While Scotland Continues

In September 2020, the then Minister for Women and Equalities, in a written statement to the UK Parliament, announced that the UK government did not intend to proceed with reform of the GRA 2004.[63] There had been a change of Prime Minister and government since the 2018 consultation and, in her statement, the Minister sought to distance the current administration from the previous one. In a somewhat selective interpretation of the consultation responses, she presented a new understanding to the effect that 'gender recognition reform, though supported in the consultation undertaken by the last government, is not the top priority for transgender people'. The government's view was that 'the balance struck in [the existing GRA 2004] is correct, in that there are proper checks and balances in the system'. Drawing a line under potential reform, the focus for the UK government switched instead to practical measures and implementation, including the announcement of investment in specialist clinics and health support.

In Scotland, meanwhile the process of reform continued with the publication in September 2021 of the *Gender Recognition Reform (Scotland) Bill: Analysis*

59 Ibid., para. 6.1.
60 Ibid., para. 23.1.
61 Ibid., para. 2.5.
62 Ibid., para. 6.1.
63 Written Ministerial Statement, 22 September 2020, https://www.gov.uk/government/speeches/response-to-gender-recognition-act-2004-consultation.

of responses to the public consultation exercise.[64] By this point, the focus for consultation had narrowed to the key details of the proposed new scheme: the length of period in which the applicant must have lived in their acquired gender; the requirement of a period of reflection before obtaining the GRC; and the question of whether the minimum age for applicants should be reduced from 18 to 16. While the questions had become narrow and clear, it was evident from the opening pages of the *Analysis* that the responses had become wide-ranging and somewhat chaotic. Respondents were categorised as fitting into one of two positions – 'either broadly in support of, or broadly opposed to, a statutory declaration-based system'.[65] Beyond that, there was a wide range of views on issues both within and beyond the detail of the Bill, with relatively little evidence of consistent alignment.

Once again, there was very little reference to the wider UK context and no specific mention of cooperation with the UK government. Increasingly the focus was inward looking, with one of the key themes highlighted being that the Scottish government was not listening. To whom they were not listening was, however, as polarised as much of the rest of the debate:

> It was ... suggested that the Scottish Government *has not listened* to the concerns and needs of the trans community, and that the Scottish Government *listens primarily* to the trans community [emphasis added].[66]

While by this point the language of the consultation process was Scotland-centric and no longer explicitly referencing the rest of the UK, the breakdown of residence of respondents suggested there was considerable wider interest and input in the Scottish process from respondents outwith Scotland. Of the 17,058 responses analysed, 55% of the respondents were resident in Scotland, 32% resident in the rest of the UK (i.e. England, Northern Ireland and Wales) and 14% in the rest of the world. It was reported, however, that 'no significant variations were found' dependent on place of residence.[67]

---

64 *Gender Recognition Reform (Scotland) Bill: Analysis of responses to the public consultation exercise*, September 2021, https://www.gov.scot/binaries/content/documents/govscot/publications/consultation-analysis/2021/09/gender-recognition-reform-scotland-bill-analysis-responses-public-consultation-exercise/documents/gender-recognition-reform-scotland-bill-analysis-responses-public-consultation-exercise-august-2021/gender-recognition-reform-scotland-bill-analysis-responses-public-consultation-exercise-august-2021/govscot%3Adocument/gender-recognition-reform-scotland-bill-analysis-responses-public-consultation-exercise-august-2021.pdf.

65 Ibid., p. i.

66 Ibid., p. ii.

67 Ibid., para. 1.28.

4. A SCOTTISH BILL BUT STILL NO ACT

On 2 March 2022, the Scottish government introduced its Bill on Gender Recognition Reform to the Scottish Parliament. Much has been said and written of the reform process in Scotland which led to the passing of the Gender Recognition Reform (Scotland) Bill and of the aftermath, but in this short chapter, only the headlines are included.[68] As the First Minister of Scotland said, on the day of the final debate in the Scottish Parliament, it was 'possibly the most scrutinised piece of legislation in the history of the Parliament'.[69] The outcome of that intense scrutiny and debate was that the Bill completed the final stage of the parliamentary process on 22 December 2022 and was passed by a clear majority of the Scottish Parliament: 86 for and 39 against.

From a shared starting point in 2016 of the need for UK-wide reform of the GRA 2004,[70] the end point in 2022 was a significant reform for Scotland alone. In the latter stages, the narrative of policy and debate had become increasingly inward looking, albeit with references to the alignment of Scotland with good practice in the rest of the world. The significance or desirability of cooperation and consistency closer to home, within the UK, had all but disappeared. There was one notable reference to the relationship between Scotland and England in the opening words of the cabinet secretary as she introduced the final debate on the Bill:

> The bill provides a new and improved route to legal recognition in Scotland, but the existing process will continue to be available across the whole of the United Kingdom. The bill does not remove the ability of someone who lives in Scotland to apply under the existing GRC process.

As she went on to explain:

> If the United Kingdom Government chooses not to recognise GRCs issued in Scotland, it will be particularly important that the existing system remains open to people in Scotland – for example, someone with an English birth certificate who lives in Scotland must have a route to be able to update that birth certificate in line with their acquired gender. I add, though, that I hope that the UK Government does not choose to take that step.[71]

---

68 A very helpful overview is provided in D. Torrance and D. Pyper, *The Secretary of State's veto and the Gender Reform (Scotland) Bill*, House of Commons Library Research Briefing, December 2023, No. CBP9705, https://researchbriefings.files.parliament.uk/documents/CBP-9705/CBP-9705.pdf.

69 Scottish Parliament, 22 December 2022, Stage 3 Debate, col. 11, https://www.parliament.scot/api/sitecore/CustomMedia/OfficialReport?meetingId=14071.

70 House of Commons Women and Equalities Committee, *Transgender Equality, First Report of Session 2015–16*, HC 390, 2016. Discussed above section 3.1.

71 Scottish Parliament, 22 December 2022, Stage 3 Debate, col. 31, https://www.parliament.scot/api/sitecore/CustomMedia/OfficialReport?meetingId=14071.

In fact, the next step which the UK government took was of much greater significance and it was one which did not appear to have been anticipated. The Gender Recognition Reform (Scotland) Bill had been passed by vote of the Scottish Parliament in December 2022 and the final stage in the legislative process would be for the Bill to receive Royal Assent, at which point it would become an Act. On 16 January 2023, however, the Secretary of State for Scotland, who is a member of the UK government, announced his intention to make a 'section 35 Order'.[72] Section 35 is a provision of the Scotland Act 1998 which provides for the Secretary of State (of the UK government) to make an order preventing a Bill (of the Scottish Parliament) from being put forward for Royal Assent if it contains provisions:

> which make modifications of the law as it applies to reserved matters and which the Secretary of State has reasonable grounds to believe would have an adverse effect on the operation of the law as it applies to reserved matters.[73]

In his Statement of Reasons for this action, the Secretary of State restated that there was no question that the issue of gender recognition was a devolved matter in which the Scottish Parliament had competence to act, but the precise detail of the Bill was such that in his view it would have an adverse effect on the operation of matters reserved to the UK Parliament, specifically matters of 'equal opportunities'.[74]

This was the first time that a section 35 order had been made and the political impact of its use went far beyond the specific topic of gender recognition. It was seen by many as an attack not only on Scottish policy and reform but on devolution itself. Its use was challenged by the Scottish government by means of a petition for judicial review of the order but, in a decision of the Court of Session in December 2023, the order was upheld.[75] Despite a range of opinions as to the reasonableness or rightness of the Secretary of State's actions and the decision of the Lord Ordinary in the subsequent judicial review, the Scottish government indicated that it would not seek to appeal. Nor, to date, has it taken any steps to revise the Bill or pursue alternative reform.

5. HARMONISATION AND DISHARMONY

> The Gender Recognition Reform (Scotland) Bill, which aim[ed] to ease gender recognition for transgender people by introducing a self-identification system, has

72 Gender Recognition Reform (Scotland) Bill: statement from Alister Jack, https://www.gov.uk/government/news/gender-recognition-reform-scotland-bill-statement-from-alister-jack.

73 Scotland Act 1998, s. 35(1)(b).

74 Statement of reasons, https://assets.publishing.service.gov.uk/media/63c68c66e90e074eecb1c26e/policy-statement-section-35-powers-Gender-Recognition-Reform-_Scotland_-Bill.pdf.

75 *Scottish Ministers, Petitioners* 2024 SC 173.

> become the single most controversial piece of legislation since the introduction of devolution.[76]

This legislation, and the whole process of seeking to reform the GRA 2004, has acquired a significance far beyond the field of trans rights and their interaction with family law.[77] The influences and interests, personal, cultural and political, are diverse and complex and, as has been seen through much of the debate, they lend themselves to multiple, often diametrically opposed, interpretations. If the various nations within the UK had worked together more closely and collaboratively on reform of gender recognition, as they did on the development and enactment of the original GRA 2004, would the outcome have been any different? It is overly simplistic to draw conclusions from the previous process which resulted in the original UK-wide legislation – which saw the domestic nations working together in response to an external prompt – in contrast to the internal disharmony and disintegration which has characterised recent attempts at reform. Nonetheless, they are comparable processes of legal reform which stand in stark contrast, with the absence of cooperation ultimately ending in blocking and veto. The repercussions are likely to be felt for some time.

For family law and family lawyers, what has happened within the UK in terms of gender recognition reform has been a stark reminder that legal reform is a complex and contested process, even among apparently similar countries and communities which have much in common geographically, culturally and socially. Far from 'harmonisation' in personal and family law being seen as a European project, which we have sometimes only observed from the edge, its potential benefits have never been clearer. The practical consequences of disharmony, when viewed at close quarters across the internal borders of the UK, have brought the importance of working together much closer to home.

---

76 F. Simpkins, 'Conservative unionism v Gender Recognition Reform (Scotland) Bill: killing two birds with one stone?' in A.P. Bonnet and R. Kilty (eds), *Towards a Very British Version of the "Culture Wars": Populism, Social Fractures and Political Communication*, Routledge, Abingdon 2024, p. 191.

77 See e.g. A. McHarg, 'The contested boundaries of devolved legislative competence', Bennet Institute for Public Policy, Cambridge, https://www.bennettinstitute.cam.ac.uk/wp-content/uploads/2023/05/Contested-boundaries-devolved-legislative-consent.pdf.

PART VII

FINAL REFLECTIONS AND SUMMARY

CHARTING THE FUTURE OF EUROPEAN FAMILY LAW

Katharina Boele-Woelki

The question of 'what family law for Europe?' served as the guiding theme for the Stockholm conference, originally inspired by my 2016 article in the *Rabels Zeitschrift für ausländisches und internationales Privatrecht.*[1] In that article, I tried to look into the future by predicting several different developments in the field of family law in Europe. Comparing them with what we discussed some ten years later, I think that some of them still hold true, but we have further distilled different themes of what might lie ahead and how we can work together in different areas. It will come as no surprise that there was a wide range of ideas. The theme of the conference provided a rich basis for discussion. Over two days we explored how European family law might develop and how we can work together across borders. The responses were varied and thought-provoking, offering insights into the future of this field.

The conference marked a significant milestone as the first of its kind in Europe, bringing together an extensive network of family law scholars. Our primary aim was to foster a mutual understanding of ongoing research, address methodological challenges, and identify the most pressing issues in our field. The organisers believe that a collaborative European approach, rooted in comparative law research, is the best path forward for advancing family law.

We took time to reflect on the achievements of past international and European collaborations. The result is something to be proud of. Through shared efforts, we have had numerous successes: from international conventions and expert meetings to joint publications and the development of Principles of European Family Law that have shaped the discipline. This history of cooperation set the stage for our discussions, particularly in the sessions examining the trajectory of Nordic family law cooperation and on revisiting the Principles of European Family Law.

The focus on Nordic family law showed that there are both convergences and divergences between the countries. Although cooperation has led to significant

1 *RabelsZ* 2018, 1–30.

progress, including in children's law, linguistic diversity is a challenge. Knowledge of each other's languages and legislation is now lower. While English can be used as a working language in negotiations, it cannot be used in drafting legislation. EU membership further complicates this dynamic, especially for Finland and Sweden, whose obligations under EU regulations have made it necessary to renegotiate the Nordic Conventions. Despite notable achievements, the political landscape – characterised by an increasing diversity of parties and interests – has led to more diverse approaches in the Nordic countries. But the Nordic model strives for equal opportunities, social cohesion, pragmatic solutions, consultation and compromise. It is a fascinating cooperation.

In our discussions on the CEFL Principles, we looked at the evolution of several key family law norms. For example, the Divorce Principles aim to simplify the dissolution of marriages by removing fault requirements, but this approach raises questions such as whether divorce is now too accessible, potentially undermining the institution of marriage. The introduction of non-judicial divorces further challenges the role of the judiciary in these matters, suggesting a tension between legal efficiency and the need for careful oversight in sensitive cases. Some similar complexities have been identified in other areas, such as parental responsibilities, property rights and the emerging legal framework for *de facto* unions.

Looking ahead, three themes emerged as priorities for future research and cooperation:

1. parent–child relationships, especially regarding assisted reproductive technologies (ART) and evolving definitions of parentage;
2. legal recognition of new adult relationships, including non-romantic and community-based arrangements like Germany's 'community of responsibility'; and
3. strengthening protections against domestic violence, ensuring the safety and well-being of children.

While these areas are promising, they require a deeply interdisciplinary approach, calling for collaboration with fields such as sociology and psychology. However, truly interdisciplinary research is time-consuming and costly, in addition to comparative legal research, and requires a commitment across different academic traditions.

In the session on vulnerable adults, we addressed the pressing issue of balancing autonomy and protection, a challenge that will only increase as populations age. Presentations from the FL-EUR project illuminated the varying approaches to legal capacity and representation, highlighting the need for further empirical research. The session also touched upon the changing landscape of private international law, where new European rules are being proposed to adapt to cross-border needs in adult protection.

Discussions on assisted reproduction technologies and the right to know one's origins raised critical ethical and legal questions. The right to access genetic information is becoming more urgent as ART practices continue to expand. These evolving technologies, from IVF to synthetic embryos, will have profound implications for family law, requiring careful consideration for years to come.

The conference concluded with a session on legal gender and identities, featuring diverse perspectives from across Europe. The topic embodies 'huge diversity'. The discussion underscored the complexities and internal inconsistencies within legal frameworks, as jurisdictions navigate the changing realities of gender identities.

Throughout the conference, one theme resonated strongly: the increasing influence of politics on family law, often to the detriment of progressive norms. Right-wing movements in several countries are pushing back against the gains made in equality and human rights, challenging the foundations of our liberal family law systems. As scholars, we must remain vigilant and ready to defend the principles of fairness and inclusivity.

The final question is how we move forward. Who will take the lead in the new research areas, and how will collaboration unfold? These are questions for each of us to take back to our respective groups, but the Stockholm conference has already provided us with valuable ideas and connections. As the chairperson of the CEFL's Organising Committee, I am proud of what we have achieved in advancing comparative family law studies. Our publications will continue to serve as a resource, and we remain open to sharing our expertise in methodology and beyond.

WHAT FAMILY LAW FOR EUROPE?

Debates and Insights at the Stockholm Conference

Charlotte Mol and Susanna Roßbach

Bringing together European family law scholars for two days not only provides for interesting presentations on a wide variety of topics, but also allows for an important forum for discussions. Insights were shared from different perspectives, in light of differing national regimes, political pressures and research experiences. The focus of this conference report is to synthesise the discussions held during the conference, in order to share these insights more broadly. For in-depth coverage of the papers presented at the conference, we refer to the preceding chapters in this volume.

The structure of this conference report follows the programme of the conference, starting with a discussion of Nordic family law cooperation, before turning to the revisited CEFL Principles and avenues for reform, the FL-EUR project on vulnerable adults, and finally topics for future collaborative and comparative projects.

1. NORDIC FAMILY LAW COOPERATION

The conference's first session focused on the success story of Nordic family law cooperation and asked whether the Nordic countries nowadays are united or separate actors. The first presentation by Lund-Andersen provided a historical overview, especially regarding the cooperation in academia. After describing the relationship between the five Nordic countries – Denmark, Norway, Iceland, Sweden and Finland – as 'five swans flying in the same direction', Lund-Andersen identified four main phases in the harmonisation of family laws in these countries. The influence of academia has varied throughout these phases, but has overall been fruitful on many levels. To describe this development, Lund-Andersen used the metaphor of a wave that started high with intense cooperation at the beginning of the 20th century, slowly sinking before then again rising in recent years.

In the following presentation, Silvola and Hartley addressed the cooperation within the Nordic (governmental) expert group on family law. Today, this group consists of government officials dealing with family and succession law from the five Nordic countries as well as the Faroe Islands, which joined in 2018. Among their main achievements is the revision of the Nordic Conventions on private international law aspects of family and succession law, originally adopted in the 1930s. Silvola and Hartley emphasised the longevity of the expert group as its special feature. Nevertheless, a challenge for Nordic family law cooperation that Silvola and Hartley pointed out, as well as Lund-Andersen before this, is how Nordic cooperation relates to cooperation within the European Union: as Finland and Sweden are bound by the EU regulations on family law and Nordic exceptions to EU regulations become increasingly problematic, the possibilities for negotiation within Nordic cooperation are nowadays limited.

The session's third presentation, delivered by Friðriksdóttir, then focused on child law in the Nordic countries. Child law, in the understanding of the presentation, includes the relationship between children and parents as well as the legal framework for the rights of children. Friðriksdóttir described that the Nordic model for child law is based on equal opportunity and the principle of gender equality, but is also defined by pragmatic solutions and compromises. Therefore, finding a balance with the best interests of the child is still a persistent challenge in Nordic laws, for example when defining factors for the allocation of parenthood or the relation of active and equal parents. Friðriksdóttir summarised that in this context 'child law has become a battlefield for gender policy'.

Finally, Sverdrup asked, in the last presentation of this session, what future cooperation in substantive family law could look like. As an example for possible cooperation, Sverdrup described a phenomenon in modern relationships: two parties act independently in the market and at the same time form a unit of work, consumption and investment. Sverdrup stated that in many Western jurisdictions only assets created during the marriage are divided equally, while premarital assets, gifts and inheritances are not divided upon divorce. At the same time, it can be difficult for the economically weaker party to invest during the relationship if the results of their consumption are divided equally. Therefore, Sverdrup raised the question whether this form of corrective justice fits within marriage and cohabitation. In this regard, Sverdrup suggested a collaborative project between legal academics and social scientists in the Nordic countries to find out how the various financial settlements in the Nordic countries work in practice.

The subsequent discussion started with a question from Lund-Andersen, who asked why the legal situation of rainbow families was not mentioned as a current topic for the Nordic expert group on family law. Silvola and Hartley explained that this had certainly been discussed, but that there was a lack of political consensus as the political landscape has changed. In their view, it is seen as a very sensitive political topic that cannot be addressed by civil servants only. Referring to this, Dethloff pointed out that it is nevertheless a highly important topic, because it is the social reality of families nowadays. Following this, Boele-Woelki thought aloud about why there is so much diversity in very important issues in the Nordic countries at the moment and asked if there are only political or maybe also cultural reasons for this.

The discussion then moved on to the topic of the property of spouses or cohabitants. It was discussed that legal resolutions in this area are often based on case law. Schrama pointed out that an obstacle for potential legislation could be that cohabitants, compared for example to LGBTQI+ persons, do not have lobbying groups to represent them. In the following discussion that revolved around care work, the significance of traditional gender roles was mentioned: women are meant to be selfless and are expected to care, such that it seems acceptable that they are not paid for this kind of work. Sverdrup made it clear that this is a deeply political issue, because it effects nearly everyone. Lastly, Scherpe pointed out that formal equality is not the same as real equality, because real equality has to recognise differences as well.

2. REVISITING THE CEFL PRINCIPLES OF EUROPEAN FAMILY LAW AND REQUESTS FOR REFORM

Following an insightful discussion on Nordic cooperation, the focus of the second session was the joint project which served as the foundation for the network of most conference participants, namely the Commission on European Family Law. The first presentation, given by Martiny, addressed the working method of the CEFL through comparison but notably also teamwork. Over a period of almost two decades, the national experts and Organising Committee of the CEFL have developed and published four multilingual sets of European family law Principles. Most recently, this has been complemented by a reflection on developments since the drafting of these Principles, revisiting the Principles and addressing expected and unexpected new trends in European family law. Martiny set out the comparative method used, addressing the wealth of information and the value of new developments while also noting the challenges that the latter raise for endeavours such as that of the CEFL.

Subsequently, Lowe and González Beilfuss shared the key conclusions of the revisited CEFL Principles. For each set of Principles, the original aim was shared before delving into emerging issues and trends since their publication. Most Principles have withstood the test of time rather well, at times also capturing subsequent trends within European family law, such as alternate residence schemes and relocation disputes in the field of parental responsibilities. In some areas unforeseen developments were noted, for example the introduction of non-judicial or extrajudicial divorces. All in all, Lowe and González Beilfuss conclude that the Principles have led to interesting academic discourse and some influence on new legislation in various jurisdictions.

In the final presentation Novak and Dethloff invited those present to join them in considering new topics and perspectives to be addressed in collaborative and comparative European family law research. Dethloff addressed potential avenues for research on both the horizontal and the vertical level of family relationships. Commencing with the latter, she suggested broad, comparative and interdisciplinary research into parenthood and all its forms. With regard to horizontal family relationships, she argued that the groundbreaking CEFL Principles on *de facto* Unions needed further promotion. New research could address new forms of family relationships for solidarity and care. In that regard she zoomed in on the new German proposal for a community of responsibility (*Verantwortungsgemeinschaft*), consisting of two to six adults. Novak advocated for future research to address domestic violence, both in horizontal relationships between partners and in vertical relationships between parents and their children. How should and can family law provide protection and what impact does it have on agreements made between (former) partners or custody and visitation rights?

The presentations set the stage for further engagement with the suggested avenues of research. Many agreed that domestic violence is an important topic to be addressed in family law, not only by criminal law. As Mair noted, it is a 'timely and overdue topic'. Where criminal scholars have 'raced ahead' in this field, family law has not. Others agreed that collaboration and cooperation should be sought between these two fields of law, both in research and in practice. Antokolskaia did stress that in doing so, it is important to keep in mind the different tasks of the criminal and civil courts: whereas the presumption of innocence is key in criminal proceedings, a family judge is tasked with taking decisions in the best interests of the child, including protecting the child where necessary. In that regard, judges in family law cases should not or might not only rely on penal law judgments in these cases. In addition, attention should be paid to the role that the police play, as they have been shown not always to take accusations of domestic violence seriously. In the same vein, in light of the definition of abuse becoming much broader, Friðriksdóttir critically raised the question of whether the broad spectrum, even when criminalised and sanctioned, should always have direct effects in family law. This question built upon a comment by Novak that the recent mentality in European family law of encouraging agreements between former partners and parents might very well conflict with the need to protect victims of domestic violence, for example through different hearings or by halting mediation efforts. Friðriksdóttir questioned whether this would always be the best course of action, especially where parents continue to exercise parental responsibilities jointly after separation and cutting them off from mediation or making agreements might not be the most appropriate route to take. Jänterä-Jareborg also noted the 'troublesome' situation in which strategic allegations of domestic violence in family law proceedings might also occur, a trend seen previously in international child abduction cases, for which no answers yet exist. Many agreed that a multidisciplinary approach would be necessary to answer the various difficult questions posed.

The politically difficult, if not sensitive, question of 'who is a parent?' was also addressed as an avenue for further European research. Boele-Woelki noted that the polar opposite views on the answer to this question between European states had been a reason for the Commission on European Family Law not to select the topic, although perhaps 'it might have been easier then than now'. The speakers raised the urgency of the topic, as also reflected by the current work of the European Commission in drafting and negotiating a parentage regulation as a private international law instrument. Research on the topic being of great importance in that regard, as Hartley underlined, it sheds light on aspects that negotiators have to take into account and the problems it may help to resolve. When Sahlin, as a philosopher specialising in medical ethics, raised further questions about parentage and its consequences pre-birth, others responded that there were sufficient challenges to address post-birth before turning to the even more controversial pre-birth discussions. The intertwined challenges of who is a parent, which rights and obligations are attached, what consequences it has for the many adjacent areas of law, such as maintenance, succession, tax law, etc., and how it relates to children's and parents' fundamental rights require an eagle-eyed view. Here too, the need for inter- or multidisciplinary research was stressed.

Finally, the discussion on future avenues for European research turned to new forms of adult relationships that provide solidarity or care outside of amorous or familial relationships. Many agreed that this would be a great topic and an urgent one in light of an ageing population and globalisation, but that it may be difficult. As Panforti noted, 'if I would have to answer a questionnaire, it would be very easy as there is nothing to fill in'. According to Schrama, this is because of the fact that the topic is not yet addressed by family law, but instead requires researchers to delve into many other areas of law, such as medical, social security and tax law. Whereas some noted that other relationships or more solidarity may need to be encouraged, the question also arose whether there is currently a problem, and if so, whether it requires a legal solution. Dethloff added that if a legal solution were required, research should consider whether it ought to be through contracts or through granting a specific status to the relationship with subsequent rights and obligations. Her proposal would be the latter. In response, Brattström was hesitant with regard to new relationship rights and obligations on the basis of status due to the very real risk of people believing they are (sufficiently) protected by the law when, in fact, they are not protected in the way that they think they are. In this regard, Ribot Igualada highlighted the option of a community of responsibilities in Catalonian law as, perhaps, inspiration for other jurisdictions.

Coming to a conclusion, a final topic was raised very briefly, namely migrant families and the effects of migration on family law. Most of those present agreed that all topics require further research across Europe and preferably in an inter- or multidisciplinary manner.

3. BALANCING AUTONOMY AND THE PROTECTION OF VULNERABLE ADULTS

The second day of the conference commenced with a session on the so-called 'challenge of our time', namely the protection and empowerment of vulnerable adults. This session consisted of two parts: first a focus on the Family Law in Europe (FL-EUR) project and its initial results in this field, and secondly, a reflection on limitations and obstacles when addressing the topic of vulnerable adults.

In the first part, Antokolskaia commenced with an introduction to FL-EUR, an academic network of experts in the field of family and law across 31 European jurisdictions. The aim, working method and choice of topic were discussed. The chosen topic addresses the paradigm shift from the protection to the empowerment of vulnerable adults, as provided for by the Convention on the Rights of Persons with Disabilities (CRPD), which all of the jurisdictions studied have ratified. This makes it a unique topic to address and Antokolskaia shared an overview of where states are in reforming their laws to meet the requirements of the CRPD along a spectrum. In the subsequent presentations, the preliminary results from FL-EUR were shared. Wuyts addressed state-ordered measures, addressing both the link between state-ordered measures and legal capacity and the powers and duties of support persons. He distinguished between different approaches to state-ordered measures amongst European jurisdictions, and delved into the decision-making by support persons. The latter is also relevant in light of empowerment: are vulnerable adults provided with support in decision-making or are decisions made for them (substituted decision-making)? Schrama presented preliminary results regarding ex lege measures. These 'relatively informal, below the legal radar' measures allow for representation by a partner or other family member. Her presentation showed a great diversity between jurisdictions on the various aspects, including the legal ground for an ex lege measure, the necessity for medical evidence, who the representative can be, and what the representative may do. Schrama stressed the need to consider demographic and societal trends when studying the need and feasibility of these measures, as well as the need for more empirical insights.

The subsequent discussion further explored this need. Sahlin promoted the use of the vast literature that is available on human decision-making in psychology. Hvidsten shared her insights from within the Norwegian Ministry of Justice, where a new Guardianship Act is being worked upon. In her experience, 'putting people in spreadsheets' can be difficult, but the numbers can be important to understand the system and how it works. In her example, while Norwegian law allows for a total limitation of legal capacity, the numbers demonstrate that this is applied very restrictively, with tens of thousands more vulnerable adults being subject to only voluntary guardianships. Wuyts agreed that it is necessary to 'dig deeper', going beyond the legal framework to the law in action. However, he noted the difficulty in doing so when empirical data is not available. Others agreed, but also noted the limits of time and money in collecting such data.

In the second part of the session, the same speakers first reflected on limitations and obstacles in the FL-EUR project. Antokolskaia shared insights into the drafting of the FL-EUR questionnaire and the difficulties experienced in trying to hit the 'moving target'. Profiting from the comparative-based drafting of the CEFL, the choice was made to draft an extensive questionnaire with detailed questions, explaining the terminology used and therefore attempting to prevent rapporteurs from straying away from the subject at hand. A functional approach was used to bridge language gaps and make comparison possible. Wuyts further explained the terminological issues at play, through the example of legal capacity. This term, which is key to measuring compliance with Article 12 CRPD, has been shown to have different meanings in different contexts. Wuyts addressed the link with mental capacity and support measures, as well as whether and how it can be general, matter-specific, decision-specific or time-specific. Schrama, the final FL-EUR contributor, discussed the dissemination of the research results. Noting that she herself did not have the answers to successful dissemination, she reflected on ChatGPT's suggestions for the dissemination of results following European academic collaborations. These included traditional methods of publication and the organisation of conferences, as well as targeting key stakeholders and public engagement. In a final presentation, Karjalainen took us on an investigation of cross-border adult protection. She focused on looking at the role of private international law in removing impediments to cross-border support for vulnerable adults, its connection with human rights standards and the potential new obstacles revealed for cross-border support in the comparative work of FL-EUR. Two intertwined issues were noted: the role of private international law in facilitating human rights protection acting as a tool for accommodating support, and those situations in which private international law and human rights may clash, in part due to differences in national laws.

In the discussion that followed, Jänterä-Jareborg posed a question to Karjalainen as to whether the cross-border recognition of partial guardianship (for example) actually works in practice and to what extent a best interests principle as it exists for children may also work for vulnerable adults. Karjalainen noted that while it might be effective in certain cases, the cross-border support and protection of vulnerable adults does not always work, in part due to practical issues, such as the additional rules that banks have in place for these types of situations. She added that there is no such best interests principle for adults, as instead the wishes of the adult should be taken into account. The rest of the discussion focused on the dissemination of research results. The value of building and maintaining connections with relevant European and national institutions, for example the EU and ELI, but also national ministries of justice, was noted. The inclusion of early career researchers in network-building and of academics and professionals from other disciplines in research or conferences were stressed as valuable avenues.

4. FUTURE PROJECTS AND TOPICS?

The conference continued in the afternoon with presentations on potential future projects for cooperation and they focused in the first session on assisted reproduction techniques, ethics and the right to know one's origin. This session started with a presentation by Todorova, who discussed what a fair balance between a child's right to know its origin and the rights of related adults can look like. According to the Convention on the Rights of the Child, every child has the right to know their parents. Nevertheless, Todorova showed that difficult situations can occur in cases of anonymous births, adoptions and surrogacy and that the legislation throughout Europe is inconsistent.

The second presentation, given by Mol, focused on child participation against the background of new frontiers in parentage law. These new frontiers can be seen as Mol described, for example, in assisted reproduction techniques or surrogacy. Because children have the right to participate in all matters affecting them, including parentage proceedings, according to international and European human rights law the question arises whether there are avenues for child participation: can there be participation if a child has not yet been born? Mol described different approaches for collective participation and for representation, as well as their inherent risks.

In the following presentation, Ribot Igualada addressed the Spanish law on assisted reproduction techniques since 1988 and asked if it is a 'troublemaker or a frontrunner'. Ribot Igualada started by providing a comparative overview of the available treatments in Europe for heterosexual couples, female couples and single women, as well as on the regulations on anonymity. It was pointed out that Spain has a high-performance private industry for assisted reproduction techniques without restrictions for single mothers or female families. Therefore, around 15% of the families in question come from abroad. This raises the question of a need for harmonising the regulations on assisted reproduction techniques in Europe, as Ribot Igualada discussed at the end of the presentation.

In the last presentation of this session, Sahlin took the conference participants on a 'road trip with five stops' analysing 'brand new ways to make babies'. The presentation discussed whether, from an ethical perspective, laws and regulations in the field of reproductive medicine are sufficient. For this purpose, Sahlin gave five examples: (1) reimbursements for egg donations in Sweden; (2) artificial eggs and sperm made out of other cells from a person's body; (3) gene editing;

(4) artificial embryos; and (5) artificial wombs. Sahlin stated that in all five areas regulations are either lacking, outdated or inconsistent.

The presentations in this session led to a lively discussion. Referring to Sahlin, Silvola raised the issue that the discussion around artificial wombs also leads to the debate on when life begins. Silvola further questioned the relation to surrogacy and asked if artificial reproductive technology may be a substitute one day. Sahlin underlined that he sees it as one of the main problems that the embryo is not connected to a mother, but can be made 'from scratch' without parents. In answer to a question from Novak, Sahlin clarified that it will be possible in the future to create a child in a laboratory and bear it in an artificial womb. Sahlin therefore emphasised that in his opinion it is important to create regulations now rather than later.

Following that, the discussion moved on to current assisted reproduction techniques. Jänterä-Jareborg stated that in Sweden donors have to undergo a suitability test and the number of donations is restricted. Referring to Ribot Igualada's presentation, she asked whether such control mechanisms also exist in Spain, as the clinics work outside the public health system. Ribot Igualada agreed that it is very unlikely for a child conceived with reproductive medicine to be born in the public sector. But although the clinics are private, controls exist. Ribot Igualada explained that the clinics even promise the 'best quality' of donors. However, Ribot Igualada also mentioned that 'pathological donors' who donate in many European countries and bypass controls nevertheless exist.

The discussion then moved on to questions of parenthood. Singer stated that it is very important for children to know their origins, but raised the question of whether there is a risk of reducing parenthood to genetics in these cases. Coming back to Sahlin's presentation, Novak emphasised that genetics are one option for allocating parenthood, but especially when using assisted reproductive techniques intention can be a factor as well: parents are those who want to have a child. Overall, all discussants agreed that regulation in this field will be necessary in the future, but that it will raise difficult legal and ethical questions. As Singer summarised: 'you must have great faith in lawyers.'

5. LEGAL GENDERS

The last session of the conference finally focused on legal genders and identities in a European perspective. Scherpe, in the first presentation of this session, described the legal situation in Germany and the Nordic countries, which are traditionally 'at the head of the curve' for queer rights. It was emphasised that Germany has a strong constitutional tradition and awareness of 'othering' people, because of its history under the NS regime. After describing the requirements to change one's legal gender under the different national laws and non-binary options that exist in Iceland and Germany, Scherpe focused in the last part of the presentation on the recognition of trans parents and asked why the legal terms 'mother' and 'father' cannot be abolished.

Subsequently, Vaigė reported on legal genders and identities in Eastern European jurisdictions. The presentation covered a total of 11 jurisdictions, all of which are now part of the European Union and were part of or heavily influenced by the former Soviet Union. These jurisdictions encompass a wide range of regulations: while Estonia has quite liberal regulations on the correction of the recognised gender, Hungary prohibits this completely. Because of the sheer amount of information, Vaigė presented an overview and highlighted particularly interesting aspects. Overall, Vaigė observed that the Eastern European jurisdictions do not provide for self-determination laws or the protection of trans minors or non-binary people.

The following presentation, given by Távora Vítor, focused on Southern Europe and covered Portugal, Spain, Italy and Malta. Those countries share the same main features, are traditionally Catholic and belong – except for Malta – to the Latin language area. Távora Vítor prepared an overview of trans rights in these jurisdictions: while Italy was one of the first countries in Europe to allow a correction of the recognised gender, Malta is seen as being at the forefront of LGBTQ rights in Europe nowadays. All of these jurisdictions share the fact that legal and (socio-)political discussions about trans rights are still ongoing.

The last presentation of the session by Mair also had a strong focus on political discussions, covering the internal disharmony regarding trans rights in the British Isles. Mair described that the British Isles are increasingly divided over internal identity politics. When, in 2022, Scotland passed a Gender Recognition Reform Bill, it was blocked by the Westminster government. The Scottish government challenged this by judicial review, but the legality of the order was upheld. Mair summarised the political process as a 'story of disharmony' and a good example of how not to do this.

In the following discussion, Mair clarified this by answering a question from Boele-Woelki that the challenge of the order before a Scottish court complies with the process and an appeal against this decision would have gone to the Supreme Court. Referring to the presentation by Scherpe, Friðriksdóttir subsequently emphasised that a clear distinction must be made between the regulations for the allocation of parenthood and, for example, the terms 'mother' and 'father' that are used.

Lastly the discussion moved on to the current decision of the European Court of Justice in the *Mirin* case.[1] In answering a question from Roßbach, Vaigė was not very optimistic that Hungary and Bulgaria would accept this new case law

1 Case C-4/23, *M.-A. A. v Direcţia de Evidenţă a Persoanelor Cluj, Serviciul stare civilă*, ECLI:EU:C:2024:385.

from the Court, because they have also not reacted to other decisions in the past. In Vaigė's view, these countries see queer rights purely as a political issue and do not accept legal arguments. Therefore, it is almost impossible to challenge their laws through European human rights law. Other participants agreed with this opinion.

6. CONCLUSION

All in all, many topics of European family law and the practice of comparative European projects were addressed in the presentations and discussions at the conference. In closing the conference, Boele-Woelki remarked on a number of overarching take-home messages. A main theme was the value of collaboration. Meeting one another face-to-face with time to discuss content, methods and new questions both during the sessions and at lunch and dinner is extremely valuable. Having the opportunity to meet (new) colleagues, to speak freely on the challenges arising in various jurisdictions and to brainstorm new areas of research provided new inspiration and impetus for collaboration. Boele-Woelki emphasised the value of this, especially in a time when political backlash in many areas of family law creates a risk of family law topics being hijacked for other aims. This trend, the pushback against human rights and children's rights, was noted on a number of occasions throughout the conference and raised concerns among many of the participants. The question was therefore also raised whether, as researchers, we ought to rely less on human rights in pushing for developments when these rights are under attack. Boele-Woelki closed the conference by asking about the 'elephant in the room': who will further engage in research on which topic and how can collaboration be brought to fruition? With many debates having been raised and new insights shared, the conference participants left with renewed inspiration to address them.

www.ingramcontent.com/pod-product-compliance
Ingram Content Group UK Ltd.
Pitfield, Milton Keynes, MK11 3LW, UK
UKHW051906290926
8980IPUK00018B/1796